Newgate Calendar

Newgate to take water at Blackfriars

THE FLOATING BROTHEL

THE FLOATING BROTHEL

The extraordinary true story of an eighteenth-century ship and its cargo of female convicts

Siân Rees

HEADLINE

First published in 2001
by HEADLINE BOOK PUBLISHING

10 9 8 7 6 5 4 3 2

British Library Cataloguing in Publication Data

Rees, Siân
The floating brothel: the extraordinary true story of an 18th-century
ship and its cargo of female convicts
1. Convict ships – Great Britain – History – 18th century 2. Women
prisoners – Transportation – Great Britain – History – 18th century
3. Women prisoners – Great Britain – Sexual behaviour – History –
18th century 4. Abused women – Great Britain – History – 18th
century
I. Title
364.6'8'082'09033

ISBN 0 7472 7286 7

Typeset by Avon Dataset Ltd, Bidford-on-Avon, Warks

Printed and bound in Great Britain by
Clays Ltd, St Ives plc

HEADLINE BOOK PUBLISHING
A division of Hodder Headline
338 Euston Road
London NW1 3BH

www.headline.co.uk
www.hodderheadline.com

Dedicated to John Rees, 1934–2000,
and my Australian family

'Not much attempt had been made to enforce discipline among the women, many of them London prostitutes, who had turned the ship into a floating brothel at her various ports of call'

M. D. Nash, *The Last Voyage of the* Guardian, 1990

'. . . the majority were London prostitutes . . . On the passage to Port Jackson the *Lady Julian* was nothing more than a floating brothel . . .'

Charles Bateson, *The Convict Ships*, 1985

Contents

Chapter One

Disorderly Girls

Winter 1788, London. Outside the royal stables, at the bottom of the Mall, where Trafalgar Square now stands, a 26-year-old Scottish prostitute staked out her space and began her night's work.

Matilda Johnson already knew William McPherson by sight as a fellow Scot. As he passed through the mews on his way from Westminster to Oxford Street, she stopped him, 'pressed me close against the wall and asked me what I would give her'. Wise to the ways of prostitutes, McPherson felt for his watch to move it into his waistcoat pocket, but it was already up her sleeve. He remonstrated; Matilda flirted and would not give it back. First, she wanted a gin in Orange Street. Next, she wanted a plate of salmon round the corner. He refused, refused again, told her nicely he was not interested that night and wanted his watch. Matilda was confident, or drunk enough to assume he would bargain it back with a glass of gin or five minutes against the wall, and disappeared into a pawnshop in St Martin's Lane, where she announced that her countryman wanted to pawn his watch to buy her a petticoat. McPherson was now late and exasperated and asked Mr Crouch the pawnbroker to search her. Realising he meant it, Matilda finally produced the watch from beneath her petticoats.

It was the pawnbroker who insisted on calling in the constable,

---

1

hoping for part of the reward. McPherson said afterwards that Matilda, by now crying, 'begged me to take the watch, and I wished to have taken it'. He would have left the matter there. When the constable arrived, McPherson turned defender rather than prosecutor and accompanied the girl to the watchhouse, where he 'begged the clerk and the constable to discharge her'. They refused. Perhaps they already knew her as a frequent offender and would not lose the opportunity of charging her on the whim of a foreigner taken in by a pretty face. Still pleading with McPherson to rescue her, Matilda was shackled, hoisted on to a cart and within hours was in Newgate gaol, a prisoner awaiting trial at the Old Bailey.

A few days later, a mother and daughter were out shoplifting among the linen-drapers of Holborn. They entered Edward Bowerbank's drapery on Newgate Street one afternoon when the light was fading and went through to the back shop. Here, they asked the assistant to show them some aprons and launched into the four-step sequence of eighteenth-century shoplifting. Step one was to 'tumble the muslins' on the counter. Step two was to divert the shopman by sending him off for scissors or change. Step three was to stuff a piece of cloth up your skirt, and step four was to leave the premises unhurriedly and without ungainly lumps. It was what every shoplifter did, and every draper in Holborn was on the lookout for it. If packaged with skill, up to 60 yards of material could disappear beneath a woman's petticoats, and tradesmen all over London were losing money to ladies fingering the muslins.

Charlotte Marsh was fussy in her choice, and there were a dozen aprons on the countertop before she chose one, paid and asked the assistant to change half-a-crown. The assistant had no change, he said, and called for Mr Bowerbank. It was a pre-arranged signal that something suspicious was going on and, sure enough, the moment the shopman turned his head Mrs Clapton plucked an apron from the counter and hid it under her cloak. As she backed towards the door, Mr Bowerbank stepped lithely across the shop and got there first, told her 'she had something she should not have' and 'wished her to produce it'.

Both women were outraged. They had taken nothing. The apron in Mrs Clapton's inside pocket? She had wanted to see it by the door in the light. Mr Bowerbank had now had time to cast a professional linen-draper's eye over the messy bundle under Charlotte Marsh's arm. Detaining the daughter while his assistant watched the mother, he unrolled an armful of lengths of calico. Both women now gave in, bargaining that they would not only buy a number of expensive items from Mr Bowerbank's shop but even sell him the stolen cloth. This might have been their mistake: the honest drapers of Holborn stuck together. Refusing the offer of a bundle of hot calico, Bowerbank sent one assistant for the peace officer and another to knock on doors around Holborn, Snow Hill and Newgate Street to identify the shopmark on the stolen cloth. When the man from whose shop they had earlier taken 11 yards of printed calico walked in, Ann Clapton pretended to swoon. The men remained stony-faced. She summoned the last of her resources, jumped back on her feet, pointed a finger at her daughter and swore 'it wasn't me, it was her!'

The peace officers did not believe either of them. They were taken to Wood Street Compter (a forerunner of the police station) to be charged and held over for appearance before the magistrates, hoping one or other of their husbands would hear what had happened and be in court tomorrow to offer a security.

A classier heist was being carried out in Soho. Ann Gallant presented herself at Mrs Underhill's apartment house as a superior sort of maidservant to a superior sort of employer. She had been sent, she said, to enquire for a lodging on behalf of her employers, a French lady and gentleman currently putting up at the French hotel in Jermyn Street. Mrs Underhill's rooms were inspected and approved. The following day Ann Gallant came back with a French interpreter to supervise personally the airing of the apartment, the making of the bed and the arrangement of knick-knacks for madame and monsieur. The interpreter bowed over Mrs Underhill's hand and spoke with a charming accent. Ann Gallant placed an order for coal and checked the inventory of linen and plate which Mrs Underhill had sat up the night before to prepare.

Madame moved in with two more servants the next day. For four days all went well. The foreigners kept themselves to themselves. Mrs Underhill had found herself a tenant with some cachet for the winter (even if the tenant had not actually paid yet) and the interpreter continued to lisp and bow. So it was a rude shock when Ann Gallant woke her on Monday morning, worried that neither her mistress nor the interpreter had returned on Sunday night. Ann Gallant may have been a bad actress or one of Mrs Underhill's maids may already have discovered that madame's rooms had been stripped. A peace officer was sent for from the Litchfield Street Compter, Ann Gallant was searched and before the end of the day she was up before a magistrate on a charge that could carry a capital sentence. Alone, unable to contact her accomplices and threatened with the noose, she confessed.

The charming interpreter was a plain Englishman, Francis Bunting. He would be found, said Ann, in the French coffee-house in Jermyn Street or at the French hairdresser's in Peter Street. Taken by surprise in Peter Street by the Litchfield Street officers, at first Bunting pretended he could neither speak nor understand English. Was this not strange for an interpreter? they asked and took him the rounds of the usual dodgy pawnbrokers of Golden Square and Brewer Street, where he redeemed some of Mrs Underhill's sheets, and then before the magistrate in Bow Street, still protesting he spoke no English. The magistrate had by now managed to work out more or less what had gone on in this whole confusing story and ordered that both Bunting and Ann Gallant be detained until 'the other woman' be found. To

Bunting's discomfiture, they were taken to a compter that boasted a constable fluent in French. Resisting to the last, he now pretended it was not *French* he spoke, but *another* foreign language, which he referred to as French because, because . . . well, why, he could not say.

Eventually, he gave in and accompanied the French-speaking constable to another Soho pawnbroker to ask for a set of silver spoons back, in English. Madame was never found. Ann Gallant and Francis Bunting naturally blamed everything on her, but either madame had covered her tracks or her two employees feared reprisals as they could or would not tell the constables where to find her. 'She went by a number of names' was all they said.

By the first week of December 1788, all these 'disorderly women' (and Francis Bunting) were prisoners of law in Newgate, London, part of a turbulent population of over 700 prisoners. The condition of the cells inside was a reflection of the crisis on the streets outside, for this was the most crowded gaol in the most crowded city of England. There had been a huge growth in the population over two generations, increased mobility throughout the country, particularly in and out of the hub of London, and a sudden rise in unemployment. The nation was gripped by royal paralysis at the top and racked by too rapid a change at the bottom. Caught in between, magistrates, parish councils and peace officers were struggling to apply old rules to communities which did not conform to old patterns. The resources of law and order were overstretched.

In 1783, overcrowding in the towns worsened acutely when a disbanded army of monstrous size came home from the wars. One hundred and thirty thousand males, equivalent to two per cent of the population, were discharged when the American colonies defeated King George's British and German forces. From one month to another, London alone had to house and employ tens of thousands of men, and the effect was visible as unemployment for both sexes rose sharply. The first wave was immediate: the streets were full of cripples begging ha'pennies. The second was slower: when the men came home from war, thousands of women found themselves 'out of a place' and out on the streets. It is a familiar post-war story. Male unemployment could be solved by giving women's jobs to men and sending women back to the home – except that in the urban world of 1780s England, many did not have homes to go to. And so throughout the decade the veterans and amputees were joined by ex-shopgirls, ex-milkmaids, ex-labourers and ex-maidservants, now disorderly girls living off gin and plates of fatty meat, scraping by on pennies supplemented wherever possible by stealing from someone marginally better off.

In London, the authorities turned more frequently to repression. One evening in November 1785, the City peace officers had arrived *en masse* in St Paul's, the bridge between the City and Westminster, and began an orchestrated drive of the prostitutes who worked there away from the City and into Westminster. The same evening, the Westminster peace officers had turned up with the intention of driving the women away from Westminster and into the City. 'In consequence of these moral proceedings,' wrote *The Times* the following day, 'these wretched women must seek an asylum in the arms of old Father Thames or starve in their wretched hovels . . . A few years ago,' it continued, 'they had arrangements in shops; it is now different; needles, ribbons and the most trifling article must be supplied by a fellow six foot high or the shop is thought of no account.' Rather than punishing those women forced out of work by unemployed men, the writer suggested a tax on shopmen working in drapers, milliners, perfumers and haberdashers, all of which had been regular employers of women until a couple of years earlier.

The same year, Prime Minister Pitt's proposed tax on maidservants over the age of 15 was, Lord Surrey told the House of Lords, deeply unfair to women 'who had no other mode of obtaining a subsistence but by their domestic labour'. He, too, proposed a tax on those 'who trespassed on the natural employment of women, such as men-milliners, haberdashers, staymakers &co, &co'. *The Times* was behind him. 'Fifteen is a most dangerous time for the female sex; that thousands will be turned out of employment at that age, there is everything to be dreaded . . . when poverty and want have no relief but from the wages of prostitution.' The tax was approved nevertheless. In July of the following year, *The Times* estimated that 'upon a very modest calculation, not less than 10,000 have been added to the number of common prostitutes by Mr Pitt's tax on maidservants.' By October, it despaired. 'The height to which female prostitution is carried', it wrote, 'and is likely to increase in this capital is truly alarming . . . There are in London and its environs 50,000 common women.'

It was an acknowledged fact that unemployed maidservants were 'one of the grand sources which furnish this town with prostitutes'. Some sought desperately to avoid this fate. One was 20-year-old Mary Anderson, in Newgate since her conviction in May 1788, for which she had been sentenced to seven years' Transportation to Parts Beyond the Seas. Hers was a brief and pathetic trial, following a brief and pathetic theft. Mary Anderson was from Bristol and had come to London to find work, perhaps because some misadventure had sullied her name where she was known, perhaps because there was no work in her home parish. Alone in the capital, she could find no place and, when her money was gone, she robbed a room in Virginia Street, halfway between the Tower and Shadwell. Today, it is a grim, dank, postindustrial mess with a motorway thundering across its northern end. In 1788, it was full of small shops and cheap lodging-houses. She snatched a bundle of clothes and household linen from a room in one of these and was seen leaving with a bulge under her apron. At her trial, the woman who had caught her told the judge 'she cried and said, if I would let her go, she would not come near the house any more'. Mary Anderson's defence was equally artless: 'my friends live in Bristol; I did take the things . . . I thought I had better do that than be a common prostitute.' The choice for women out of work was bald.

Reasons for the rise in female crime and female poverty were half-known and half-expressed. Society could not yet make the leap from acknowledging that the cause of her crime might lie outside a female's control to accepting this as mitigation of her guilt. Deserving of charity, yes; compassion, certainly; some minor change in the enforcement, wording, even aim of legislation to curb the excesses of sentencing perhaps; but rehabilitation, no. It was a regrettable fact that disgraced females found 'their character is utterly gone, may never be retrieved', whereas disgraced males 'after many errors, may reform and be admitted into that same society and meet with a cordial reception as before' – but there it was, nature's way, God's will, human nature. Female crime was like terminal illness, terribly sad, sometimes brought on by circumstances outside the victims' control, but irreversible. When the number of women offending rose, as it did in the 1780s, there was not only a lack of gaol space to accommodate them but no means to absorb them back into society. 'Society' in the 1780s referred to a far smaller portion of the nation than it does now; among themselves and their own kind, more prosaic attitudes to disorderly women prevailed. But for now it was 'society' that judged them and recorded its judgements.

The problem of how to regard female offences lurked in the background in December 1788. More important was finding some way to prevent them, and nobody seemed to know how to do this. It was not that the authorities were unaware of the problem. At every level, their workload increased. Lowly peace officers were recording the effects of the post-war maladjustments in laborious longhand entries in their compter books each night. At Poultry Compter, on the edge of the City of London, one disorderly girl after another was taken up for 'wandering abroad crying in the Open Air', 'having no visible way of living and lying in the Open Air on the streets', 'running away with a Watchman's Lantern', 'making a great Noise and Disturbance', 'making use of approbrious language' and once, with greater spirit, 'chasing a Bullock down Poultry'. When the compter books, with their miserable record of disorderly lives, were brought into court at 11 o'clock prompt each morning, it was the turn of the magistrates to deal with the pickpockets, shop-lifters, prostitutes and bagsnatchers who told some pathetic and predictable story of want suffered and opportunity seized. And when the magistrates had sifted the misdemeanours from the felonies and shut their books for the day, responsibility passed up to the judges, who would have to decide how to punish this endless stream of petty criminals, with their numbingly similar stories of life lived in unremitting insecurity.

Among the women who passed each month through the courts of the Old Bailey, some had lived with family, friends or some other human connection which anchored them to a place and a social group. But many, like Mary Anderson, had lived alone, on their wits, drifting from city to city and place to place, single and cunning, left by or leaving whatever family they had, passing through friendships and partnerships which lasted a night or a week until one or the other wandered off, often picking her partner's pocket as she went. Throughout the City, Westminster, the Borough, the Ratcliff Highway and the docks of London, the 'common lodging-houses' – a combination of inn, flophouse and brothel – were full of these people. Drunks, nursing mothers, thieves, immigrants, out-of-work servants, labourers down on their luck and thousands of other unfortunates on the margins of City life slept here in dormitories, sheds, stables, lean-tos and even the privies in the yard. Beds were let by the night to singles, couples, triples or however many it took to come up with the bed-rent, sleeping head to toe in garrets where the mattresses were made of damp straw and the windows were stuffed with rags to keep out the cold and keep in an air rank with nights of foul breath, farts and copulation. A bed in a dormitory might cost 6d, 4d a head if sharing. Downstairs in the yard, it cost 3d to sleep in the straw next to the privies – the sort of money the cheapest prostitutes were backing themselves against the wall for.

Sleepers in these houses were prey to cold, damp, disease and the depredations of fellow lodgers. On 26 September 1787, Elizabeth Ayres, 28, and her friend Ann Wood, 23, had a casual lodging arrangement in a house in Goldsmith Alley (now Goldsmith Street), a tiny street connecting Gutter Lane and Wood Street, off Cheapside. They agreed that one James Roach, labourer, could share their bed for the night. He assured the court that this was for sleeping purposes only. Roach paid the women a shilling as his night's fee, undressed and climbed into bed. They waited until he was asleep, took his clothes and ran. Round the corner, Ann Wood paused to pull Roach's breeches on under her skirt and then ran on with his coat over her arm. They got as far as Plumtree Street (now Court) at the far end of Newgate Street when they were noticed and stopped by Constable Cornelius Harrigan. Why were they running with a man's coat? the constable asked. It's my husband's coat, Ann Wood told him, and I'm taking it to be mended at the tailor's. What did her husband do? He was a hackney coachman. Surely hackney coachmen did not wear that sort of coat? *My* husband is a tailor, announced Elizabeth Ayres, taking a hand. Harrigan collared them both and took them in to Edward Treadway, constable of the night at the nearest compter and a familiar figure in the Old Bailey. Officer Treadway examined the coat and decided tailors and hackney coachmen were both irrelevant as the coat did not need mending. He then examined the women and discovered Ann Wood's breeches. Both women were now in Newgate, both sentenced to Transportation to Parts Beyond the Seas.

Sleeping arrangements like Elizabeth Ayres' and Ann Wood's were normal for much of the city's population, and it was not only the possessions of the men brought back to rented beds which went missing in the night. One petty thief commonly stole from another, and a woman who had just relieved her bedmate of his watch and seals might stuff them under the pillow and find someone else had removed them in her turn by morning. It was hard for a woman who lived from bed to bed to keep even the clothes she wore safe from the gentle fingers of a stranger sharing her mattress. Coins were sewn into seams or swallowed for safety, then retrieved with a good laxative, graphically known as an 'opening medicine'. One Welsh magistrate recalled another hiding place 'in the hair . . . where decency forbids to name'. He knew of a woman who had stored 30 gold sovereigns there. But not everything could be swallowed or inserted, and necklaces were taken from around necks, coins unsewn, shoebuckles sliced off with a razor, shifts, shoes and aprons undone and removed by strangers in the night.

One step up from this squalor were private lodging-houses, such as the one from which Mary Anderson had stolen in Virginia Street. Thousands of slightly better-off transients rented furnished bedsits by the week for four or five shillings in houses like this. A few were run purely as businesses. Others were the family homes of tradesmen, shopkeepers or widows earning a second income by taking in lodgers. The ground floor was commonly taken up with trading premises and the 'one pair of stairs' (first floor) occupied by the tradesman's family. Upwards and downwards of this, the house was stuffed with tenants, each floor and room let at a graded rent and attracting a minutely differentiated clientele. A single lady eking out a pension might share the 'one pair of stairs' with the landlady; in the 'two pair of stairs', a couple of servants might double up for a week while looking for work in town; in the garret above, a servant who had been out of a place a little longer and was running short of funds might sleep for a lower rent. Cellars were the cheapest and nastiest of all. These were not basements with steps to the street, but underground rooms entered through a trapdoor in the pavement outside. If this were opened to let out cooking fumes, steam from a mangle, or the stench of a chandler's wax, drunks would regularly crash through, to the great inconvenience of all.

Women newly out of work, or newly arrived in the city, would take rooms in these houses. Renting a room, using up savings, failing to find work, pawning the furniture in order to meet the rent and then falling into ever more hopeless debt was a story heard at every Old Bailey Sessions. Some lodgers truly intended to redeem the items pawned when they were back on their feet and earning a little more. These tenants often, and mistakenly, believed that as long as everything was there when they moved out, they could pawn as they wished in the meantime.

Widow Ryan was a typical landlady of a private lodging-house, living on the one pair of stairs in her dwelling-house in Short's Gardens, Seven Dials, and renting out the other rooms by the week. Elizabeth Gosling took a room there in August 1787 at three shillings a week. If she had come from out of town, or had just left one place and was looking for another, she had chosen a hard month. Many families were away, living in their summer lodgings in Bath and Cheltenham. By mid-September, she was unable to meet her rent and first pawned a quilt worth 18d, then a sheet worth 6d. Elizabeth Gosling did not deny pawning the bedclothes to the constable who arrested her, to the magistrate or even to the judge in the Old Bailey: 'I never gave up my apartment till she took me to the office,' she told the court, clearly under the impression this exonerated her. She was wrong. She, too, went down for seven years' Transportation to Parts Beyond the Seas and by December 1788 she had been in Newgate over a year.

Among the several other women convicted of similar offences now in the cells with Elizabeth Gosling were two who had been prosecuted by the same landlady. Mrs Martha Davis owned one lodging-house in Broad Street, Bloomsbury, where Mary Stewart rented a furnished room at five shillings a week, and another in Little St Andrew's Street, Seven Dials. Like Elizabeth Gosling, Mary Stewart stayed a couple of months and then started pawning the furniture bit by bit to a pawnbroker in West Street, close to Mrs Davis's Seven Dials house.

Mary Stewart also thought that if a lodger did not leave and continued to pay the rent, she could pawn things in the meanwhile. She told the court that Mrs Davis had said she could pawn what she liked as long as everything was there when she left. This was common in Davis's houses, she said: in Little St Andrew's Street 'there is not one that has got a pair of sheets'. In fact, Mrs Davis kept a pawnbroker's shop 'and takes in the things herself; the things were pledged to pay her the rent'. Mrs Davis denied it. It may have been that she was fed up with lodgers selling her movable goods and then pleading innocence. Elizabeth Kearnon, alias Price, and her partner had moved in to Little St Andrew's Street in October 1786 and within 48 hours had pawned an iron frying-pan, a flat-iron, three blankets, a pair of linen sheets, a bed quilt, a copper saucepan – as Mrs Davis testified, 'everything in the room but the chairs and tables'. When caught, they used excuses which in the cases of Elizabeth Gosling and Mary Stewart might have been genuine but were less likely to be so for the Kearnons, whose crime shows signs of professionalism. Certainly, not all lodgers were down on their luck but with good intentions for the future. Some landladies were only a few steps up from the poverty of their tenants and could not afford to lose a flat-iron or a pair of curtains every time a room changed hands.

In lodging-houses like Mrs Davis's, landladies were not the only victims – as in the slummier common lodging-houses, tenants frequently robbed each other. A huge volume of human traffic passed through these places. New faces were constantly seen on stairs and landings; people wandered in and out and petty opportunistic theft was rife. Hannah Wigfall sublet half her bed in a St Sepulchre bedsit to Ann White for a shilling a week, then invited her friend Elizabeth Johnson, alias Lee, round. Under cover of chat, Elizabeth Johnson stole Mrs White's box from under her bed while she lay trying to sleep; she, too, was now waiting in Newgate for the authorities to decide what to do with her. In another boarding-house let out in single rooms, 17-year-old Ann Bone, alias Smith, went to visit her sister in November 1788, popped into someone else's room on her way out and took goods worth 50 shillings. An apron was identified when she was taken up the following day, tied round her waist under her petticoats so no one else could pinch it in their turn.

Elsewhere in London at the end of 1788, Charles Marsh arose at 4.45 one morning to go to work and, leaving the house through the yard, 'heard a woman's voice in the necessary'. This turned out to be Esther Curtis, 18 years old and thoroughly drunk. He asked her what she thought she was doing in his privy. She had fallen over the night before, she said, slept on the steps and was now relieving herself before moving on. It was a common enough scene, and Marsh let her go about her business. Later, he discovered she had robbed him of nearly 20 shillings' worth of clothes. He wrote off the theft to experience, reminded himself to keep the lavatory door locked in future and would have forgotten her if Esther herself had not turned up sitting on the doorstep the following day, once again blind drunk and this time without her shoes on. Marsh went for the watch. Esther's defence in court was as confused as her actions in Marsh's yard. She had met a man . . . somewhere . . . he told her to go to his lodging . . . where she had gone . . . and to take off her shoes because the landlady was ill and should not be disturbed . . .

Both common and private lodging-houses were regularly used by prostitutes, turning tricks among the sleeping clientele. Any woman could rent a bed or a room for the night and share it with others, turn and turn about as the customers came. A prostitute with a customer and nowhere to go might displace a friend from a rented bed for half an hour in return for part of the fee – or, notoriously, in return for part of the profit made by stealing and pawning his watch or breeches. Stories of prostitutes emptying the pockets of their clients and passing the contents to a friend in the shadows were as common in the Old Bailey as stories of lodgers pawning the quilt.

Not all men who lost their breeches in the night were as coy about their sleeping arrangements as James Roach (see page 10). The case of Nimrod Blampin was an outright farce, which must have cost him as much in dignity as in lost possessions. He admitted openly in court that he had picked up Rachel Hoddy on the 'cooing seats' of St James's Park when drunk and gone back with her to her lodging in Gravel Lane for a supper of salmon and beer before taking her to bed. Shortly afterwards, he turned his face to the wall and slept it all off – until seven o'clock in the morning, when he awoke to find himself naked, locked in from the outside and robbed of all his clothes and money. It was June – the situation was embarrassing rather than critical. Naked, he smashed down the door with a poker and persuaded a soldier lodging below to lend him some clothes. By the time he got to the nearest compter, Rachel's fellow lodger, Ann Hardiman, had been taken up by an alert officer of the night on her way to the pawnshop with Nimrod's shirt over her arm. She had already placed the rest of his clothes with three different pawnbrokers along Fleet Street. Once in the compter, Ann Hardiman confessed that the clothes were Blampin's, passed on by Rachel during the night, but that 'the things were given [Rachel] in lieu of cash'.

Nimrod Blampin and James Roach escaped with some damage to their dignity but with their clothes back and no personal injury sustained. They were lucky. In the rougher parts of town, a prostitute with one hand in a man's pocket often used the other to punch him in the head, or summon a partner to do it for her. Then, it was known as 'assault on the king's highway'; now, as mugging. The area most notorious for this was the Ratcliff Highway, a long, straight road leading east from the City of London to Limehouse packed with lodging-houses which sheltered gangs of prostitutes and muggers. Picking up a prostitute here was a risky business, especially if a man were alone and drink-fuddled. The whisk of dirty skirts round a corner, down an alley and into a court where a dozen vicious slum-dwellers waited to defend their own was a common experience. If prudent, the man would cut his losses and back away.

An official 'Report on Common Lodging Houses' commissioned in 1788 went into some detail on traps for the unwary punter. In particular, it described a situation repeated nightly up and down the Ratcliff Highway: 'when a prostitute has decoyed a man and robbed him, the mistress of the house has half the pay and half the plunder.' In October 1788, Mary Anson decoyed Benjamin Solomon into a house owned by Elizabeth Underhill. Underhill was a woman to make a man tremble, although Solomon, without his breeches and ready for love, was particularly vulnerable. Not only did she have the muscle to threaten him physically, but she also had the imagination to make her threat truly foul. Twenty-three-year-old Mary Anson must have been more alluring, at least in the dark streets of Shoreditch, where she picked up Solomon on his way home from a convivial evening in Hoxton Square. First he gave her a penny for a candle, next he laid out a shilling to buy her a drink, and by the time they reached St Paul's Alley, he was committed. Solomon made the grave mistake of being the first to undress. When naked from the waist down, his jingling breeches were snatched from his hand, pretty Mary Anson disappeared and in her place was Mrs Underhill. She 'demanded to know what I wanted there', he told the judge, and then threatened magnificently to 'smother me, if I talked, under six or seven load of nightsoil . . . emptied from the necessaries . . .'. Faced with death by sewage, Solomon agreed to silence. His breeches, no longer jingling, reappeared and he was shown the door, loose about the knees as his buckles had been part of the price of freedom.

Cowed, but not to the point of complete capitulation, he flapped away to find the patrol. Mary Anson was tried at the Old Bailey and sentenced to seven years' Transportation to Parts Beyond the Seas. Mrs Underhill had been ordered by the judges to be held over until the December Sessions for trial as 'accessory to the fact'. Both women were in Newgate.

Another East End twosome currently in Newgate under sentence of Transportation to Parts Beyond the Seas were Poll Randall and Mary Butler. These two had committed an even more audacious raid on Joseph Clark at a lodging-house or brothel in Cable Street owned by 25-year-old Elizabeth Sully. On the night of 10 November 1787, Joseph Clark was strolling down Cable Street with the extraordinarily incautious sum of £40 in his pocket and half a cheese on his head. When he found himself seized from behind by Poll Randall and Mary Butler and dragged into a house, it was, he explained to a bemused court, care for his cheese which prevented his putting up any resistance. Inside, his cheese was snatched and this, he went on, was why he could not leave. A wiser man might have abandoned a few shillings' worth of cheese and saved £40 in cash.

Joseph Clark held out for his cheese during half a pint of gin, a game of cards, a further half of gin and supper, although he did object as supper was suggested that 'I only want my cheese and to go home'. But suddenly the mood changed. Poll and Mary hauled him upstairs – 'you could not resist at all?' asked an incredulous judge – and forcibly undressed him. 'She threw me on the bed!' he said in his defence. 'I cried out, for God's sake do not use me ill!' It was only when Poll demanded the banknotes in his pockets that Clark realised they were not just after his cheese. Even at this dramatic point, they all had another round of beef

17

and gin, Clark still tucked up in bed. The girls were prepared to humour him for a while, but at a certain point Poll Randall ran out of patience – she wanted a drink: 'She took both my hands and put them behind me; I was afraid to make any resistance!' Both Poll Randall and Mary Butler were 13.

Five months after their trial, they were joined in the cells by Mother Sully herself and another of her brood of chicks. Sully seems to have specialised in teenage prostitutes – Mary Bateman, convicted with her in May 1788, was 14. She and her friend Elizabeth Durand had picked up James Palmer in Wellhouse Square as he returned to his lodgings in the house of a Limehouse biscuit-maker after a night getting drunk in the Minories. Palmer bought the girls a half-pint of gin each at a Wellhouse Square inn, struck terms and went with Mary Bateman to Mrs Sully's house, where they had sex. Although in court he testified 'how I went out [of her house] I do not know, I was so much in liquor', he sobered up back on the street outside when he realised he had been robbed of coat, cash and a watch worth £3, and went for the constable of the night, Joshua Grey.

The time it took Officer Grey to reach Cable Street was enough for the women to hide the watch so well that his search of Mary Bateman's room turned up nothing. However, the theft of a watch worth £3 on his patch, especially in a house as notorious as Mrs Sully's, was too serious for the constable to leave the matter there. Sometime over the next couple of days, Grey managed to get little Elizabeth Durand on her own and bully or bribe her into giving him information. Acting on this, he went back to Cable Street, brought the women in for questioning and frightened them into making a clean breast of it. He may have offered them a reduction in the value of the theft stated in the indictment to reduce it from a capital to a non-capital offence – but only if they co-operated now. Mary Bateman took Grey back to the house and showed him the watch, stuffed in Mrs Sully's mattress.

The overcrowded city of London was a curious place in the 1780s. Some areas were decidedly grand; others were irredeemably squalid. In many middling districts, the lodging-houses where strangers slept head to toe existed side by side with the respectable households of tradesmen, clerks and smaller merchants. There was a continual shifting overlap between them: the servant maid down on her luck in a Seven Dials flophouse might, with a stroke of good fortune, be maid of all work to a respectable butcher in Smithfield next week. The widow of a shopkeeper with a small private pension might lodge next door to a pickpocket or shoplifter. Even out of the world of the lodging-houses, people lived in constant intimate contact with strangers, whether tenants, fellow lodgers or servants – and this gave rise to opportunities for another of the commonest stories of female felony heard in the Old Bailey: the maidservant who pinched the silver.

'The offence of servants, in general, robbing their masters . . . is a crime which so entirely cuts up every bond of civil society that it is the duty of the Courts of Justice at all times to punish it with severity.' These were the words of the Recorder of London, James Adair, who had sentenced many of the women currently in Newgate to Transportation to Parts Beyond the Seas in his capacity as judge. His view of servant–employer relationships bore less and less relation to what really happened. Amid Georgian concerns about the number of people out of a place, there are glimpses of an almost Elizabethan fear of masterless men. However, insistence on the old bonds of duty and obedience to the master and mistress, with their financial and moral protection as quid pro quo, was becoming obsolete in this shifting world of casual employment. Few family retainers passed through the High Court; the stories told in the Old Bailey came from a world where people moved from job to job with their possessions in a box on their back, looking constantly for an extra sixpence a week, a warmer bed or better food, where

strangers were taken on as servants with a minimum of prelimi-
naries and given intimate access to the household – and dismissed
again with the same lack of thought, replaced by other floating
unknowns when necessary.

The most usual time for a maidservant to be 'turned off' by a
wealthy family was late spring, when the household prepared to
pack up the house in London and move to summer lodgings out
of town. Skeleton staffs were sometimes maintained in London,
but employers knew it would be easy to restock the attics with
maids when they returned in the autumn. Those who practised
this economy also knew that the few days between dismissal and
departure were a time to keep a specially close eye on the family
valuables. There was little surprise in Grosvenor Square in April
1788 when a local pawnbroker knocked at the door of Sir Henry
George Little, Baronet, with a crested silver tablespoon and a
description of the skivvy who had been turned off the day before.
The butler, who deposed, could not tell the court why Catherine
Hounsam had been dismissed. One can almost detect the lift of
his eyebrows at the suggestion he should be familiar with the
affairs of a kitchenmaid. Catherine comes over as slightly simple-
minded. She had taken a valuable and easily identified spoon to
a pawnbroker just round the corner and told him it had fallen off
the back of a dustcart. Off the back of a dustcart? Yes, off the
back of a dustcart, and the dustmen said that 'I might have it to
eat my porridge with'. Even the jury thought her a little lacking.
The value and circumstances of the theft required the death
sentence be passed, but the jury humbly recommended her for
mercy, 'being very young and ignorant'. In fact, she was 30 and
proved more canny in later life than one might suspect from the
ineptitude of her crime.

Catherine probably grabbed the spoon to tide her over until
she found her next place scrubbing out the scullery, and the
situation in which she, and thousands like her, found themselves
was well understood. Elizabeth Gale had done the same –

although with rather more stealth than Catherine. She was indicted of stealing goods worth the enormous amount of £17 but convicted of theft only to the value of 9d. She had been maidservant to Alexander Annesley for 16 months and, he said, was 'going away the day after the robbery'. This had occurred at night, when Gale herself woke the family and called the watch. They found the 'sideboard stripped' and, damningly, 'a neighbour's coachman under the prisoner's bed'. In her box was 9d-worth of children's clothing, and during her interrogation she admitted to having let four other men sleep under her bed during her time in service. The theft of the silver could not be pinned on her, but the theft of the clothing was enough for her to be sentenced to seven years' transportation.

There was some sympathy for dismissed maidservants as there was for the shopgirls replaced by soldiers. However, they were tarred by two brushes at once – irredeemable female and thieving servant, for there were many other servants out there stealing not because they had to but because they could. The eighteenth-century mistress of the house carried that great bunch of keys round her waist to guard against inside jobs more than outside menace. Employers who forgot to lock the tea chest or the parlour door were considered fair game, and pilfering by domestic staff was endemic in households of all sizes.

Elizabeth Parry was 21 and claimed to be freshly down from Lancashire when she went knocking on doors round the fields north of City Road in May 1787, looking for work 'in the milk business'. She struck lucky with Mrs Attewell, who took her on as cow-keeper, and she moved into the Attewell household with her box as soon as the deal was made. During the eight days she spent there, she never milked an Attewell cow or dirtied her boots in an Attewell field, as within two days she had fallen sick and taken to her bed. Mrs Attewell attended the girl in her room, paid for the attentions of an apothecary – including bleeding at thruppence the time – then came home one afternoon and found

Elizabeth gone, her own box robbed, and the money set aside for her other cow-keepers' wages stolen. Susanna Attewell might have been a poor judge of character but was experienced enough to know that if she did not get a constable to Elizabeth Parry within hours, the girl would disappear into the sea of bonnets and brown cotton gowns which swirled up and down the City Road. She moved swiftly and within a couple of hours Elizabeth Parry had been taken up. In court, she was feisty, interrupting Mrs Attewell's testimony with 'I never said any such thing!', pointing out that her mistress had also gone out the day before and the things could have been taken then and making a defiant final defence: 'the things are my own and as for money, the prosecutrix had none!'

Elizabeth Parry was a girl on the make, Catherine Hounsam a woman in distress, Elizabeth Gale somewhere in between. The story of another servant in Newgate with them was more ambiguous. Twenty-seven-year-old Rachel Turner had worked for Cleophas Comber, a wax and tallow chandler in the parish of St Martin's. He was prosperous enough to employ Rachel, two menservants and, during his wife's confinement, a nurse as well. It was when the nurse came to live in that certain clothes, linen and sauceboats went missing. Comber suspected Rachel, he later told the court, but did not wish to confront her himself and sent for Beadle Parsley. Mr Parsley listened to the master's suspicions, then questioned the maidservant and insisted on seeing her box. Inside were the silver sauceboats, and Rachel was told to fetch her cloak. A list of stolen goods was drawn up in the watchhouse before the constable, to which Rachel 'made her mark' before the judge in the Old Bailey in December 1787.

She had employed a well-known counsel, Mr Garrow, and his principal line of defence was attack: Rachel, he said, had been framed. Harassed by accusations from his wife that he was sleeping with Rachel, Cleophas Comber had hit on this solution of getting rid of the girl. She had worked for Mrs Comber blamelessly for six months. The 'curtain lectures' to Cleophas must have begun when 'the good woman was in the straw' (and, being pregnant, inclined to hysterical fancies) and only when the nurse ('always a gossip') arrived, and began insinuating that the master was getting up to no good with the maid in the back parlour. Did Mr Garrow invent this entire story or did something Rachel Turner told him put it in his mind? Nothing clear emerges from Cleophas Comber's version of events, but he is a rather shamefaced figure in Rachel's downfall. It would not be the first time a husband, especially a husband whose wife was pregnant, went knocking on the maidservant's door one night and tried to buy her off with a hasty gift off the mantelpiece the next morning.

Chapter Two

Fair British Nymphs

One of the most popular characters in late-eighteenth-century literature was the fallen woman. The girl of good family seduced and betrayed by a plausible villain was particularly fascinating. Chapbooks published collections of *True Stories!* with a historical or moral twist which were the staple reading material of the literate lower-middle classes. They used the fallen woman as their single most frequent character. The sixteen 'histories' of one chapbook include two seduced-and-betrayed heroines; two morality tales ('The Happy Negro' and 'Sunday School Ben') and two loosely truthful fifteenth-century bodice-rippers. Blue-Eyed Patty Freelove, who dressed as a soldier to follow her lover into the Botany Bay Rangers, represents another contemporary obsession: female cross-dressers masquerading as marines or soldiers in order to accomplish heroic deeds feature in three of the sixteen stories.

The fictional story of Louisa Harewood, published in another chapbook, was affectingly recounted in the form of a confessional letter to her parents on the eve of her departure for Botany Bay and followed by a little verse:

> Ye fair British nymphs of beauty and fame too
> listen to my story, beware of my fate too
> once like you I was happy, like you I was blest,

though now I am wretched with sorrow oppresst
oh! pity my sorrows! ah, me, well-a-day,
as a convict I'm forced now to Botany Bay!

. . . and all because of a chance meeting with Lieutenant Henry Harris at the home of the local squire. One thing led to another with the handsome lieutenant and 'one fatal evening I resigned, with my virgin innocence, the peace of my soul, your care and protection and intailed a series of lasting miseries on myself' when Henry persuaded her to elope. After only a few blissful weeks, he was called to his ship at Portsmouth and left, swearing 'eternal constancy' and a promise 'to transmit me money and at every opportunity to write to me which, alas! he never fulfilled'. At length, Louisa spent her last money on the coach to Portsmouth, found lodgings and sent word to Henry. They had another two days together before she learned his ship was under way, a shock which sent her into a decline from which she emerged 'mistress of only four guineas'. Forced to pawn her clothes and then '(though with the utmost regret) to make free with the furniture of my lodgings', she was prosecuted and sentenced to seven years in Botany Bay.

It is easy to mock moralistic tales like Louisa Harewood's, bursting with repressed sexual excitement – so easy that it is a shock to realise how closely they could conform to the truth. One young girl, whose story could have been the model for Louisa Harewood, was in gaol 250 miles north of London. Mary Rose and another girl who was to become her best friend, Sarah Whitelam, were natives of Lincolnshire, a long, flat, fenny county in the east of England. They were among a handful of disorderly girls sentenced to Transportation to Parts Beyond the Seas by the judges of the Norfolk Circuit in 1787.

Lincolnshire was too far away and too uncompromisingly rural for its affairs to be of much interest to the cities, especially the capital, but in 1788 it had achieved a claim to fame. This was the year that King George III suffered his worst bout yet of insanity, and the doctor brought to attend him where he raved at Kew was a Lincolnshire man. The hopes of Prime Minister Pitt and the king's party rested on Dr Willis's method of plain speaking and hot poultices. Dr Willis, however, was of low birth. Premier Lincolnshire bigwig of the age was Sir Joseph Banks of Revesby Hall, President of the Royal Society, sponsor to geographical and botanical missions all over the globe and, almost two decades earlier, gentleman passenger with Captain Cook on the voyage of exploration and discovery which took him to New South Wales in 1770.

Neither Dr Willis nor Sir Joseph Banks had ever heard of Sarah Whitelam, 18 years old and recorded only as 'spinster of Tealby' at her trial at the Kesteven Quarter Sessions of April 1787 and now in Kesteven Gaol. She had been convicted of stealing, 'with force and arms', an enormous haul, including: 'One Raven Grey Coventry Gown, One white Ground Cotton Gown with Red and laylock Stripes, One Norwich Crape Gown, one pink quilted pettycoat, 7 yards of Black Calomanco, 1 pair of Women's Stays, One Black Sattin Cloak, One Red Duffin Cloak, 1 Fine White Lawn Apron, One Chocoloate Ground Silk Handkerchief, One red and black silk handkerchief, One Black Silk handkerchief, One Women's Black Silk hat, three White Linen Aprons, two Check'd Linen and Cotton Aprons, one pair of leather Shoes and one Pair of Plaited Shoebuckles' worth a total of 51 shillings. Any records illuminating the circumstances in which she stole have not survived or have not been found. She probably committed one of the eighteenth-century staples: robbed her mistress or broke into the room next door in a lodging-house. Not much can be inferred from 'force and arms'. This could cover anything from shoving someone out of the way to get to the door to fully fledged axe-wielding. She cannot have been carrying any very threatening weapon or this, combined with the fact that the value of her theft was over 39 shillings, would have brought a death sentence.

In Lincoln, Mary Rose – aged 16, according to some records, 20, according to others – was preparing to spend her second Christmas in the city gaol. Mary Rose's situation was rather different from Sarah Whitelam's for, by December 1788, Sir Joseph Banks of Revesby Hall was taking a personal interest in her case. He had been alerted to it by other local worthies, all, it seems, distressed by the story of this real-life Louisa Harewood with the pretty face, the romantic name and the story of love betrayed.

In the *Lincoln, Rutland and Stamford Mercury* of 26 December 1788, one of them had an extraordinary poem published:

On MARY ROSE, a young girl about 16 or 17 years of age, a prisoner in Lincoln City Gaol . . . for a petty offence:

> When clustering clouds deform the sky,
> And winter reigns in all her might,
> When biting winds with keen-edge fly
> And stop the river's rippling tide,
> O then, ye truly good and great,
> Ye Howards of old Lincoln Town,
> O think upon the prison-grate
> Where Horror dwells with dismal frown.
>
> To chace light slumber far away,
> The pearly morn which shines so bright
> Did beam around a double ray
> Upon the sable breast of night.
> 'Twas then my wandering thoughts did bend
> To Lincoln prison-dreary cell
> Where weeks and months, without a friend,
> A ROSE, distress'd, is forc'd to dwell.
>
> Alas, poor girl, thy lot is hard

On straw to rest, from year to year.
The cheerful sun from thee is barr'd
Thy only solace is a tear,
Thy prison-seat, a cold, damp stone,
Thy dwelling-place, a murky cave.
Give me, kind fate, a better home.
That place of rest – a silent grave.

Until her mid- or late teens, it seems Mary Rose had lived blamelessly at home with her parents, part of a close family of middling income, working the land in Lincolnshire, destined for marriage to a son off a neighbouring farm and a tranquil life similar to the one her mother and grandmother had led, no different from dozens of other farmers' daughters all over the county. This all changed when she met an officer who was temporarily stationed there.

For some reason, marriage was not possible. She may still have been under 16. It could be that her family disapproved or thought she was too young. More probably, it was his family or senior officers who disapproved of a match between a young gentleman and a farmer's daughter. Perhaps the question of marriage was never raised at all if the social differences between them were great, but Mary was persuaded her officer would look after her nevertheless. They (or certainly she) fell in love and one night she eloped from the family farm to lodgings in Lincoln.

Her parents woke to find her gone. Whatever they did on discovering her absence, they had to do it immediately – within hours their little girl would be an irredeemably fallen woman and the family disgraced. Mary Rose was not a penniless maidservant with tuppence and a spare shift to her name. With a personal income of £20 per year when she turned 21, she represented some considerable property and a respected local name. Presumably, her family mounted a frantic early-morning search throughout the farm, the lanes and the fields on their neighbours' lands and sent farmhands galloping into the village to enquire if anyone had seen her pass through. At some point the realisation that she had run off with that officer occurred. Her family must already have known of his existence; they had probably entertained him to family meals and musical entertainments in their own farm parlour and seen him at dances and the more genteel inns of Lincoln on market day. It cannot have taken long for the Rose family to guess what Mary had done.

The only thing that would have saved her from scandal was immediate capture or immediate marriage, and neither of these happened. Within days, possibly hours, of leaving her parents' house, Mary Rose had shared a bed with her officer. Perhaps he truly meant to marry her, and her flight was a means of forcing her father's hand; possibly he had always meant to abandon her later. Either way, his own hand was now forced by events as, within weeks of their elopement, his regiment was posted abroad and he left his teenage mistress in lodgings to await his return. It seems he behaved decently, leaving money with the landlady to cover the expense of Mary's board and lodging until he should return. The officer emerges from the story ambiguous but with his honour more or less intact. The landlady turns out a real villain.

However Mary and her lover passed themselves off to Anne Kestleby, landlady of their Lincoln lodging-house, she quickly summed up the situation. Mrs Kestleby's behaviour towards Mary when her officer had left reveals how much consideration could be expected by a girl who threw away respectability for love. As far as the landlady was concerned, she had forfeited her right to the protection of her family, had chosen to become a moral outcast and, with her only male protector on his way to France, would have to take what was coming to her. Mrs Kestleby had her eyes on the cash the officer had left, and what easier way of getting rid of the girl than accusing her of stealing furnishings from her lodgings? The accusation would be immediately plausible to a magistrate, especially when he was made aware of the girl's circumstances. Mary Rose was charged and taken before a magistrate who, faced with evidence of a felony and a witness, had no choice but to hold her over for trial by a High Court judge at the next Assizes of the Norfolk Circuit. She was taken into the cells of Lincoln City Gaol to wait.

What had happened to Mary Rose is what happened to Louisa Harewood and Lydia Bennett, and the frequency with which this plot-line is used in everything from chapbooks to Jane Austen indicates the fascination exerted by sexual downfall. Lydia at least fled from Hampshire to London with her handsome schemer, where nobody would recognise her, and the family was given some time to react. The Bennett family was also – and crucially to the plot – blessed by Mr Darcy, who beat up his caddish stepbrother and saved the day. No one came forward to save Mary Rose from Lincoln City Gaol.

Mr Justice Heath entered Lincoln late one afternoon in May 1787, escorted by the sheriff's men in full livery. He was welcomed by Sheriff Theophilus Buckworth, accommodated in an inn and called on by the good and the great of the county. The Lent Assizes opened the following day with the usual pomp. There were only ten accused felons to be tried in the Lincoln courthouse, but the ritual of calling the names of every member of the commission of peace, followed by the names of every mayor, coroner, steward, bailiff and constable took place in Lincoln with the same heavy dignity as in the Old Bailey, where hundreds of felons were processed each Sessions. The members of the Grand Jury filed in, those lumpen middle-aged men of property on whose intelligence and disinterest the entire system ultimately relied. They were charged and sworn in, the judge intoned some rambling, generic homily on the greatness of the English constitution, the common law, George III, liberty, property and morality, and then they filed back out into a private chamber to hear the Sessions Clerk read the bills of indictment.

This was all rather dull for the audience assembled on rickety benches in the public galleries. 'The weather being fine, drew a greater number of people to this assize than has been known for many years', the *Lincoln Mercury* reported. They fidgeted and passed refreshments. If there was a man of consequence on the Grand Jury, some handsome landowner or young squire whom the middling sort rarely got a look at, this enlivened the early tedious hours of the Assize, but what they were really waiting for was the thrill of seeing felons in irons stumble up from the gaol and tell their stories. If these involved violence or illicit passion, so much the better. It may not have been the fine weather that drew such a crowd to the Lent Assizes but rather the particularly juicy selection due to stand at the bar: two murderers and one fallen female of good family.

The prosecutors and witnesses in each case were now summoned before Justice Heath to be sworn and then led into the Grand Jury's room, where they gave their evidence away from the public. Finally, the ten accused felons from the City and Castle Gaols were all brought in together. The public galleries sat up straight and commented on their appearance and prospects. Any whose indictments the Grand Jury had already dismissed were removed; the rest stepped forward, one by one, raised their hand to acknowledge their name, were asked how they pled, and replied.

'How will you be tried?' the clerk asked William Rawby.

'By God and by my country.' It was the only possible answer.

'How will you be tried?' he asked Mary Rose, John Lee and John Thompson.

'By God and by my country.'

Now a petty jury of 12 men was assembled and sworn, and finally the public galleries stopped chatting as the sad, compelling stories of the prisoners were told. It was the high point of the day, but brief: hearings were conducted at a cracking pace, and if the accused was in the slightest slow-witted, he would be pronounced innocent or guilty before he realised his case was being heard. Character witnesses could be called by the defendant, but it is unlikely Mary Rose had anyone 'to her character' in May 1787. Anne Kestleby, the spiteful landlady, told her story, Mary Rose stood, probably silent, at the bar, the jury went into a brief huddle, emerged, was asked its verdict and pronounced her guilty. The public buzzed. She was removed from the courtroom. If this Assize followed the normal pattern, when verdict had been pronounced on all ten cases, Mr Justice Heath left the bench and was entertained to a dinner as guest of the sheriff. They discussed the affairs of the county and its notables, the health of the king and probably the state of the county's finances with reference to how many felons it could afford to keep in its gaols. The prisoners waited. After pudding, the judge re-entered the courtroom, belched and passed sentence.

'Can you offer any reason that judgement should not be passed upon you?' he asked.

'No,' they replied.

Sentences followed. John Lee and John Thompson, housebreakers, and Mary Rose, thief, seven years' Transportation to Parts Beyond the Seas. William Rawby, murderer of his maidservant, execution on the morrow.

By four o'clock, it was all over. Justice Heath left town to judge the felons of Nottingham and Stafford, and the farmers in from the villages got back in their carts and drove home. Mary Rose was taken back to the cells of the Lower Gaol. She must have despaired. She would spend the next 20 months in the City Gaol, four decaying cells in the basement of a house next door to the Guildhall, three steps below street level. Her only light came from small grated windows through which people outside could kneel on the pavement and hand in food and liquor. Two cells were for males, two for females. As in all gaols, debtors and felons were kept separately when space allowed, and Mary was probably alone for much of her first months in the City Gaol.

Female felons here were few. It gave her a little more space; it meant the bucket in the corner contained no one's waste but hers, but it also meant loneliness and time to dwell on her future.

Two months before Mary Rose was incarcerated in Lincoln and Sarah Whitelam in Kesteven, several gaols in the county of Lincolnshire had expelled a part of their long-term population. Felons sentenced to Transportation to Parts Beyond the Seas had been taken south for embarkation on the first fleet to Botany Bay in New South Wales, the latest savage isle approved for the exile of British convicts. William Douglas, from Horncastle; Mary Groves, a Lincoln girl who stole a bag containing 13 guineas; Mary Harrison, who had stolen bills of exchange out of a letter in Gainsborough post office; John Irvine, alias Aderson, alias Law, a quack and nostrum-monger (a seller of spurious medical recipes), sentenced in 1784 for the theft of a silver cup; Paul Page, condemned to hang for housebreaking and reprieved on condition he go to Botany Bay; pickpocket George Robinson from Market Rasen; Thomas Saunderson, shopbreaker; James Stow, thief; John Mowbray, who had stolen a silver watch; William Sands, who had stolen a mare; Mary Pinder, of whom nothing is known; and Rebecca Bolton, wife of Thomas, and her eight-month-old baby all embarked on the ships in London. Mary Rose and Sarah Whitelam had missed the boat by weeks.

During the early months of their time in gaol, the two girls may have been glad of it. A week after Mary Rose's trial, the *Lincoln Mercury* published a cheerful passage:

The ships bound to Botany Bay have carried off near 1,000 felons . . . This mode of transportation is to take place once a year, when all felons convicted within the period will be assembled and sent off together . . . The transportation to Botany Bay has the advantage of the former mode of Trans-portation to America, in securing the kingdom from the dread of being again infected with these pernicious members of society. From the mortality which has already taken place on the transports, it is supposed not more than 1 in 5 will survive the voyage; and should the remainder live to the expiration of their sentence, they can never pay the expence of a passage home.

It would become clear during the dreary year and a half which Mary Rose and Sarah Whitelam spent in Lincolnshire gaols that this tidy plan for annual expulsions was not going to work. In November 1787, the *Mercury* still believed all was proceeding smoothly with the next fleet: 'the ships bound for Botany Bay', it reported (on information from London) 'are expected to sail at the latter end of next month.' In February, the ships had still not sailed, but seven male prisoners from Lincoln Castle Gaol had been conveyed in prison-wagons to Portsmouth in readiness. In mid-June 1788, five more men joined them from Oakham Gaol. By December 1788, the ships for Botany Bay were still in the yards of Deptford, the felons taken south in February and May were living aboard prison ships in Portsmouth Harbour, and Mary Rose and Sarah Whitelam had served 18 months of their seven-year sentence of Transportation to Parts Beyond the Seas without leaving Lincolnshire.

Sarah's family lived in Lincolnshire and had not abandoned their daughter. They would have brought her gifts of food, clean linen, small things to palliate the discomfort of her communal cell. Women in country gaols like Sarah's were let out on parole during the summer to help with the harvest on the local farms, returning to the cells or the custody of a trusted farmer each night. No records of any petition for remission of her sentence have survived, and it is unlikely that any was made: she had been found guilty of a crime that carried the death penalty and had been sentenced only to transportation. She would not receive more clemency than this.

Mary Rose was suffering badly. Transportation to Botany Bay

had been a dreadful prospect in spring 1787, but by December 1788 it had apparently become preferable to life in the City Gaol. Something of Mary's desperation can be imagined. Her family seemed to have abandoned her; her officer was clearly not coming back; in 18 months she had had no fresh air, or any exercise beyond what a cell no larger than 13 square feet allowed; she was a girl with a sexual history, the natural target for sexual insult and possibly attack by the turnkeys.

However, someone from her former, relatively privileged life must have remained in touch with her as, during 1788, Mary collected sponsors. She was a determined lass, or a very lucky one, because Sir Joseph Banks had taken up her cause. At Christmas, a Mr Vanniel went to call on her, apparently at the request of the mayor, possibly himself responding to a letter from Sir Joseph. There seems to have been no request pending for a pardon whose progress he wished to discuss, nor scheme to farm out the city prisoners to open cells in the country towns which she might have wished to join, so it seems most likely he went to sound her out about being among the first candidates for transportation on the second fleet to Botany Bay, New South Wales.

Sir Joseph Banks had been closely involved in the establishment of the New South Wales colony. As a young and ambitious man, he had spent three years with Captain Cook on a voyage that took him to the islands of the South Seas, New Zealand and then to the strange southern continent which went by a variety of names but was most often known as New Holland. The explorers named the eastern part of this country New South Wales and claimed it for Britain. The Dutch had not revisited the unfriendly shore to which they had given their name for over a century; it was unlikely they would dispute possession. Botany Bay was also given its European name during this voyage, in honour of the variety and exotic nature of the specimens Sir Joseph collected there. Some of these were displayed in hugely popular exhibitions when the explorers returned in 1771. The voyage and exhibitions had made Banks's name, and since then he had vigorously promoted himself as an expert on antipodean affairs. It had been partly on his recommendation that the Secretary of State for Home and Colonial Affairs, Lord Sydney, had plumped for New South Wales as a suitable place to send felons sentenced to Transportation to Parts Beyond the Seas 15 years later.

In 1786, the Banks–Sydney project for a penal colony in New South Wales was approved and, the same month Mary Rose and Sarah Whitelam were convicted in Lincolnshire, 11 ships left Portsmouth for New South Wales with the first batch of convict labour aboard. By the time Mr Vanniel called on Mary Rose in Lincoln City Gaol, a second fleet of convicts should already have joined the first but still no lists of names had been drawn up and only one transport had been commissioned. Nevertheless, the possibility of including some of the Lincolnshire felons among those on the next ship out, with a little behind-the-scenes pushing from Sir Joseph, may have been what was discussed between Mr Vanniel and Mary Rose in December 1788. 'She seemed eager to go to Botany Bay', wrote Mr Vanniel to the mayor on 28 December; indeed, 'she is very willing to go any where sooner than remain in that horrid place.' A week or so after this meeting was reported to the mayor, thence to Sir Joseph Banks, her case was discussed at a parish or city council meeting. Mentions of Sir Joseph and Botany Bay were made on one side, a hint at the desirability of using local influence to get some of their felons off parish expenses and on to national ones. The other side pointed out that getting the girl south to London for embarkation would cost the parish £10.12s. for the coach and the services of a turnkey to accompany her. Someone also mentioned darkly that according to his information Mary Rose was 'a bad one'. All this was reported back to Banks, who overrode objections by offering personally to contribute to the cost of Mary's transport. By February, the decision was made and the Lincoln council was waiting for the official order from Lord Sydney to bring her south on the first leg of her voyage from Lincolnshire to New South Wales. Meanwhile, 'a trifle of pocket money' was being raised for her.

Thirteen thousand miles away, the convicts who had left Lincoln in March 1787 had arrived in New South Wales with the rest of the first fleet in January 1788. Nobody back in England yet knew it, but their camp was not at Botany Bay, for the land here had been found barren and exposed. Instead, the colonists had settled round a small bay a few miles down a river that had also been spotted during the 1770 voyage. They named it Sydney Cove. Here, the soil seemed more fertile, the waters of the creek at the head of the cove were plentiful and clean and the sea shelved sharply away from the land, which would allow future ships to come close in to a future wharf.

By December 1788, Sydney Cove was a British garrison town at the edge of an Aboriginal continent, a labour camp worked by convicts, guarded by a military presence of 250 men, governed by a handful of civil appointments reporting to Britain's newest colonial governor, Arthur Phillip. From their base camp, some of the settlers had penetrated 15 miles inland and founded a village, named Rose Hill, at the head of the river. Others had sailed 1,000 miles north-east into the Pacific to found another on Norfolk Island, also noted by Captain Cook and Sir Joseph when they sailed past 18 years earlier. A 5,000-mile round trip of at least four months' sailing separated the garrison from its nearest European neighbours, the Dutch, who had trading settlements at Batavia (Jakarta) to the north and Cape Town to the east. Unknown thousands of miles of earth hung above them. No more isolated European settlement existed on the globe.

The first fleet to Botany Bay had left England with food supplies calculated for six months at sea and one year after arrival, a promise from Secretary Sydney that relief would arrive within that year and the expectation that before then they would have achieved some measure of self-sufficiency. The plans had gone awry. They had brought livestock with them to breed, but many animals had fallen sick between Cape Town and New South Wales or had disappeared into the bush. They had also brought seed from the Cape, but it had germinated at sea and was useless on arrival. The soil among the little huts they had built on the slopes of Sydney Cove was infertile. Earth on the adjoining headland and the islands in the river had been turned and sowed but could not be made to produce sufficient greens to support the camp. The land immediately around them lacked natural fertility and could only have been made fertile with buckets of manure, for which they needed animals and, indeed, buckets, and ploughs, hoes, axes, carthorses, carts, gardeners and agricultural labourers, people with some knowledge of horticulture and husbandry, people who could yoke a horse and knew what use to make of its dung. Governor Phillip had none of these. What he had was gangs of male city-dwellers who had picked pockets in Covent Garden and Shoreditch, or stolen the furniture out of lodgings in Bristol and Hull, yoked into carts made of green wood with wheels imperfectly round, bumping along dirt tracks around the cove. He had gangs of female city-dwellers, who had grabbed from shops in Holborn or stolen the mistress's silver in Liverpool, now grubbing along the shoreline for bits of oyster shell to grind into lime to hold their huts together. He had squads of sullen military who squabbled among themselves over questions of precedence and honour and considered the duties of camp guard below their dignity.

The little colony at Sydney Cove was the latest in a series of camps manned by unsuitably dressed Europeans beating their way into the bush of an unknown continent. European governments had been sending colonial advance parties overseas for more than two centuries, to encourage trade, rid the home country of undesirables and prevent another country from getting there first. Sydney Cove was established for these three classic reasons, and in December 1788 it was suffering the problems of all young, male-dominated colonies far from home.

When the settlement was first promoted in the 1770s, officials had to calculate how to keep the place supplied until it became self-supporting. Discussions were not limited to seed, cattle and bricks. Provision of women was also vital, to keep up numbers and safeguard against dangerous urges. 'Without a sufficient proportion of that sex, it is well-known that it would be impossible to preserve the settlement from gross irregularities', wrote a prim functionary. Governor Phillip took a ferocious view of potential 'irregularities': he thought that anyone caught pants down in the act of sodomy should be taken to New Zealand and handed to the Maoris to be eaten. 'The very small proportion of females', Phillip wrote in one of his first dispatches home, 'makes the sending out an additional number absolutely necessary.'

The difficulty of finding sufficient females had been debated with some imagination. In 1786, advisers to Lord Sydney had suggested they be obtained from the Friendly Islands (now Tonga) and New Caledonia 'from whence any number may be procured without difficulty'. Both Sydney and Governor Phillip had originally agreed that a procurement of dusky beauties would be the happiest arrangement to keep the colony pure in deed, and the plan was incorporated into Phillip's official instructions (although with the proviso that no 'compulsive measures and fallacious pretences' be used to obtain them). By the time Phillip sent his first letters home from the colony in 1788, he had revised his opinions: 'to send for women from the Islands, in our present situation, would answer no purpose than that of bringing them to pine away in misery.' Sydney Cove was not the tropical paradise suitable for girls in grass skirts that had been optimistically assumed in London.

Of the 1,079 people on the 1787 fleet to Botany Bay, 259 were officials or marines, 35 of whom were accompanied by their wives. Women convicts numbered 193, insufficient to prevent irregularities among the governing classes, let alone to iron them out among the convicts. If the settlement were to grow, male emigrants and emancipated convicts had to take a long-term interest in its future and, if this were to happen, females had to be available. It was neither a new problem nor a difficult one to solve. The transportation of women felons from the mother country was the traditional answer. Steady supplies had been crossing the Atlantic and Indian Oceans to older colonies for decades, through established routes and dealers, principally to the Americas and the East Indies. Sixty thousand men and women from the British Isles had already left the mother country as transported felons to these plantations and trading stations before New South Wales was established. It would be easy to transfer the American system to the new colony. Once there, the women would provide the essential stabilising influence of femininity, as wives and concubines. The new colonial government in New South Wales was quite clear as to their role. It would not be long before some of the male convicts already in the colony were emancipated; to keep them there, and productive, they would require land, assistance in clearing and tilling it, assigned labour from other convicts who still had time left to serve, and a wife. It had been decided, therefore, that if a man married, he would be entitled to 50 acres of ground, with ten extra for each child born. If he remained single, he would be entitled to only 30. As a plan to ensure steady colonial growth, it was sensible and pragmatic, but it required a stock of pliant potential wives.

It was not planned that all incoming females become certified wives. There was a place for the unmarried mate in the colony. Lord Sydney had estimated that 200 women from the islands of the Pacific would 'suffice as companions for the men', and by 'the men' he meant other ranks, not convicts. As the islanders were staying put on their islands, an alternative source of comfort women had to be supplied. What now seems an astonishing piece of Georgian hypocrisy was all utterly normal to men like Commodore Phillip and Secretary Sydney. They were versed in the ways and needs of young colonies and familiar with the warped colonial version of the household. The role of colonial comfort women was so well established that many commentators would refer to them, especially to those appointed to servicemen of rank, as 'wives' – which, a visitor to Sydney Cove would write in five years' time, 'every officer, settler and soldier is entitled to and few are without'. Sydney Cove had immediately followed the social model of colonial garrison towns elsewhere in the world, of unions neither partner expected to be permanent. Already there was scarcely a marine in the colony who did not have his 'wife'; nor officer, clerk, surgeon, surgeon's assistant, or anyone in any position that carried privilege. The only exception in the colony seems to have been the governor himself – and this may be due to gaps in the records rather than chastity in the big house.

Governor Phillip believed that encouraging convicts to marry among themselves would be conducive to decency and good order also in the lowest section of society. However, he was aware that marriage would not mop up the sexual energy of a male-dominated colony and that young men do, after all, have those undeniable needs. One of the suggestions he made to Lord Sydney before setting off overseas was the creation of a whores' ghetto staffed by 'the most abandoned' – whom he seems to have thought would soon reveal themselves – where they would be 'permitted to receive the visits of the convicts in the limits allotted to them and under certain restrictions'. This would allow the rest, strictly virtuous, to be kept under wraps pending wifehood with convicts or concubinage with the military.

These letters from Governor Phillip outlining the breeding prospects of the new colony and other matters for the attention of Lord Sydney were, in December 1788, aboard two separate convoys. Of the 11 ships that had taken the fleet out in 1787, two were to remain permanently in the colony and the other nine would return to England. Three had been contracted by the Admiralty only as far as Sydney Cove; thereafter, they were under contract from the East India Company to return via Canton, where they would pick up a cargo of tea. They left Sydney Cove in May 1788. The next ships would return to England direct. They left in July and, by December, had rounded the Horn and were off the coast of Brazil, heading north. Each convoy of ships, as it left for home, took with it heartfelt dispatches from Governor Phillip. He described baldly the state of the colony and less baldly his fears that it would have to be closed down unless it were better supported in this earliest and most vulnerable stage of its development. Phillip was a believer in New South Wales: he believed the soil would yield, the timber would fall, the savages would become friends, the seas would give up fish and turtle, and that British men of war and traders would within very few years be nestling side by side in Sydney Cove. But he knew these ambitions could not be realised using the material supplied him by the British government when it filled the holds and decks of the first fleet in May 1787. His dispatches state over and over again his basic needs: more food, more skilled men, and more females, in that order.

Chapter Three

Gaol Fever

By December 1788, 151 female convicts were living in three female cells in Newgate, which had been built to house a maximum of 70. They lived on rations fixed for that theoretical maximum and not for the number actually confined. Each cell had one window opening on to an interior well. There were no beds. Instead, there was a ramp at one end of the room with a wooden beam fixed to its top end which served as mattress and pillow. To sleep on the ramp and beam was a privilege, to be paid for weekly. To rent a blanket woven of raw hemp cost extra. Those who could afford neither curled up together on stone slabs awash with saliva and urine. Before the cells were opened each morning, turnkeys would drink a glass of spirits to keep them from fainting, for the 'putrid stream or myasma' was enough to knock them off their feet.

The population of Newgate was malnourished, debilitated, cold, inadequately clothed, and infested with disease-bearing lice. Its cells were a happy home for typhus. For some time Mr Simpson, surgeon to the gaol, had been personally subbing gaol funds to pay for medicines and employ extra apothecaries. There was nothing new about this in the 1780s: the gaols went into crisis each winter and generally staggered through until spring providing nothing terrible happened. But the winter of 1788 was exceptionally severe; the gaols were hopelessly crowded and there were not enough funds in the pot to pay for food, let alone medicine.

One morning in November 1788, Surgeon Simpson was summoned to the wards. A prisoner was displaying unmistakable signs of 'the fever'. The surgeon backed out and reported straight away to the governor. Given conditions in the gaol, both knew they could have an epidemic on their hands.

During November and early December, while gaol staff struggled to contain the fever among prisoners already in the cells, new prisoners were being brought in by harassed peace officers and constables of the night from compters all over London. Ann Clapton and Charlotte Marsh came in on the Wood Street Compter wagon on 5 December. Mary Arnold, caught picking pockets among the livery stables of Long Acre, and Mary Oakley, caught doing the same thing on Holborn, came in from Poultry. 'Housebreaker' Esther Curtis, who had got drunk in the privies, was brought in from Tothill. Ann Bone, alias Smith, Ratcliff prostitute Jane Walters and her boyfriend John Dearman, and fraudster Ann Gallant and her accomplice Francis Bunting all arrived at the end of the month from City compters. They had been 'cast for law' at the next Sessions at the Old Bailey, due to begin on 10 December.

The previous Old Bailey Sessions had finished six weeks earlier. Newgate was now housing not only those who had since been brought in to await trial but all those who had been sentenced to execution or transportation during the previous Sessions. Throughout 1788 the overall number in the gaol would rise to a peak between each Sessions as anything from 75 to 200 new prisoners were brought in. About a fifth of these would be the newly convicted; the rest were prisoners for law brought in for trial. A part of this prisoner for law list would be convicted after each Sessions, its names transcribed on to a different list in the prison's vast registers, and become part of the gaol's long-term population which, month by month, had grown to its present unsustainable level.

The final tally of felons at the end of October 1788 was: 18 awaiting execution, 1 sentenced to transportation to the Americas, 4 to transportation to Africa, 4 to transportation to New South Wales and 279 to Transportation to Parts Beyond the Seas. To these were added the long lists of debtors who made up more than half the gaol's population. By 10 December, 141 prisoners for law had been brought in for the next court Sessions and there were over 800 people in the cells. The gaol population now exceeded the number for which it had been built ten years previously by almost 300 per cent. The situation was unmanageable, and still the disorderly girls, the debtors, the petty thieves, and the muggers arrived each day, requiring space, bedding, food, air.

It was in these alarming conditions that the last Sessions of 1788 opened in the High Court of London. The courts backed directly on to Newgate. These two institutions ran the entire length of Old Bailey, the north–south alleyway connecting Holborn and Ludgate Hill at the ancient boundary of the City of London. The gaol was connected to the High Court by Dead Man's Walk, an underground passageway down which prisoners were led to the bar. Yards from the courtrooms, at the other end of this passageway, the fever was rampant. Over four days, in the worst of the winter weather, judges, jurors, witnesses and court officials sat or stood in courtrooms whose doors and windows were kept wide open to the snow and pelting rain for fear of infection from the prisoners brought up from the cells. The courtrooms had been washed with wine and vinegar, and herbs were burned throughout the day on open braziers. Small amounts of sulphur and tobacco were exploded into the rooms. Juries, counsel and judges chewed on garlic, citrus peel, cardamom and caraway seeds to prevent infection from the prisoners' breath.

The first day of the December Sessions was raw. Prisoners for law huddled and coughed on the stairs leading up from Dead Man's Walk, where a Bible, a prayer book and a candlestick were chained to the walls. At nine in the morning the Lord Mayor, in robe, hat and chain, was driven from the Mansion House to the Old Bailey, attended by the Recorder of the City of London, the Serjeant at Arms, carrying his mace, the Sword Bearer, bearing his sword, and the City Marshal. At the Old Bailey they were ceremoniously received by Mr Bloxham, Sheriff of the City of London, and escorted inside. The Lord Mayor entered Courtroom One, the largest of the three, and arranged himself beneath the Sword of Justice. The other two judges were taken by the aldermen and sheriffs to Courtrooms Two and Three. Juries were sworn and penned into wooden enclosures.

When the courts finally opened for business, justice was brisk. Mary Dowling, for shoplifting on Holborn – transportation; Mary Oakley, Matilda Johnson and Mary Arnold, for picking pockets – transportation; Ann Bone, alias Smith, for stealing an apron – transportation; Charlotte Thomas Marsh and Ann William Clapton, for the theft of calico on Snow Hill – transportation; and Ann Gallant, for theft in a dwelling-house in Soho – transportation. Back into the cells they went, for the clerks to transcribe their names on to a different list.

The penal code of the late eighteenth century was an inadequate and crude instrument by which to regulate the country's affairs, even in the view of contemporaries. It had been built up haphazardly and piecemeal over the centuries, with sudden splurges of law-making whenever there was a crime wave. Theoretically, capital crimes (or double felonies), as formally summarised in the written report on each Old Bailey Sessions, were:

Arson, Burglary, Beast-Stealing, Coining, Forgery, Highway Robbery, House-Breaking, Horse-Stealing, Murder, Manslaughter, Privately stealing, Rape, Robbery in a Dwelling-House, Robbing the Mails, Robbing the Post Office, Rioters,

Stealing in a Dwelling-House, Shop-Lifting, Sheep-Stealing, Stealing on board a Ship or Barge, Treason, Unlawfully shooting.

However, it was not as simple as this. Most thefts came under the heading of single felony but became double felonies in certain circumstances regarding value and location of the offence. These had been decided on by previous generations and bore diminishing relation to conditions and values current in the 1780s. In most cases, stealing to above the value of 39 shillings was a capital offence. This was true, for example, of 'stealing privily' in a private house, which covered theft from employers by servants, theft by lodgers from landlords, and some theft in shops. In some cases, the value could be lower than 39 shillings, but the theft would nevertheless be a capital offence because of other aggravating circumstances. Housebreaking (breaking and entering) was a double felony whatever the value of goods taken. When 'stealing privily' meant picking pockets, as was the case for nearly all prostitutes, theft of anything to a value of more than a shilling became a capital crime.

This legislation was unworkable. Juries, judges and prosecutors were no longer prepared to send people to the gallows for a theft of a few pence. With the connivance of the whole courtroom, women indicted of a double felony were routinely found guilty of a single felony and sentenced to transportation instead of death. Even when a death sentence could not be avoided, female offenders were rarely hanged; a petition for pardon would be drawn up by the sentencing judge and the sentence commuted to transportation to 'Parts Beyond the Seas', the vague name given to the rest of the world by the Elizabethan Transportation Act, introduced when the world was less well known and unnamed continents lurked at the edge of charts. If the judges had been sticklers in sentencing according to the evidence, many of the women who ended up in Sydney Cove would have been hanged in England.

It would be a shock to those Australian observers who comment with smug horror on the barbarism with which the Brits treated their convicts to discover how their European neighbours regarded the British judicial system. Prussian Baron Johann von Archenholz wrote with perplexity in his *Picture of England* that in this country 'an infraction of [the laws] . . . is punished without any respect to the rank or fortune of the culprit' and even 'if the chief magistrate should depart from the line of conduct prescribed to him by the laws, he is obliged to submit to justice like one of the meanest citizens'. To a European aristocrat, this was an outrageously democratic way to run a country. 'Nothing is more astonishing than the mildness and humanity with which criminals are treated, whether they be thieves, murderers or incendiaries', he went on. 'Even if their guilt is evident, the bar, the jury and the judges all seem to conspire for the acquittal; the counsel defend the culprit with zeal and the witnesses against him are questioned with much strictness and sometimes with much severity. His own confession is never demanded . . . a strange contrast to the practice of those tribunals of which torture is the grand resource.'

While merciful compared with the death sentences that could have been handed down had the law been strictly observed, the frequency with which judges resorted to the one-size-fits-all sentence of Transportation to Parts Beyond the Seas for women felons illustrates the severe limitations on sentencing. Even had they wanted to hand down a more lenient sentence, they could not: there was nothing else to hand down. For this reason, there appear cruel anomalies. Elizabeth Sully ran a pack of teenage prostitutes and routinely robbed and threatened the men they picked up. She got seven years' transportation. Esther Curtis got drunk in the lavatories – and got the same sentence. Justice was still a blunt stick.

The English social reformer Jonas Hanway described the situation that had provoked admiration in von Archenholz from a different angle and put his finger on the problem this 'lenity' created. 'The punishments now in use are not equal to the evil', he wrote, noting that brutal corporal punishments were no longer used in England as 'the gentler spirit of modern times has softened these rigors . . . whipping is in few cases deemed politic . . . and we do not think it a right measure to put all such persons to death . . . as have forfeited their lives to the laws. What then shall we do?' It was the question of the decade.

Sarah Dorset, 19 years old, was one of the prisoners sitting out her transportation sentence in the packed cells of Newgate. She had been arrested at a chophouse in the City of London one afternoon in October 1787, although she seems originally to have come from out of town. She had eloped from her family home with a man but 'had not been with the villain who ruined her above six weeks' before he abandoned her and 'she was forced by want upon the streets', where she turned to petty theft. She came to London, presumably because she would no longer be able to find work in her own parish or because she did not want to embarrass her parents further. She certainly kept in touch with her sister Mary, who was with her in the chophouse. The two girls took a seat in the parlour and ordered something to eat and a glass of beer. The landlady, Mrs Davidson, went off to draw two pints, leaving the sisters alone. When they made to leave, Mrs Davidson realised a coat, which had been hanging from a hook on the parlour door, was missing. She grabbed Sarah, thrust a hand under her cloak and found it. 'The coat fell from the settle on my arm and the gentlewoman had me taken up,' said Sarah. 'I know nothing of the matter,' said Mary. Mary was found not guilty; Sarah received the usual sentence of seven years' transportation.

There is a mystery in Sarah Dorset's story which begins here in the chophouse. Mrs Davidson was backed up in court by her servant, one William Powell, who agreed that, yes, the coat had been there, yes, it had been found under the girl's cloak, and, yes, she had taken it. It was partly on his evidence that Sarah Dorset was convicted. William was an extremely common first name in England at this time and Powell not an unusual surname. An English William Powell, known to his friends by his second name of Edward, would later play a role of great importance in Sarah Dorset's life. We know little of William Edward Powell beyond the facts that he was a Lancastrian by origin, a farmer who later went to sea, probably pressed during the American wars. He may be a different man entirely from the William Powell who worked in a London chophouse in October 1787; or he may not.

Sarah Dorset had been on the Common Side of Newgate for over a year, with 150 other women. There was another block in Newgate, however. The Master's Side offered more comfortable accommodation for those who could afford the half-crown weekly rent. The Common Side was for those who could not. A single week's rent on the Master's Side was beyond most women, let alone the many half-crowns that would be necessary during the months, sometimes years, which elapsed between conviction and discharge. The majority of disorderly girls brought in as prisoners of law and detained as felons lived on the stone slabs of the Common Side. The few who could afford the Master's rates were, apart from one, high-class shoplifters who had clearly stashed away a good few pounds before being caught. For those prepared to play for high stakes but with no training in specialist trades such as forgery – a very high earner – shoplifting was definitely the crime of choice. Alice Haynes had been convicted of stealing lace in a Fleet Street haberdashery; clearly previous crimes had been more successful as she was now paying her way on the Master's Side. Thirty-year-old Mary Higgins, eight months pregnant when she moved in in January 1789, stole blue lutestring in Cranbourn Passage worth £7 – roughly equivalent in value to the annual wage of a maidservant.

The cleverest of the women on the Master's Side was forger and businesswoman Nelly Kerwin. She was tried as 'Eleanor

Kerwin, alias Karavan, widow', who had for several years run 'a house of entertainment for sailors, not in the public but in the private line' in Gosport, near Portsmouth. She was a familiar figure on board ships in Gosport Harbour. Her principal line of business was 'bomb-boating', extending credit to cash-hungry sailors against prize-money or wages due. She also acted as an informal employment agent for captains who were ready to sail but lacked a full complement of crew. Her story in court was that she had procured 14 or 15 seamen for a Captain Urmiston in 1781. Among them was Samuel Druce, for whom Nelly had already paid several pounds' worth of lodging and entertainment, in cash, both in her lodging-house and at another one nearby. He may have been a boyfriend who turned into a sponger with whom she had become irritated. She arranged a job for him with Urmiston and, before he went, wanted a will made out to her which she would hold in security against his wages. However, when Druce went aboard he signed up on the muster as James White and, under this name, drew up another will, witnessed in all innocence by Captain Urmiston, in which he left wages and future prize-money to his mother. The Admiralty would issue wages in whichever name appeared on the muster. Nelly had been cheated. The implication of the case for the prosecution was that she decided to forge the will she had been promised and, if Druce died overseas, would then disprove the legitimacy of any will signed by 'James White'.

It took the jury an hour to decide Nelly's guilt on the counts of which she was indicted: first, of forging, or causing to be forged, the will, and, second, of 'uttering this will, with intention to defraud our Lord the King'. She was found guilty of the second and sentenced to death.

If Nelly was the cleverest of all the Master's ladies, the most flamboyant were Elizabeth Barnsley and her partner, Ann Wheeler. Among the shoplifters these two were queens: Barnsley had the pedigree and Wheeler had the class. Even the officers of the court referred to them, apparently without irony, as 'ladies', and Mrs Barnsley would in future months leave no one in doubt as to her rights and privileges.

Ann and Elizabeth stole from the best addresses: the 18 yards of muslin Wheeler tried to hide beneath her 'white silk cloak, trimmed with furr' and behind her 'large muff', came from Hodgkinson, Warrener and Percival of Bond Street. Like Mary Higgins, they were uninterested in thefts worth shillings and pence: that muslin was worth £6 and Wheeler proffered a £10 note in payment for her piece of Irish linen. The first part was beautifully performed, but one or other of them fumbled the vital act of whipping the cloth off the counter, shoving it up her dress and sailing out with a confusing rustle of skirts. As the ladies turned to leave, they were challenged by a brave shopman. His courage did not fail even before their outrage at his impertinence. Wheeler enquired frostily if he did not recognise her as a lady who patronised the establishment regularly for both her own and her servants' needs? And was, clinchingly, an intimate of Lady Spencer? Elizabeth Barnsley backed her up, but the shopman refused to back down and the ladies were bundled off to Newgate, protesting their connections. Both had been receiving visitors in their Master's Side apartments since they were sentenced to seven years' transportation in February.

The presence of 15-year-old Sarah Roberts is more of a mystery. Her theft of calico on Holborn Hill had neither yielded great value nor been carried out with great flair; moreover, she, too, was in the early stages of pregnancy. Some anonymous benefactor was paying to keep her on the relative comfort of the Master's Side.

There was easy communication between the Master's Side and the Common Side of Newgate Gaol. In fact, in the second half of 1788 there was too much communication for the authorities' liking, for mutiny was rumbling. In August, discipline in the women's cells had all but broken down under the seditious influence of a man sharing the Master's Side with Mrs Barnsley, Mrs Higgins and Mrs Haynes. Lord George Gordon was the embodiment of *fin de siècle* radical chic, godson to the king himself but also darling of the London mob. It was he who had incited this mob into the anti-Catholic riots of 1780, during which a previous Newgate Gaol had been burned to the ground. (It was rebuilt during the 1780s.) In 1787, Lord George was convicted of stirring up mutiny among the convicts about to sail in the fleet to Botany Bay. He (or, rather, his footman) had distributed a pamphlet among the prisoners of Newgate which, it was said at his trial, 'excites the subject [felons condemned to transportation or death] to rise in defence of those whose lives and liberties are forfeited'. Found guilty of sedition, Lord George Gordon was sentenced to imprisonment and entered Newgate Gaol. He immediately set himself to become Prisoners' Friend, or, in the eyes of the authorities, to make trouble among the convicts sentenced to sail in the next fleet. He was daily to be seen in the women's cells, discussing their cases, advising on their petitions and distributing food and money. Gordon's ability to spin publicity for himself and his protégées was fearsome. So was his following among convicts, sailors, pro-Americans and other dangerous elements for whom his support was not restricted to encouraging words. Favoured prisoners were given a 'pension', which they came to collect from his apartments on the Master's Side each week. It may well have been Lord George who paid for accommodation for Sarah Roberts: 15 years of age, pregnant, and under sentence of transportation, she was a natural object for compassion. His appeal was a dangerous mixture of fanaticism, charisma and money, and the governor and sheriff considered him a serious threat to stability within the prison.

His Majesty had recently been called on by his Cabinet to speak against the increase of crime on the streets, of heavy drinking, gambling, prostitution, failure to observe the Sabbath and general moral decline. His proclamation had been published throughout Britain. Already one of the most famous speeches of the year, it became even more so when the women of Newgate, under Gordon's influence, attempted to turn it to their own advantage. That summer, petty thief Arabella Stuart appeared in the Old Bailey and astonished the court with the uppity claim that God's Holy Law, as referred to by the king himself, required that 'for all manner of trespass . . . whom the judges shall condemn . . . shall pay double unto his neighbour'. Therefore, she said, she should pay back double the value of what she had taken but to banish her to Botany Bay would be to go against the word of the Lord. She was hanged.

Arabella was only the first of Lord George's convict friends to use this line. It bubbled beneath letters and petitions leaving the gaol through the summer. In August 1788, *The Times* reported a mass petition to His Majesty, claiming again that transportation was contrary to Holy Law as defined by His Majesty's own proclamation. It was signed by 82 women; all 82 were among the women who would be sent to New South Wales on the first ship out. Eight years previously, Lord George Gordon had raised a crowd of 60,000 which had threatened the Bank of England and the Tower of London. He was too dangerous to be allowed free access to convicts whose connections extended to some of the most skilful criminal operators in London. Sheriff Bloxham and Governor Akerman confined him to the Master's Side of the gaol and incipient mutiny on the Common Side was quelled. It was here that George Gordon died of gaol fever in 1793.

But crisis followed crisis. It might be mutiny, hunger or gaol fever, but the root cause was always the same. A hundred and fifty-one women, on three ha'pence-worth of bread per day, living in foul conditions and with an utterly uncertain future, would not long remain submissive.

Chapter Four

Galleons Reach

Far-fetched plans had been promoted for several years to deal with the pile-up of felons in the British gaols. They could be made an annual present of to the Empress Catherine of Russia, currently failing to persuade her own subjects to inhabit colonies in what were described by *The Times* as the 'dreary, inhospitable regions' of the Caucasus, from which 'escape is impossible'. They could be eliminated by sending them to 'Algiers, Tripoly and Tunis and exchanging them for unfortunate Christian slaves, in the hands of those Barbarians'. They could be employed as galley-slaves, as in France, as slave labour, as in the German states, or as miners, as in Sweden and Denmark.

These European methods of dealing with an overabundant lowlife did not appeal to the British government, which continued to favour a penal colony over all other solutions. Even after America declared its independence and switched from convict to slave labour, the British government clung to the idea that somewhere in the New World someone would accept British felons. New World dumps were attempted further north, but by now even American loyalists no longer wanted convict labour from the Old Country. In November 1785, it was reported that Halifax, Nova Scotia, had started to turn back British transport ships.

Five years after the American wars had ended, a 'Transportation to America' list still appeared in the Newgate prison registers, the one convict under this sentence duly entered and re-entered each week. A separate list existed for those sentenced to transportation to Africa. The African coasts kept coming back as a penal option, and kept failing. In 1782, an advance party of 200 had been reduced by sickness and desertion to 50 in under a month when they were transported to Cape Coast Castle. In 1783, another bunch was sent out, utterly unprovided for, and landed at Goree, where they were landed 'naked and diseased on the sandy shore'. Those who survived were shipped out later in the year. In 1785, a prison hulk in Portsmouth was set aside specifically to hold convicts awaiting transportation to Africa. This was the *Ceres*, whose inhabitants were shortly to be carried over to a privately run settlement on the River Gambia. The Recorder of London emerged from talks with Secretary Sydney in February of that year and confidently told the City aldermen that the government had taken up a ship, 'formerly employed in the Guinea trade [i.e. the slave trade] with double barricades & co.', which was being fitted out in Deptford 'to carry over some felons to the coast of Africa'. There was space for 200 aboard; the Recorder had extracted a promise that at least 100 would come out of Newgate Gaol. The courts latched on to this option, as in 1787 they would latch on to Botany Bay and in 1789 to Sydney Cove. In April 1785, 100 convicted felons were taken from Newgate to the Woolwich hulks in preparation for the voyage to the island of Lemano, in the River Gambia. They never sailed; instead, they remained on the *Ceres*.

A feeble attempt to set up a penal colony in Africa popped up again in 1786, when the Bay of Das Voltas received a visit from British surveyors and swiftly repelled them – but not before the government at home had once again jumped the gun and promised everyone that up to 1,000 convicts were about to be shipped off to the new African prison camp.

In December 1786 a further African project loomed, this time to the new settlement for the black poor at Freetown, Sierra Leone. A bizarre twist was thrown in. Those sent over 'would be slaves for life', ran this extraordinary plan, 'to attend upon black masters that settle in the new colony going to be settled there, which, it is thought, will be a greater punishment than death'.

Even now, Africa was not written off as a possible home to a penal settlement, and judges continued to sentence a few criminals to transportation to Africa, *faute de mieux*. These felons sat in the cells, along with those sentenced more vaguely to exile in Parts Beyond the Seas. The African option seems to have been reserved for felons of a peculiarly depraved nature. Frightful descriptions were made of the horrors they would meet. 'The country on each side the [Gambia] river', wrote *The Times*, 'is peopled by warlike negro tribes, who sacrifice to their idol deities, such white men as fall into their hands and whose bodies they devour, which will prevent their deserting . . .'

Africa turned out fever-ridden and infertile; America would no longer accept British felons and nothing had been heard of Commodore Phillip's fleet to Botany Bay for over a year. His ships had last been seen by Europeans leaving the Dutch settlement of Cape Town in November 1787. Since then, no news of them had been received in England. As *The Times* said in August 1788 – and then hastily denied – 'it is probable we may never hear more from our Botany Bay convicts.' The islands of the southern seas were littered with the bones of unfortunate mariners, and as the months passed gloomy suspicions grew that those of Phillip's fleet were among them. The Dutch had more up-to-date news, for Captain John Hunter, one of Phillip's senior officers, had arrived back at the Cape in October 1788 to buy supplies for the desperate colony. The dispatches he had sent on to England from there had not yet arrived.

One last, half-hearted attempt at Transportation to Parts Beyond the Seas was made in the summer of 1788. This time the destination was Quebec, where transported felons would act as servants 'for menial and Laborious offices'. For a couple of months the planners were optimistic. If the convicts could be embarked swiftly, there was still time to get ships across the Atlantic and up the St Lawrence River before it froze over for the winter. Through July and August, prison wagons rumbled off to Gosport bearing male convicts for the transport ships. But by the time the fleet was ready, the last date at which the weather would allow them to complete the passage safely had been passed. Some small relief was gained temporarily by the London gaols, at the expense of the prison hulks in Portsmouth harbour where the convicts destined for Quebec spent most of the next year in conditions of utter squalor.

There were men in the Home Department and the Admiralty who knew that Commodore Phillip's fleet to New South Wales had been ill-conceived and poorly equipped. They did not know whether he had even arrived in Botany Bay, let alone managed to survive once there, but by late 1788 New South Wales seemed their only remaining transportation option. Assembling another fleet to follow the first was a gamble; at stake were the lives of the convicted felons whom the government planned to remove from its bursting gaols. All other means of disposing of the prisoners who clogged the cells seemed closed.

And so, '. . . regarding the affecting state of the Gaol of Newgate', wrote Lord Sydney on 20 December 1788, 'I find . . . the Ship in which they are to be embarked is now nearly, if not altogether ready for their reception . . . I am led to suspect that 150 of the Convicts will be taken away, which will give great relief to the Goal [sic] . . . as to prevent the spreading of the dreadful Disorder which . . . has made its appearance.' In this way, before anyone knew whether those on the first fleet to New South Wales were alive or dead, the officials of courts and gaols up and down the country were informed that a second fleet to New South Wales was finally to be assembled.

The ship hastily commissioned by the Admiralty to convey

felons from Newgate Gaol to New South Wales was the *Lady Julian*, 'a fine, river-built vessel [i.e. built on the Thames], the first ship that was taken by the Americans on her passage from Jamaica to London and was afterwards retaken by a man-of-war and conveyed to England'. She was 'barque-built', three-masted and two-decked. Her specification does not survive, as she was built before the underwriters of Lloyd's began their Green Book, recording tonnage and dimensions of new ships. However, the specification does survive of the *Scarborough*, the two-decked three-master that had been fitted at the same dock two years previously as part of the Fleet to Botany Bay. The *Scarborough* was of the same dimensions as the *Lady Julian* to within ten registered tons – 411 to the *Lady Julian*'s 401 – and presumably of similar dimensions.

She was 110 feet long and 30 feet wide at her widest point, with a height between her decks of about four feet five inches. Each of her three masts – foremast, mainmast and mizzen, moving from bow to stern – was rigged to carry three square sails. Stay sails hung between each mast. At the bow, one, two or three foresails could be attached and a bowsprit projected some 25 feet. The sternmost part of her deck, the quarterdeck, was raised above the rest. It was enclosed by a rail and was the preserve of officers only, whose accommodation was built into the area below. The foremost part of the ship, between the mainmast and the bow, was known as the forecastle. The accommodation of the ordinary seamen – the 'ship's company' – was built into a raised area on this which mirrored the officers' quarters at the stern. The bottom deck of the ship was the orlop, usually reserved for well-insulated cargo. This was where Deptford carpenters were currently at work to turn the *Lady Julian* into a prison ship. Partitions were erected to create three self-contained areas on the orlop deck. Forward and aft were stores, and the middle section, anywhere between 1,500 and 2,000 square feet, was allotted to the 150 expected felons. The hatches which led into this space were fitted with gratings that could be bolted down from above. Wide shelves, sleeping between four and six people each, were attached to each side of the hull.

By December 1788, the *Lady Julian* was at Galleons Reach in the Thames. She was intended to carry over 150 female convicts and 100 male marines to New South Wales on an Admiralty contract, then sail north to Canton and bring home a cargo of tea for the East India Company. Captain Aitken, of whom little is known, had been appointed to command the ship. He was a less colourful character, and had less direct impact on the women who would come aboard the *Lady Julian*, than Lieutenant Thomas Edgar, who had been appointed to the double role of master and government agent. Edgar was better known as 'Little Bassey' – 'little' for his stature, 'bassey' for the speech impediment which had his favourite curse – 'Blast 'ee' – emerge thus. He took up his post early in 1789.

A seaman who accompanied Thomas Edgar on his next commission, in 1794, described him with some affection as a 'strange and unaccountable being . . . a good sailor and navigator, or rather had been, for he drank very hard, so as to entirely ruin his constitution'. By 1794, he had been sadly brought down by liquor and spent the voyage getting steadily drunker, forgetting to carry out orders. 'Edgar, you are drunk,' the long-suffering captain would say. 'No sir, bass me if I am,' Edgar would reply.

In 1776, Edgar had been a bright young officer appointed to the commission of a lifetime as master of the *Discovery*, one of two ships which sailed on a four-year voyage to the Antipodes and back by way of Cape Horn and the South Seas under command of the greatest seaman of the age, Captain James Cook. The other of the ships on this third and last of Cook's great voyages of exploration and discovery was commanded by William Bligh.

Thomas Edgar's part in the fracas in which Captain Cook died is unclear. He emerges not dishonourable but impetuous. It was partly his action, the day before Captain Cook was clubbed over the head on Hawaii in February 1779, that created the ill-feeling between seamen and islanders which would break into violence. Tools from the *Discovery* were snatched by an islander visiting on board, and Edgar set off with a few *Discovery* men after his canoe. Both he and the British sailors on shore, who saw what was going on and joined in, failed miserably to catch the giggling Hawaiians, who slipped into the palm banks and led them in circles. When the tools were handed back by a third party at the end of the day, an exasperated Edgar tried again to seize the thief's canoe and a scuffle broke out in which both sailors and islanders were hurt. In revenge, the islanders stole the *Discovery*'s cutter early the next morning, and when Cook went ashore to demand it back a far more serious fight broke out in which the captain was killed.

Edgar had been lieutenant then, in 1779, and he was still lieutenant now, a decade later. Others among Cook's officers had been promoted through a series of commissions. William Bligh had been chosen to command the latest Cook-like voyage of trade and exploration sponsored by Sir Joseph Banks and had been given the prestigious commission of investigating the collection of breadfruit from Tahiti to feed the slaves in the Caribbean aboard HMS *Bounty*. However, Lieutenant Edgar's experience in navigating long Pacific voyages made him an obvious candidate for the post of master of the *Lady Julian* and, as an old Cook man, he may have been recommended by Sir Joseph Banks.

Edgar's role as government agent on the *Lady Julian* was administrative rather than technical. The appointment of a decent man as agent was of prime importance to the convicts. Their wellbeing during the voyage to New South Wales depended on the honesty and humanity of this officer more than any other on board. It was the agent's task to ensure that the terms of the contract made between the Home Department and the shipping agent who owned or leased the transport ship were observed. It was he who would ensure – or not – that the shipping agent supplied in full any rations specified in the contract and did not short-change the convicts on quantity or quality. It was he who would ensure – or not – that the captain and crew allowed the convicts sufficient fresh air and exercise on deck while at sea. It was he who would ensure – or not – that the surgeon would perform his medical and surgical duties and that the sailors and officers would not maltreat the convicts.

It is tempting to think that Lieutenant Edgar sought romantic refuge in the bottle from the torment of guilt over his part in Cook's death and the brake this had put on a promising career. In truth, however, he seems to have been a carefree chap; a fat, jolly, wheezy little man who drank for the pleasure of it rather than to escape his ghosts, and still a competent seaman in 1789, able to take decisions when necessary. His honesty and care for the convicts in his charge were exemplary. He was one of the few naval agents whose kneejerk reaction to his powers was not to defraud the Naval Board and skim a private profit from the rations meant for those in his charge but to ensure that those rations were of the best quality. His steward on the *Lady Julian* described Edgar as a 'decent, kindly man', and he performed his duties well, treating the convicts in his care with compassion.

Another *Lady Julian* appointment made at the beginning of 1789 was that of the surgeon, Richard Alley. The character of the surgeon would have almost as much effect on the health of the convicts as that of the agent. The agent was the superior officer, and on those ships where an agent was cruel or negligent it fell to the surgeon to fight the convicts' corner against him for decent food and enough exercise. On ships where neither agent nor surgeon gave consideration to the sufferings on the orlop, the consequences were dreadful. Naval surgeons were popularly portrayed as incompetents and drunks. A first fleet marine recalled one surgeon 'left the Ship for Drunk-ed' before they had left England; the drunkenness of the surgeon who had left the year before with William Bligh would be cited the following year in the captain's explanation of the mutiny aboard his ship. Alley does not seem to have suffered from drunkenness, and his treatment of the convicts in his care was such that the government would promote him to agent on a later transport ship and send him out to New South Wales again. The women on the *Lady Julian* were fortunate in having men of decency appointed to both the positions which most influenced the conditions in which they lived on board.

The convicts sent on board transport ships in the Thames had already undergone a cursory medical examination to test their survival prospects on the voyage and, theoretically, their ability to contribute to the life of the colony. These examinations, depending on which doctor made them and how much pressure there was to get the convicts out of the gaol, could easily allow the sick and the frail to slip through the net. There were three women over 60 on board the *Lady Julian* who could not reasonably be expected to aid the colony either by producing babies or by hard labour. Almost half the women had come on board straight from a gaol crawling with typhus, and many of them must already have had the pox. It was impossible to eliminate all women infected with some form of sexually transmitted disease, current or dormant. According to the most respected writer on syphilis and gonorrhoea, Dr William Buchan, 'there is one class of society among whom this disease may be said to have its stronghold: I mean that description of females commonly called women of the town . . . Very few of this class of patients ever get thoroughly well.' It would not have made much difference to the colony anyway, although nobody in England knew that in spring 1789 – Sydney Cove was already riddled with the clap.

Several members of the crew were also already on board the ship at Galleons Reach, and at least one of the ship's tradesmen. This was 34-year-old John Nicol, who would act as both steward (officers' servant) and cooper. The only known first-hand account of the voyage of the *Lady Julian* is in John Nicol's memoirs, dictated over 30 years later to an Edinburgh journalist. He had been back in Britain for only three months when he went on board the *Lady Julian*, and had already spent 20 years at sea, travelling most of the known world on one ship or another since leaving his home in Borrowstowness in the Scottish Lowlands.

John Nicol had been on board in the river for three or four months when a ship homeward bound from Canton sailed slowly up the Thames in the first week of March 1789. She was the *Prince of Wales*, the first ship home from Botany Bay. The destination of convicts in gaols all over the country was finally confirmed. Sydney Cove, Port Jackson, was in the news; accounts of the colony were splashed all over the press. Papers authorising the movement of prisoners piled up as fast as the prisoners themselves, and the inky fingers of prison clerks struggled to keep their records up to date. Within days, dazed women who had been sentenced to Transportation to Parts Beyond the Seas were being shunted across the country to London, the Thames and the *Lady Julian*.

From eastern England, a coach arrived from Lincoln in the charge of the Castle Gaol turnkey. He was familiar with the procedure: he had brought down 11 felons and a baby three years before for embarkation with the previous fleet. This time, 14 exhausted women were roped to the outside seats. The irons riveted round their wrists in Lincoln Gaol remained in place throughout the journey south. Here they had sat for 36 hours, exposed to an English March and the curiosity of every groom and potboy aroused by fallen womanhood in chains. Among them were Sarah Whitelam and Mary Rose. When finally they were rowed across the Thames and aboard the *Lady Julian*, the women were dirty, wet and weak from cold and hunger. It was John Nicol who pulled them and their few belongings over the side.

Despite these sordid circumstances, the attraction was immediate – at least on his side. Even in the lamentable condition in which the authorities had delivered Sarah Whitelam on board, she was still sufficiently personable to make an impact. The first thing Nicol did was to free the hateful manacles round the women's wrists, paying the Lincoln turnkey his half-crown-a-head fee, and let them get their balance. The exhausted women lined up obediently in front of his blacksmith's anvil and held out their hands, Sarah among them. 'I first fixed my fancy on her the moment I knocked the rivet from her irons upon my anvil,' wrote Nicol. It was an unusual way to start a courtship.

As Sarah recovered from the journey in the relative warmth and safety of the ship, she recounted her story bit by bit to the besotted steward. The tale she told him was one of betrayal and misfortune. It seemed to go like this: she had been living in Kesteven before her trial, working for a local family and sharing lodgings with other young women. As was normal among girlfriends, they freely used each other's clothes and possessions, none having enough money to dress herself with the variety she would have wanted and filling the gaps in her toilette with items borrowed from the others' boxes. All had gone well for some time; she had made a decent living and lived a decent life. And then she had borrowed a mantle from one of the circle of friends and returned it the next day – nothing unusual there. But for some reason she had never known, she was accused a couple of days later of having taken it without permission. At first, she thought that she must have given offence unknowingly; perhaps she had stained or torn the mantle without realising and upset her friend by not offering to repair or replace it. But the friend would not listen to reason and Sarah found herself being accused of an offence that from day to day escalated from abuse of friendship into felony, for now another girl was accusing her of having deliberately stolen the mantle. She was thus caught up in the dreadful situation of being prosecuted by this 'false friend', as she defined her to John Nicol, to the point where one day she stood before the magistrates, was pronounced guilty of a crime she had not committed, and sentenced to seven years in Parts Beyond the Seas.

At 17, her life lay around her in ruins. Her family apparently could not help her and her employers, perhaps convinced they had been tricked by a pretty face and winning ways, would not. From being a lively lass with good prospects, she had become a convicted felon sleeping on rancid straw in a country gaol, destined for exile. This was the story John got out of her during her first weeks on the river, recovering from the rigours of Kesteven Gaol, and the one he repeated in his memoirs 30 years later. Appalled by the tragedy that had befallen her, entranced by her prettiness, determined to alleviate her distress, the ship's steward fell hopelessly in love with this 'girl of a modest, reserved turn, as kind and true a creature as ever lived'. Still a teenager and sentenced for a crime she had not committed to the thieves' colony in the company of rogues, she seemed worthy of Nicol's deepest compassion. And he was the first man Sarah had met in two years who had not disbelieved her, despised her or known the truth about her. So she reciprocated – more slowly, but nevertheless with increasing trust and affection. 'I courted her for upwards of a week', wrote Nicol. It was clearly quite a long time in his scheme of courtship, but long before the ship left Galleons Reach, Sarah had left the convict quarters in the orlop hold and was sleeping in the comfort and privacy of Nicol's bunk on the 'tween deck. By the end of April she was pregnant.

Chapter Five

Life in the River

The *Lady Julian* was now home to over 150 women, with more arriving each week, sent from gaols throughout England to what John Nicol called 'a colony in great want of women'. Plans that she should carry a cargo of male and female convicts, or females accompanied by a marine corps battalion to relieve the garrison in Sydney Cove, were both dropped, and it was decided she should carry a full complement of women. This may have been to maximise the number of females in the colony as fast as possible; it may have been because of pressure on the female cells in Newgate Gaol, or it may have been because it was not possible to raise a corps of marines swiftly enough.

By far the largest group of women came out of Newgate Gaol. On 12 March 1789, 108 women and two infants were brought out of the gaol at dawn, loaded into lighters at Blackfriars Bridge and rowed down the Thames to Galleons Reach. Among them was Sarah Dorset, whose petition for mercy had been turned down by James Adair in July 1788, when he also reported on Esther Abrahams, former cellmate of Nelly Kerwin who, by the time he dealt with her petition, had already been in the colony for six months and was pregnant to a marine officer. Three of the 108 had been shunted off the 'transportation to Africa' list the week before and switched to New South Wales. All 82 of the women who had signed Lord George's summer petition to His

Majesty in August 1788 were rowed down the Thames that day.

Even at this early hour of the morning, the river was crowded. The Port of London was one of the busiest in the world. The City, anxious to preserve its huge income from licences, refused to allow the construction of wharves and docks further east for another decade, despite huge congestion in the Pool of London. With as many as ten tall-masted ships there at one time, side by side, it was an obstacle course for the lightermen. For miles to the east, ships milled about for days waiting for a berth to become vacant. A haze of coal dust from the colliers hung over the docks.

Their route took the women past the north bank of the Thames, where half the *Lady Julian*'s cargo had lived and worked among those they had robbed and assaulted. In Fish Street Hill, 13-year-old Mary Cavenor had attempted to snatch a piece of cloth from the doorway of a drapery. On the other side of the Monument, in Lombard Court, Mary Hook had raided her mistress's bureau and stolen the household's wages when she should have been boiling lobsters in the kitchen. Bett Farrell had run into a constable in Blue Anchor Yard, just past the Tower, who, 'knowing her, stopt her and asked her what she had in her apron'; it proved to be stolen laundry from a house in East Smithfield. 'Bett, this is £40 for me,' he told her, and turned her in. Three turnings down, in Virginia Street, Mary Anderson had robbed a house because she did not want to be a common prostitute. And behind the house she had robbed, Mary Butler and Poll Randall had enticed Joseph Clark and his cheese into bed and run off with his money, and Mary Bateman and Elizabeth Sully had lured James Palmer into a lodging-house and stolen his silver watch.

The Ratcliff Highway almost touched the bank at the curve in the river between Wapping and Limehouse. It had been home to many in the lighters. Sophia Sarah Ann Brown had worked 'in Mrs Foy's house as a girl, an unfortunate girl' on the Highway

and robbed her drunken client of nine guineas, three shillings
and a watch. Jane Walters had robbed her client, also drunk, here
just two months ago when he fell asleep in a room rented by the
hour. Ann Morgan had picked up an inn porter here with the
words 'Come along with me, Ned', picked his breeches pocket in
the first clinch and told him 'She would poke my bloody eye
out . . . and though she was a woman she had fought a better
man than I' when he tried to get his half-guinea back.

As the lighters turned south down Limehouse Reach,
they came into less familiar waters. Where the wharves of the
City ended, ship-fitting and ship-building basins began. At
the southern end of Limehouse, in the docks of Deptford, fitting-
out basins to accommodate naval and merchant shipping lined
both banks of the river to the east. Here, the man-of-war,
HMS *Guardian*, had just been taken out of reserve to be fitted as
store ship for the colony in Sydney Cove. At Woolwich, the huge
Royal Artillery Barracks was still a building site, the barracks
half-completed.

Dotted around the waters of Deptford and Woolwich were the
prison hulks, worn-out shells of naval ships no longer fit to go to
sea. When it had seemed that transportation to America had
stopped only temporarily, prison hulks were used as a stopgap
solution to overcrowding in the prisons during the years of
colonial disobedience. As pressure on conventional prisons had
never eased, they had never been scrapped. By the time the *Lady
Julian* convicts were rowed past them, some had been there for
over a decade, with hundreds of male convicts aboard each one.
They slept in fetters, meagrely fed, continually prey to fever and
kept at heavy labour from dawn to dusk in the government dockyards. When the air was still and the weather warm, the smell of
them could pollute the river from bank to bank. Hulk after hulk,
festooned with bedding, clothes, weed and rotting rigging, lined
the river like a floating shantytown. As the lighters rowed among
them at dawn, the chain gangs were being loaded into similar

boats to be rowed ashore and start the day's labour, catcalling their sisters in irons as they went.

From now on, a couple of lighters would draw up to the *Lady Julian* each week bearing cold, damp women to be hauled aboard. Eighteen women were brought down from Warwick, ten came down the Thames from Maidstone, three from Nottingham, three from Reading, ones and twos from all over the country: pig-thief Sarah Gregory and her baby daughter from Hertford, a 68-year-old shoplifter and an 18-year-old milkmaid from Northumberland, a maidservant and a mugger from Chelmsford, a housebreaker from New Sarum reprieved from death. It was John Nicol who received them, helped them over the side, stowed their chests and boxes below and took them down to their new quarters. His uppermost emotion was chivalrous sympathy: most, he wrote, were 'harmless, unfortunate creatures, the victims of the basest seduction'.

In April, a lighter made its way towards the *Lady Julian* bearing a single occupant. Four women should have been in it: Elizabeth Barnsley, Ann Wheeler, Sarah Roberts and Alice Haynes. Ann Wheeler was too sick with gaol fever to be taken from the Newgate infirmary. Alice Haynes had been kept back at the last minute while a petition for her release was being considered. Sarah Roberts had been 'detained upon a representation from Mr Akerman that she was big with child, and near the time of her delivery, so that she could not be removed to the Vessel in the River without considerable danger and hardship'. Elizabeth Barnsley, neither sick, pregnant nor suitable material for clemency, was alone in the lighter when she allowed herself to be handed up by John Nicol and introduced to Agent Edgar. It did not take long for either man to realise that the *grande dame* of the *Lady Julian* had arrived.

Elizabeth Barnsley soon made her mark on life aboard. It was her boast that her family had been highwaymen for over a hundred years. Highwaymen were the gloryboys of eighteenth-century crime, dashing figures on black stallions with lace about the cuffs and a winning way with the ladies. Certainly, Elizabeth's brother, who often visited her on board the *Lady Julian* in the Thames, made an impression on John Nicol. Even 30 years later, he remembered with uncharacteristic awe that he was 'well dressed and genteel in his appearance as any gentleman' – and sufficiently devil-may-care that he did not mind his sister's advertising his profession. Elizabeth certainly had cash of her own, and fine clothes in trunks in the hold. Within hours of her arrival on ship, she had requested Agent Edgar's permission to exchange her vulgar convict's uniform of brown serge for something better fitting in which to receive her friends and family. He refused, but promised she could wear her finery once they had put to sea.

Mrs Barnsley was not the only woman receiving visitors aboard the *Lady Julian* at Galleons Reach. During the spring months, the decks of the ship were scenes of constant activity. There were parents who had been present in the courtroom, had visited in prison and were now desperately petitioning the authorities to have their daughters pardoned, pleading youth and ignorance and pledging themselves as security against the girls' release. There were families from outside London, who had undertaken a long and expensive journey by coach to bid farewell to a daughter or a sister whom they doubted they would see again. There were friends and relations bringing letters to an officer of the marines currently in Sydney Cove by someone who had known someone who had once met someone else who knew him, in the hope they could win their wife or mother more food, less hard labour, a better hut. There were parents who had pawned their last possessions to provide their daughters with a few guineas which might buy them an earlier release or an easier life in the colony. There were journalists and illustrators searching for stories and touching pictures. Until the day before the *Lady Julian* set sail, relations, advocates and well-wishers worked against the clock and the odds to secure a pardon or a reduction of the sentence, concocting letter after letter to persons of influence with whom they had even the vaguest connection who might be persuaded to help, hoping desperately as departure day crept nearer that someone would relent and save them.

It is likely that Sir Joseph Banks paid a visit aboard. When he was not at Revesby Hall, Lincolnshire, he spent most of his time in his London house at 34 Soho Square, from where he kept a finger in several expeditionary pies. In August 1788, just before he had intervened in the affairs of Mary Rose, he had been setting up an expedition to penetrate the interior of Africa through Sierra Leone. It was to be led by his friend Mr Lucas, another gentleman passenger of Captain Cook's on those early formative voyages in the 1770s. In April 1789, his interest had switched to Sydney Cove, and he had been called on to advise on the fitting of the *Guardian* store ship.

By April 1789, the little fleet of two ships was advancing. Lord Sydney's office had been giving some thought to the specific requests in the dispatches written by Governor Phillip and delivered by the returning ships of the first fleet. The *Guardian*, a sleek frigate of nearly 900 tons, would make a swift passage and had the capacity to carry supplies for many months to Sydney Cove. Twenty-five male convicts with some skill in horticulture or agriculture were being selected from the Portsmouth hulks, promised special privileges in the colony and prepared for embarkation on board the *Guardian*. A handful of non-convict superintendents on a salary of £40 per annum were also to sail. These were the men intended to supervise the public works on which the convict gangs were engaged in Sydney Cove. They were an eccentric and heterogeneous bunch. Two of them had been hand-picked by Sir Joseph from among the royal gardeners at Kew. Another was a widowed Hessian soldier, Philip Schaffer. He had been one of the mercenaries bought in by George III from his ancestral German territories to fight in the

American wars. He spoke little or no English and relied for translation on his ten-year-old daughter, Elisabeth. There was a flax-dresser called Andrew Hume who, it was supposed, would whip the Norfolk Island hemp industry into profitable shape; a farmer named Thomas Clarke; Philip Devine, already super-intendent of convicts on the Woolwich hulks; James Reid, 'form-erly an American planter', presumably kicked out of a previous colony for his loyalty to the Union Jack; John Barlow, ex-army officer and surveyor who had been 'employed as an engineer in Jamaica'. There was also a middle-class black sheep who seems to have been quietly advised it would be a good idea if he left the country for a time, John Thomas Doidge.

Yet another of Cook's old officers was given command of the *Guardian*. Edward Riou was 13 years old and a midshipman when he sailed on Cook's final voyage, serving under both Lieutenant Edgar on the *Discovery* and Lieutenant Bligh on the *Resolution*. He was now 26, a rising naval star whose personal acquaintanceship with the guru of the Antipodes made him a natural choice for the commission. The *Guardian* was to carry plants to start up the colony's plantations, and Sir Joseph, at Riou's diplomatic invitation, personally supervised the construc-tion of a special plant cabin on her quarterdeck. During the first week of June, Banks visited the ship with a piece of chalk in his hand to draw up lines across the timbers for the shipwrights to work to, large enough to accommodate 93 pots of fruit, herbs and vegetables from Kew for the colonists to use 'in food or physic'. His protégée Mary Rose was on board the *Lady Julian*, at Galleons Reach, a quarter-mile away.

The other compassionate gentleman with a penchant for protégées and an interest in Botany Bay had not forgotten the women he had supported in Newgate. At least four of the women on the *Lady Julian* were still receiving their pension from Lord George Gordon. John Nicol went to Newgate once a week on their behalf 'and got their allowance from his own hand'. During one of these visits, he found 'decent-looking' people waiting for him in the gaol guardhouse. They had come to the capital to seek news of their lost daughter and had tracked her as far as Newgate. The gaoler had recognised Sarah Dorset's name and told them to wait for John Nicol on his weekly visit to Lord George. 'The mother implored me to tell her, if such a one was on board', and it was Nicol's unpleasant task to break the news to Sarah's parents that, although the girl was alive and well, she was bound for Sydney Cove. 'The father's heart seemed too full to allow him to speak,' he wrote, 'but the mother, with streaming eye, blessed God they had found their poor, lost child, undone as she was.'

John took them to the river and had them rowed on board the *Lady Julian*. He put them in his own berth and went to find Sarah so the family could be reunited away from the curious or derisive stares of the others. When Sarah, disbelieving, entered his berth and saw her parents there, she fainted and then 'in the most heart-rending accents, implored their pardon . . . She . . . had not been from her father's house above two years . . . so short had been her course of folly and sin'. Sarah was one woman on board who held out no hope for a pardon, with or without her parents' help. She had already petitioned Lord Sydney in 1788 from her cell. To Sydney's request for a summary of her case, the judge who had sentenced her advised him dourly that she 'appears to me a very proper subject for the Colony at Botany Bay'. There was nothing further she could do. The day John Nicol rowed her parents aboard in April 1789 was the last time she ever saw them.

Sarah Dorset was not the only convict on board the *Lady Julian* whose petition had been turned down. The recorder had remained stony-hearted to a petition for mercy from Catherine Wilmot of Chelmsford. The character references which had accompanied her petition were from the keeper of a livery stable who had known her for two years as 'quiet and Industrious' and who believed 'she got her living by selling hardware and going to

Fairs', and from a victualler, who had known her one and a half years as a woman who 'travels and sells hardware in a Basket'. They were not inspiring. A marginally more encouraging one came from the parishioners of St Mary's, Whitechapel, who reported Catherine 'always behaves herself as becometh' and that she had four children by her husband, absent at sea during her trial, 'disconsolate, scattered at present and in real distress'. James Adair was not convinced. 'A felony of very serious and general consequence . . . The Prisoner was not a new Offender . . . I see no reason to change my opinion, nor to think that her children will be prejudiced by not being brought up under such a Parent . . .'

Nor was Sarah Dorset's the only story to hint at extraordinary connections. Thirty years after the voyage, only those women whose history or characters were most remarkable remained in John Nicol's mind. One of them was a young, anonymous girl whom he remembered not for her character or her crime but because all on board believed her to be an illegitimate daughter of the Prime Minister, William Pitt. 'She herself never contradicted it,' he said. 'She bore a most striking likeness to him in every feature and could scarce be known from him as to looks.' We do not know which of the convicts this was – Nicol, maddeningly, did not name names.

Prime Minister Pitt had a 14-year-old cousin, Thomas, who was sent to school at Charterhouse in January 1789, ran away after nine days and begged to go to sea. His father gave in – the boy would only run away again if sent back to school – and a midshipman's commission was arranged for him on HMS *Guardian*. He would sail to New South Wales alongside the transport ship which carried a female convict commonly believed to be his uncle's by-blow. Was there a link? If she truly was an illegitimate daughter and had at some point been supported by a connection of Pitt's, perhaps some cottage on a Pitt estate, young Thomas could have met and been intrigued by his cousin –

wished to follow her abroad for affection, curiosity, childhood friendship or a romantic attachment.

To most contemporaries participating in or discussing the great adventure of the convicts for Sydney Cove, their fate was a terrible one. This, certainly, was how much of the establishment wished it to be considered, for of what use was a penal settlement which was not a terrifying deterrent to crime? However, some women on board the *Lady Julian* regarded their fate more as an escape from intolerable conditions in their country of birth than a punishment. 'Numbers of them would not take their liberty as a boon . . . "We have good victuals and a warm bed," ' they told John Nicol:

> We are not ill-treated, or at the mercy of every drunken ruffian, as we were before. When we rose in the morning we knew not where we would lay our heads in the evening, or if we would break our fast in the course of the day. Banishment is a blessing to us. Have we not been banished for a long time and yet in our native land? . . . We dared not go to our relations whom we had disgraced. Other people would shut their doors in our faces. We were as if a plague were upon us, hated and shunned.

All these remembered conversations are a little suspect, as so many years passed before Nicol wrote his memoirs. Clearly, many women were relieved to be in any place of safety where they no longer had to struggle every day to feed and defend themselves. Certainly, some of the women who talked to John Nicol expressed feelings of relief, or at least resignation. Those who had been beaten into wretchedness by several years of intolerable poverty and ill-treatment may well have felt this way. What could women like Esther Curtis expect from life except more nights falling down stairs and sleeping in the lavatories?

If some were relieved to be leaving behind a life of wretchedness, thinking any future, even penal servitude on the other side of the world, must be better than what they had gone through in the last few years, others were still struggling to avoid what fate and His Majesty's judges had decreed.

Chapter Six

Capital Convicts Condemned

There were other ways to clear the gaols of convicted felons than to transport them or send them to the hulks. Not all those who had committed a capital offence found their jurors and prosecutors limited the damages so they could escape the gallows or had their petitions for clemency answered. Among those on the Capital Convicts Condemned list in Newgate Gaol, waiting for the date of their execution to be made known, were Catherine Heyland, 34, and Christian Murphy, 19, convicted separately that they 'one piece of false, feigned and counterfeit money and coin, to the likeness of one shilling, falsely and deceitfully, feloniously and traitorously, did forge, counterfeit and coin'.

In March a year since, the Westminster Forum debating society had discussed the following motion: 'is not that Law cruel and unjust which inflicts the punishment of Burning alive on a Woman for the same Offence which subjects a Man only to the usual forms of execution?' The law alluded to decreed that women guilty of high treason went to the stake, whereas men guilty of the same crime went to the gallows. The timing of the debate was apt.

In the same Westminster parish where the Forum debated the justice of one sentence for a woman and another for a man, two people were surprised in a garret in March 1788 by Peace Officer

Treadway and two colleagues, acting on information that 'bit-culls' (coiners) were at work. When they got to the top of the stairs, they found that the keyhole had been stopped, put their ears to the door, listened and burst in.

'The prisoner James', claimed Edward Treadway, 'was rubbing something in his fingers.' Seized by Officer Meecham, William James, alias Levi, put his fingers to his mouth. Meecham immediately squeezed him by the jaw, but he had swallowed the evidence and only black foam squirted down the officer's sleeve. In the window, there was a saucer of wet sand and a heap of old sixpences, two finished counterfeit sixpences and a pipkin. With them was a file, some 'scowering paper', a piece of cork, some 'black stuff' and a pair of pliers. By the fire, the officers found a crucible and 'over the garret window, outside, between the cieling [sic] and the roof' an iron flask, or 'fossil'. On the mantelpiece there was a phial of aqua fortis (nitric acid), a vessel to carry the metal to the mould, brass scales and white arsenic. It was a complete coiners' kit. If this were not conclusive enough, a fellow lodger now entered the room unaware there were peace officers there, carrying clean shirts for James. In the pocket of one they found false money and, stuffed down the bodice of Catherine's dress, they found two bags of bad sixpences.

John Nicholls, monier of the mint, was called on in the Old Bailey in April 1788 to identify a good and a bad sixpence. The use of the equipment was unfamiliar to the jury, if not to the more experienced judge, and an expert witness was asked to explain it. The flask, he told them, was the mould used to take an imprint of the good coin in coarse, wet sand, first one side and then the other. After this, the pores of the coarse sand were filled with finer sand 'otherwise what is cast would come out in little spotty holes' and it was smoked over a fire until dry. When set, the casts were filled with brass or tin which had been melted in the crucible and screwed together. The molten metal was refined to resemble copper or silver – copper by mixing it with white arsenic, which turned it one shade whiter, 'to what we call East Indian copper, or tutteneg', and silver by adding aqua fortis which, mixed into any compound containing a trace of silver, 'brings the silver to the surface and throws it white'. Once the false coin had set, it was smoothed, first with the file and then with brown paper and cork. As the expert witness testified, William James and Catherine Heyland had the 'complete apparatus for coining'.

There could be no doubt that coining had been going on in the little garret on Weston Street, nor that the coiners would be sentenced to death. For William James, the only thing that mattered during the hearing was that the judge and jury should be convinced that the guilt was his alone, and Catherine merely a bystander or, at worst, an unwilling accomplice. Throughout the trial, he interrupted judge, prosecutor and witnesses to challenge their evidence of Catherine's involvement. The court did not believe him.

Catherine and William were not the only coining couple to be tried during the April 1788 Sessions. Coiners Jeremiah Grace and Margaret Sullivan were also found guilty and, on Monday 23 June 1788, all four returned to the courtroom after a month in the cells to be told the date of their execution. William, Jeremiah and Margaret had no hope of mercy. Catherine, however, had found a sponsor in Mr Bloxham, Sheriff of the City of London. To his mind she was innocent – or, at least, not so guilty that she deserved the sentence he feared would be pronounced when she went back to the bar in June. As Sheriff of the City, Mr Bloxham was called on to participate in the ceremonies that attended executions in the Old Bailey. He had seen countless hangings and, in June 1786, had seen the coiner Phebe Harris tied to a stake and burned to death outside Newgate Gaol. It was not a sight easily forgotten.

Judge Adair dealt first with the men. William James, alias Levi, and Jeremiah Grace would be hanged that Wednesday outside Newgate Gaol. Then he turned to the women. Catherine's execution was to be stayed by a month. But Margaret Sullivan, a woman and guilty of treason, was to be burned at the stake. She had two days in which to prepare herself.

The next day saw the first of *The Times*'s attacks on the barbarity of Sullivan's sentence. 'Must not mankind laugh at our long speeches against African slavery... when ... we roast a fellow creature alive, for putting a pennyworth of quicksilver into a halfpennyworth of brass?' its writers asked.

Margaret Sullivan spent Tuesday night in prayer with a Catholic priest. She refused the gift of strawberries sent her by Sheriff Bloxham's wife. The prisoners in Newgate Gaol could hear the first signs of excitement from the early hours of Wednesday morning as people began to congregate in St Paul's Churchyard and the inns of the Old Bailey. At six o'clock, St Sepulchre's bell began to toll and a riotous crowd thronged the alley where Sheriff Bloxham's men were assembling the apparatus of execution. First, a covered-in walkway from the Debtors' Gate; next, steps leading on to the portable scaffold, which towered to three times a man's height above the crowd. People struggled for the best view; young men climbed to the balconies of the houses facing the prison. The King's Head and the Four Kings, the two inns closest to the execution place, did roaring business; at the Magpie and Stump, miniature gallows were on sale as mementoes.

At seven o'clock, William James and Jeremiah Grace came through the Debtors' Gate. They were hooded, with their hands tied behind their backs. They were led to the scaffold, the noose went round their necks and there was a roar of 'Hats off!' from the back of the crowd. And then, for 45 minutes, the chaplain made his pious and inaudible speech. Just before eight o'clock Catherine Heyland, inside the prison, heard the noise of the crowd as the platform dropped and William kicked at the end of his rope. The crowd refreshed itself. Fifteen minutes passed before Margaret Sullivan, clad in penitential white, emerged with the priest. She was taken to the stake, made to stand on a stool and faggots were placed around her. With ceremony and deliberation, the sheriff's men appeared with flaming torches, and the body of Margaret Sullivan, guilty of treason, was ritually turned to ash before the crowd in the street and the dignitaries of the City, Sheriff Bloxham among them, on a viewing platform specially erected for the occasion.

London was shocked. It had been two years since the last woman had been burned at the stake; two years since the sickening smell of human meat had floated down Newgate Street to the City and down the Strand to the Thames. Margaret Sullivan's execution was seen as savage, senseless, utterly out of step with enlightened thinking and abhorrent in its application to women only. 'It has been the boast of the country, that there was no barbarity annexed to our punishment of criminals. Is the burning of a woman no torture? Shame on such barbarity. The very savages in the wildest parts of the world pay respect to their females, whilst Great Britain selects their tender bodies as the only objects fit for excruciating torture.' *The Times* on this occasion spoke even for the hardline string-'em-up brigade.

If for many it was a week of shame and protest, for Catherine Heyland, under sentence of the same execution, it was the start of a month of terror. Now began the cat-and-mouse game of respites. She was due to burn in four weeks' time, on 21 July. Parliament was in recess, and the men who could save her, the secretaries of state and those who had access to them, were in the country for the summer. Three and a half weeks passed without word from them.

By the last of the evening light on Sunday 20 July, men were at work outside the prison walls preparing the equipment for her execution. A stake was secured; faggots placed around its base. Inside, Catherine was with the chaplain. Gifts were sent her by well-wishers, notes brought in from the outside world.

Sheriff Bloxham was not there. He was desperate that a woman he believed innocent should not die in so dreadful a way. It had become clear earlier in the day that the requested reprieve was not going to arrive and that another woman would burn unless he took immediate action. While Catherine prayed, the sheriff was galloping towards the country house where the secretary of state was spending the weekend. He arrived at three in the morning, demanded to be taken to His Lordship's bedroom and within an hour was galloping back to London with the paper in his hand. Already the crowds were gathering in St Sepulchre's yard. Two hours before the torches were due to light the faggots, Catherine Heyland was allowed a further four days of life.

The stake was dismantled, the faggots carted away. On Monday, the secretary of state was back in London, importuned before he could draw breath by Sheriff Bloxham to extend Catherine's reprieve. On 24 July, when orders had already been given to erect the stake and bring in the faggots, a paper arrived which reprieved her from her dreadful penalty during His Majesty's pleasure. She was still alive, but her future was a terrible blank.

By March 1789, Catherine Heyland had been on the Capital Convicts Condemned list for almost a year. She was one of 25 women under sentence of death (there were 74 on the equivalent list for men) all waiting for the date of their execution to be announced or for a pardon to be granted. Six days after 108 women left Newgate for the *Lady Julian*, the ghastly performance of the stake and the faggots was repeated. This time the female coiner was 19-year-old Christian Murphy; again the male accomplice was hanged first and again Catherine Heyland heard the crowd enjoying a spectacle in which one day it could be her turn to star.

The following month, however, an event occurred whose impact was felt throughout England but which had particular effect on Catherine Heyland, Nelly Kerwin and 20 other women on the Capital Convicts Condemned list. It led to a sensational trial in the Old Bailey. It was in April that King George III officially regained his wits and a national day of thanksgiving was celebrated. 'Such a day of joy was never known nor felt in any country', wrote *The Times* loyally, describing the fireworks, floats, lights, street parties and traffic jams around St James's and St Paul's, the singing, the bells, the volleys of gunfire across the river. Courtiers, socialites, merchants and honourable members fought to hold the most magnificent party. Eight hundred people attended a City assembly gala at Merchant Taylors' Hall, where a 'cold collation and soupes' was followed by creations in sugar, including a four-foot-high triumphal arch etched with statements of loyalty. A procession from St James's to St Paul's was planned for a thanksgiving service in the cathedral. People paid tuppence each through the week to see the dais being erected in the cathedral and turned out in tens of thousands to see the royal family smile and wave.

Provincial towns expressed their delight, and the *Lincoln Mercury* reported the celebrations for weeks. In Gainsborough they fired a cannon, in Lincoln they had a county dinner, in Louth a morning of thanksgiving was begun by the ringing of bells. In Swinhead, a church band paraded through the streets and ale was brought out in milk pails. In Corby, citizens processed from the Roe Buck Inn to the market cross 'playing "God Save the King" with an occasional doxology'. At Melton Mowbray they had fireworks, in Wymondham they had a bonfire, at Falkingham they roasted several whole sheep, at Thurlby rejoicings were made with 'a large quantity of liquor given by every farmer in the town'; in Houghton-on-the-Hill, every child received a penny loaf and the women were all treated with tea. To this 'liberality and condescension towards the lower class of people' was attributed much of the peaceful nature of these celebrations. Dr Willis was brought back to receptions and balls throughout the county where 'his adulation is indescribable'. In

Wisbech, a four-foot figure of Britannia on a lion couchant illuminated the Ship Inn; in Stamford, they held an 'elegant ball and cold collation'.

In London, some of the convicts condemned to die were to be pardoned as part of the general thanksgiving and, at the Old Bailey Sessions of April, this caused a fight almost literally to the death. During the five-day Sessions, some of the disorderly women in the dock became such a *cause célèbre* in London society that the closing stages of their trial were graced by two more successful members of the sisterhood, the Duchess of Cumberland and Mrs Fitzherbert, sitting in the public gallery of Court Number One.

The usual thieves and muggers appeared in the usual succession of brief hearings and swift judgements from 20 to 23 April. On 24 April, the female Capital Convicts Condemned were brought up from their cell, 'put to the Bar and informed that His Majesty's Pardon was granted to them on the following Conditions, viz: Lydia Jones, Elizabeth Shakespear, Esther Thornton, Catherine Heyland, Ann Steel, Elizabeth Smith, Mary Wade, Jane Whiting, Jane Tyler, Sarah Mills, Sarah Cowden, Sarah Storer, Martha Cutler, Eleanor Kirwin alias Karavan: *transportation for the term of their natural lives.*

'Margaret Wood, Sarah McCormick, Mary Kimes alias Potten, Sarah Chasey, Sarah Young, Mary Hook, Elizabeth Goldsmith, Elizabeth Hounsum [this should have been Catherine Hounsam]: *transportation for 7 years.*'

'Do you accept the terms of the pardon?' asked the recorder.

'Yes,' said Catherine Heyland and 15 other women.

'No,' said the remaining seven, and the fight began.

Catherine Heyland was no longer under sentence of the stake. She and the others who had accepted were taken back to the cells to be re-recorded under the 'Transportation to Sydney Cove' list. The others remained at the bar.

'I will die by the laws of my own country before ever I will go abroad for my life,' said Sarah Cowden. 'I am innocent and so is Sarah Storer.'

'Before I will go abroad for my natural life, I will sooner die,' and, 'I will not accept it, I am innocent,' said Martha Cutler and Sarah Storer.

The other three women who refused, forger Nelly Kerwin, mugger Sarah Mills and maidservant Jane Tyler, were professional criminals. But Martha Cutler, Sarah Storer, Sarah Cowden or all three of them may genuinely have been innocent of the assault on the king's highway for which they had been sentenced to hang in December 1787.

Henry Solomon, resident in the Jewish area of Whitechapel, was already known to these three women and their unidentified male accomplice. They called him by name as he passed the entrance to Gun Alley on his way to the barber, so he turned up the court towards them. At the far end, Sarah Storer knocked his hat off his head and slipped inside an open door. Three or four others surrounded him, taunting and jeering, daring him to get his hat back and finally shoving him in after her. Once inside, 'all three of them together threw me down on the bed'. Cowden 'laid upon me', Storer 'held my mouth fast' and Martha stood 'with her back against the door'. Storer rifled his pockets and passed 14 guineas and 10 shillings to Martha, who disappeared. The other two then kicked him out, threw his hat after him and told him 'I might go about my business'. Outside, in Gun Alley, a passing couple had heard the scuffling and looked through the window to see what was happening. They were on the point of calling the watch when Solomon came staggering out. It was principally on their evidence that the three women were convicted.

In the dock, all three had had excuses which rang tired and unconvincing: Cowden was only visiting, not there at the time of the offence; Storer had heard Solomon come in and, 'says he, I have been robbed and the first I meet, I will make suffer for it';

Cutler claimed Solomon was taking his revenge for some un-specified wrong. They were defences heard day in, day out, and Justice Rose was unimpressed.

Odds on, they were guilty. But some may have been guiltier than others, and it was on Solomon's word alone that the sum stolen was determined as 14 guineas and 10 shillings, over the capital limit. The watchman who took Martha up within half an hour of the offence found only three shillings on her. Half an hour was long enough to disembarrass oneself of illicit cash or goods, but what causes a qualm about the verdict was the passion with which they were still fighting back 14 months later.

The recorder, taken aback by this stony-faced rejection of His Majesty's graciousness, warned the other women at the bar that 'if you do not accept of the king's pardon now, it will be too late hereafter; you may depend upon it, that every woman who now refuses to receive the king's pardon will be ordered for immediate execution'. It was only a month since 11 men and Christian Murphy had been executed outside in the street. 'Immediate execution' meant within days. But the others, too, did not hesitate in their rejection of the terms offered. 'I will go to my former sentence,' said Sarah Mills. 'I had rather die than go out of my country to be devoured by savages.' Jane Tyler, too, preferred to 'die first. I think I have suffered hard enough to be in gaol three years for what I have done.'

Clever Nelly Kerwin was more circumspect in her approach, but of the same mind: 'I hope this honourable Court, nor any of the Gentlemen in company, will not object to what I shall say . . . I do not intend to object to my sentence but I am not in a situation to go abroad; if I was, I would go . . . I have two small children . . . I have no objection to confinement for life . . . I cannot live long . . .'

'If you do not accept it now,' the recorder told them, 'I have no power if you should wish for mitigation of your sentence; but after you have accepted it, you may apply further for mitigation . . . but if you do not accept of these terms . . . you . . . will certainly be ordered for execution and it will be too late to recall your opinion.' It was bluntly put: both stick and carrot used in an unashamed attempt to coerce them into acceptance. The government was determined to clear the cells as they had not been cleared in the haphazard run-up to the departure of the first fleet. In 1786 several convicts had managed to escape boarding through one device or another and had hung around ever since, clogging up the cells. This could not be allowed to happen again.

Nelly put in a final plea: 'If you think proper to give me time 'til Mr Simpson pronounces me fit to go . . . but not to send me away in a day or two . . .'

The insistence of the seven on 'going to their former sentence' was not due only to the terror of exile among savages. It was also a calculated gamble, and this was why the court was insisting so brutally on the inevitability of immediate execution.

Nelly Kerwin had been in Newgate since July 1786. She should already have been executed, or transported on the first fleet to Botany Bay which left in May 1787. However, at the end of October 1786 a panel of matrons had confirmed her to be pregnant. Her cellmate, Esther Abrahams, was also pregnant and in March 1787 had given birth to a daughter. Nelly's baby was due in June 1787, but in mid-April she miscarried. When Esther and her month-old baby went aboard the *Lady Penrhyn* for transportation to Botany Bay with the previous fleet, Nelly was still in the Newgate infirmary. Within three weeks of losing her baby, her sentence was reconfirmed but her execution was 'to be staid until His Majesty's pleasure should be known'. His Majesty's pleasure could not be known until the next Old Bailey Sessions – which took place two weeks after the departure of the fleet. On 23 April 1787, a prison clerk has automatically written 'pregnant' by Nelly's name, as he had done every week for seven months, and then, remembering, crossed it out. Two years later,

Nelly was gambling that ill health, small children and three years in gaol would get her an unconditional pardon.

The court of April 1789 would not allow such cases to remain in gaols where space was so desperate that every extra body counted. She had to die or go. So on 24 April, Nelly and the other recalcitrant women were taken back to the cells to think about it overnight. On 25 April, they were brought back to the bar and asked again if they would accept the terms of their pardons. The recorder once more made the government's intentions brutally clear:

Your not being inclined to accept that pardon arises from a hope that you shall not be sent off so soon as the other Prisoners . . . This sort of conduct will be considered as an aggravation of your offences and if you have any hopes that your sentence will be altered, you had much better accept of the King's pardon now, and try what interest you have to get that sentence mitigated but if you go from the Bar now, you will remain under sentence of death and you may depend upon it that you will suffer death with the first culprits, at the next execution.

Twelve hours' contemplation had not altered the women's resolve. All of them refused, the recorder lost his temper and there was uproar in the courtroom.

'Let these women be confined in separate cells and fed on bread and water!' he shouted. They could think it over in solitary confinement and on a punishment diet until the June Sessions came round.

Successive scheduled departure dates for the second fleet to New South Wales had come and gone; transportation lists had to be finalised and the women embarked. The pardons, petitions, pleas of sickness and pregnancy, movements on board the ship and off again all became too much for the prison clerks to keep up with. Records fell into disarray. Women released or too ill to travel were not cancelled from the Transportation Register; women who arrived at the last minute were never added. Surgeon Simpson had written another letter to Lord Sydney in March, acidly outlining the situation in which prisoners such as Ann Wheeler and the other unfortunates were living and attaching a petition for the immediate release of ten women for whom 'a further continuation of . . . confinement will be dangerous to their lives'. Lord Sydney did as he was requested and sent a pardon to Sheriff Bloxham. Among the women released back on to the streets were two names later transcribed on to the Transportation Register of the *Lady Julian*: maidservant Elizabeth Metcalfe, who had stolen shoes from her shoemaker master and had been in prison for six months, and Jane Williams, who had deceived her landlord into letting her a room with a sob story about an injured husband and had then stolen his furniture.

Turnover through the cells was now more rapid, but the total number in gaol was still too high for safety. The same week in which Christian Murphy was burned and her lover was hanged, Ann Thomas was robbing her mistress and Ann Rock was robbing her master, prostitute Elizabeth Jones stole the kneebuckles from a sailor's breeches while he slept in her bed on the Strand, Maria Israel stole two pieces of muslin in Prince's Street and Mary Jones took clothes from a house in Turnmill Street. All were brought in for the April Sessions, which saw Nelly Kerwin and five others sent to the cells on bread and water. Two days later, Sarah Roberts was brought to bed of a male child in the Newgate infirmary, where she remained until she was pardoned in October, although the clerks never got round to removing her name from the embarkation list.

Maidservant Ann Aborough was already on board the *Lady Julian* when her petition was finally forwarded to Lord Sydney. As Ann waited helplessly in the river, her mother had been working with determination to bring her home. First, she had gone to Lord Loughborough to plead her daughter's case. Then she acquired a 'certificate' from 'the churchwardens and other respectable inhabitants' of the parish to back up the petition sent, with Lord Loughborough's recommendation, to Lord Sydney. This stated that Ann was the only child of respectable parents, who had been 20 years in the parish and who were 'willing to take her home and provide for her'. 'Under these very favourable circumstances,' wrote Sydney, 'I cannot but feel myself impelled to recommend her to His Majesty's Royal Mercy as an Object of Free Pardon.' On 26 May, weeks before the ship sailed, a pardon was issued and Ann Aborough was taken home joyfully by her parents. Her name remained on the list of those who sailed.

At the end of the month, the women who had refused His Majesty's mercy were brought back to the bar in the Old Bailey. Clearly, a starvation diet had had some effect. There were listless replies to the recorder's question from Jane Tyler ('Yes, I will') and from Martha Cutler ('Why, I must'). But then the recorder came to Sarah Cowden, 21, headstrong and convinced of her own and her friend's innocence.

'I am willing to accept of whatever sentence the King passes upon me, but Sarah Storer is innocent . . . I will accept it if that woman's sentence is mitigated.'

'You have nothing to do with the case of any other person but yourself.'

'I will accept of my sentence willingly, if this woman's sentence is mitigated.'

There was another burst of temper from the recorder: 'Remove all the women from the court but Sarah Cowden!'

When Sarah was alone facing the bench, he let rip. 'You will attend to this. The government of this country will not suffer the mercy of the King to be trifled with . . . If you refuse . . . you must prepare to die the day following, you shall be executed the day following.'

'I hope I shall have more mercy shewn me than ever I had at this bar,' replied Sarah bitterly.

'If you are sufficiently prepared to die on Thursday next, the court will give orders accordingly.'

'That I am.'

'Let her stand committed to the cells and let the sheriffs prepare for an execution on Thursday morning. Take her away.'

Sarah Cowden was led back into the prison to uproar from the public gallery and pleas from both Counsel Garrow and Mr Villette, the ordinary (prison chaplain), to be allowed to reason with her. Reluctantly, and still simmering, the recorder dismissed the men into the cells. In the meantime, Sarah Storer, the object of Sarah Cowden's solicitude, and Sarah Mills once more faced a furious recorder and a public gallery on the edge of its seat.

'If at any future period the King would incline to grant you any further remission of your sentence, your submission to his will will be an additional motive . . . you have done wisely.'

Finally they accepted, but were clearly not going to go quietly and the recorder, determined to avoid another outburst, ordered the women to be taken away immediately. Sarah Storer left the room wailing 'but not for my life, I never will, I never will . . .'

It was now that Garrow reappeared to beg the recorder to allow Sarah Cowden back to the bar to accept her pardon. He and Mr Villette had been with her a bare quarter of an hour but had managed to turn her from passionate defiance to listless acceptance. Possibly the news that Sarah Storer had herself accepted transportation for life had been brought into her cell and she no longer had reason to sacrifice herself. Possibly the arguments the recorder had put to other women, that mitigation of a sentence was always a possibility – provided one was still alive – had been put more urgently and forcibly to her by Garrow. Possibly the ordinary had told her horrific tales of hangings gone wrong.

When eventually Sarah agreed to her conditional pardon, Mr

Garrow raced back into the courtroom as the others were being led away. The dignity of the recorder's office, however, had been too far offended for him to allow the woman back into his courtroom. 'I do not think the King's mercy should go a-begging . . . I can show no indulgence to those who treat the mercy of the King with contempt.'

'I only ask the Court to consider the order not to be irrevocable.'

'As to me, it is irrevocable. I shall order the execution.'

Ignoring Mr Garrow standing before him, the recorder then donned the customary black square and read out the death sentence on ten men who had come up before him during the Sessions. As he came to an end, Garrow tried once more, begging his indulgence, on behalf of 'a very miserable wretch who deserves now, having seen the folly of her behaviour, humbly to intreat, that she may be permitted to accept that pardon of His Majesty's'.

His plea was finally accepted and Sarah Cowden, too, was removed to the transportation cells.

It was not until two weeks later, in mid-June, that the secretary of state got round to reading the petitions for clemency on behalf of Charlotte Marsh, on board the *Lady Julian*, and not until 30 June, when the ship was on the point of leaving, that he decided she had acted under the evil influence of her mother, now dead of gaol fever, and that, as her husband was prepared to offer securities for her for the period of two years, he could take her home. Charlotte's six-month ordeal was over, and she left the ship two weeks before she sailed.

Apart from those conducting vigorous campaigns by any means open to them to be granted a pardon, there were more reckless souls on board, who, abandoning any attempt at legitimate release, escaped the night before they were due to set sail. This was one of several escape attempts while the *Lady Julian* lay in the river, but the only successful one. Many must have thought that they had little to lose and much to gain from trying, and, if they did not try now, the opportunity would be lost for ever. These women were also the friends and lovers of people on shore who were the best around in orchestrating a hit, breaking hatches and doors, planning getaway routes, distracting guards, finding venal boatmen and locksmiths and other criminal techniques.

The four who escaped went over the stern and into a boat their friends had waiting for them below. It must have taken nerve to wait for the night immediately before departure and to keep the secret hidden that long, but it paid off. The night before sailing there was the traditional party: heavy drinking among the crew, barrels of gin rowed out to the ship from the inns along the riverbanks and the sailors and their girlfriends carousing below decks from an early hour of the evening. The watch, posted on the quarterdeck and resentful he had drawn the short straw and could not join the frolics below, was an easy target. The women offered him gin, flirted, offered him more gin and, when he was senseless, slipped over the side and away. Their loss was not discovered until the morning, and then it was too late to wait for them to be rounded up and brought back on board.

As records of who was aboard were hopelessly out of date, the exact number of women who sailed on the *Lady Julian* when she left London is unknown. John Nicol, the steward, remembered there having been 245; the Transportation Register lists only 172, as none of the women from outside London had been entered on it. Sarah Whitelam, Mary Rose and the other Lincolnshire women are listed as sailing aboard the *Neptune* (a transport that sailed four months later) when in fact they sailed on the *Lady Julian*. Ann Wheeler, Elizabeth Barnsley's fever-struck partner, is listed as sailing on the *Lady Julian* when in fact she sailed on the *Neptune*. There are many other mistakes. Ann Clapton and Charlotte Marsh are both listed; the first was dead, the other pardoned. Another pardoned shoplifter, Alice Haynes, also appears on the list, as does Sarah Roberts, who was nearing her confinement in Newgate Gaol when the *Lady Julian* sailed. One consequence of this muddle is that the identities of three of the four women who went over the side are not known.

The one escaper whose identity *is* known was 24-year-old shoplifter Mary Talbot, who fled the ship with her baby William. She was later retaken and received a death sentence which was commuted to transportation for the term of her natural life in December 1790. She left for New South Wales aboard the *Mary Ann* in 1791 and died on arrival in the colony. Whoever the other three were, the *Lady Julian* sailed without them.

Chapter Seven

Leaving London

In the first week of July 1789, the *Lady Julian* left her mooring at Galleons Reach and sailed down the Thames with the tide, out to the coasts of Kent. She was making for Portsmouth and would anchor on the Mother Bank outside Portsmouth harbour. Like the Thames at Woolwich, Portsmouth harbour was crowded with prison hulks. Aboard some of them were men who had thought they were off to Quebec the previous summer; aboard others were men from Lincoln and Oakham gaols, brought south the previous year. The *Ceres* and *Dunkirk* hulks had once been ships of the line, engaged in battles against the Americans. They were now fallen on hard times and home to 600 male felons, among them a handful intimately connected to women aboard the *Lady Julian*. Thomas Higgins, partner or accomplice of London receiver Grace Maddox, was held here. Bristolian James Saney, aboard the *Dunkirk*, was known to four women who had boarded the *Lady Julian* in the Thames or would do so in Plymouth Sound: his 18-year-old sister Elizabeth and three members of the Fidoe family, mother and daughters, one of whom seems to have been responsible for shopping him. George Simpson had been on the *Ceres* for two years. He was brother, cousin or husband to Charlotte Simpson, alias Hall, with whom he had been tried in 1787 for the theft of a handsaw and a smoothing-plane. Also on the *Ceres* was William Pimlott, partner to Sarah Carter, with whom he had been convicted of stealing six cloth coats, a pair of sugar-tongs and 47 shillings in cash two years previously. Thomas Gregory of Hertfordshire had both a wife and a child aboard the *Lady Julian*: his wife Sarah had embarked with their infant daughter Elizabeth. William Bramsden, another thief, and husband of Sarah Young, had arrived in July 1788, six weeks after his wife had been arrested in Swallow Street for stealing nine yards of muslin and been sentenced to death. Bramsden himself was sentenced to transportation and sent to the *Ceres*, where he had received the news that Sarah had been pardoned on condition of transportation in thanksgiving for the king's recovery. On 25 August, a month after the *Lady Julian* had left Portsmouth harbour, a petition would arrive on Secretary Nepean's desk from Bramsden, begging to be sent out on the first ship to Sydney Cove to rejoin his beloved 18-year-old wife.

Thomas Barnsley, also on the *Ceres*, had been waiting for his sentence of transportation to be executed since 1785. In 1786, he had gone aboard the hulks, first in the Thames, then in Portsmouth, and Elizabeth and their small children had moved from Reading to London to be near him. Two petitions had already been addressed to the magistrates from the *Ceres*, probably delivered by Elizabeth. Thomas, like his wife, possessed self-confidence and imagination. His petitions (or hers on his behalf) portrayed him as an honest man, educated, a musician by profession, reduced to penury by circumstance and forced to steal to keep his wife and children from the greatest distress. He protested strongly the way in which men of breeding like himself were 'herded like animals' with men of the lowest class. The Barnsleys did not lack contacts, or persistence – Thomas had managed to avoid sailing with the first fleet and Elizabeth had got his petitions signed by an alderman and two City merchants. The magistrates did not budge. Stealing an entire trunk of tea off the back of a coach to Bristol did not conform to their idea of a man who turned to crime to feed his starving babies. The

Barnsley marriage was a union of two clever and resourceful personalities; despite a separation of four years and an end to Elizabeth's visits aboard the *Ceres* since her own arrest in February 1788, the bond between the two had survived.

Lieutenant Edgar had allowed visits on board at Galleons Reach and was to countenance, possibly encourage, visits on board at every other port of call on the voyage out. The sympathy John Nicol noted in him for the women in his care would have inclined him towards permitting a last meeting with their men or, at the least, the opportunity to send them a message. On the other hand, they had just lost four over the stern in the Thames, and it might have seemed a better idea to keep the women in strict isolation until out of British waters and away from dangerous contacts. Nor did it depend solely on Edgar whether the women of the *Lady Julian* and the men on the hulks were allowed to make contact; it also depended on the superintendents of the hulks, men not noted for their compassion. At the least, written messages of farewell were probably rowed from one ship to another by seamen. Mrs Barnsley certainly had enough money to bribe someone to run errands, with or without the permission of Agent Edgar.

Portsmouth was Nelly Kerwin's home town, although she had not been here since 1786. There is no record that her children were with her in Newgate Gaol, so they may have been boarded out in Gosport for the last three years. This was her opportunity to say goodbye.

The *Lady Julian*'s stay in Portsmouth was brief. The Mother Bank, just outside Portsmouth harbour, was a traditional gathering place for convoys of merchant or military shipping. Back at the start of the year, it had been optimistically planned that the *Lady Julian* would be only one of a fleet of transports to Sydney Cove which would gather here and sail in convoy, guarded by HMS *Guardian* and a corps of marines. Confusion, countermanded orders, a change in agent from William Richards to the slavers Camden, Calvert & King, a change in secretary of state when Sydney handed over to Evan Nepean had all delayed departure. The *Guardian* had sailed from the Thames to Portsmouth a few days before the *Lady Julian* but because of more delays taking on stores and a full complement of seamen she did not sail on with her from Portsmouth. The other three transport ships that would sail that year, the *Neptune*, *Scarborough* and *Surprize*, had only just been commissioned. The *Lady Julian* sailed late in the season and alone; no convoy joined her off Portsmouth.

Just before the *Lady Julian* left, a harbour official's boat drew up alongside with a document for Agent Edgar. It contained orders for the last-minute release of one of the women aboard. A petition lodged in May on behalf of Susannah Bray, alias Gay, a 22-year-old shoplifter from London, was being considered. Pending a decision, she must leave the ship and be taken back to London. Susannah's chest came up from the hold, she made brief farewells and left. The *Lady Julian* sailed from Portsmouth minus one, piloted around the shoals of the Isle of Wight before heading westwards down the Channel. One more woman was to leave the ship before the ship left British waters. As John Nicol wrote of her 30 years later:

The poor young Scottish girl I have never yet got out of my mind. She was young and beautiful, even in the convict dress, but pale as death and her eyes red with weeping. She never spoke to any of the other women or came on deck. She was constantly sitting in the same corner from morning to night . . . my heart bled for her – she was a countrywoman in misfortune. I offered her consolation but she heeded me not, or only answered with sighs and tears. If I spoke of Scotland she would wring her hands and sob, until I thought her heart would burst . . . I lent her my Bible to comfort her but she read it not; she laid it on her lap after kissing it and only bedewed it with her tears. At length she sunk into her grave of no disease but a broken heart.

Because the embarkation records do not list women from provincial gaols and records drawn up in Sydney list only those who disembarked, the 'poor young Scottish girl' cannot be identified. However, she was dead before the ship left British waters, of malnutrition, exhaustion, lingering gaol fever and lack of the will to live. The ship hove to and she was buried in the Channel in a rough coffin made for her by the ship's carpenter. Someone, perhaps Captain Aitken, said prayers and the convicts bowed their heads. Then the sailors went back to their tasks, the ship turned west and they got under way once more.

By the last week of July, the *Lady Julian* was one of a throng of vessels in Plymouth Sound. This was one of the busiest ports in the country. The Sound itself, Cawsand Bay, Cattewater, the Tamar River as far up as Calstock and the dockyards of Devonport were full of working craft – East Indiamen, private merchantmen, pilot boats, delivery boats, the fishing fleet, His Majesty's men-of-war. The shores were occupied by yards, workshops and market gardens whose produce supplied ships of a dozen nationalities. Along the fringe of the Mount Edgecumbe estate, a battery of guns pointed seawards towards the French. In July, the icy-cold, indigo-blue Cawsand water was scarcely visible among the mass of shipping crammed into the bay. This was the last provisioning stop before the Canaries for those sailing for Africa, the Indies, the Azores, or America.

The first task of a ship's company newly arrived in port was to water the ship. Arrangements for watering varied in sophistication and cost from harbour to harbour and country to country. In Plymouth, water was collected from Drake's Leat, the conduit built for Sir Francis, scourge of the Spanish in another century's wars, which brought sweet water from Dartmoor down to the Sound to be casked for shipping. Rowing casks ashore, filling them, getting them back on board and stowing them safely was a full day's work or more for the men.

Meanwhile, Lieutenant Edgar was pacing the government

abattoirs in Stonehouse Creek for beef, pricing up meat on the hoof at cattle markets on Plymouth Hoe and visiting agents for the Tamar Valley market gardeners to negotiate the price of greens. Most supplies and materials for the voyage had been commissioned directly by the Admiralty, whether collected in London or Plymouth, but fresh food had to be marketed at each port against a cash advance signed for in London. There seems not to have been a purser on the *Lady Julian*, and the purser's usual book-keeping duties were part of Lieutenant Edgar's brief, probably with the help of John Nicol. Nicol, as cooper, was responsible for ensuring that food was properly preserved and rations fairly distributed, while Edgar was ultimately responsible to the government for ensuring that the ship's supplies remained within budget, including the women's food allowance. The work of going ashore, placing orders and handing over cash was done by Edgar and whichever of the officers or tradesmen he trusted most. Nicol would have been one of them. He was honest and experienced and he had an interest in ensuring that all goods coming on board were properly casked – if they were not, he would get the blame when the food went rotten. So the ship remained at anchor in Cawsand Bay while Nicol rowed Lieutenant Edgar across to the Hoe each day with a pencil behind his ear and a scrap of paper for sums. They came back each day with orders placed and some smelly delicacy in the pocket of John's breeches, for Sarah Whitelam was now three months pregnant.

The quantity of shipping in port, and the relative clumsiness of a large vessel under sail, meant that sailing across the Sound to pick up supplies was impracticable. Either the ship manoeuvred herself alongside the government stores in Stonehouse Creek and took everything aboard there or, more likely, Edgar employed lighters to sail across to Cawsand Bay. While he and Nicol were placing orders for live meat ashore, the carpenter and his mate had been building cattle pens on the foredeck and poultry cages behind the wheel. Livestock had probably not been taken on in London for the short trip along the south coast but for a voyage to the Canaries, thence Cape Town, it was time to get the cows aboard. The animals were penned into lighters – a small herd of cows, some goats, poultry, a few hogs and a flock of sheep – and brought across the Sound. The lighters came alongside, the smaller animals were passed up, then the cattle were forced into a canvas sling and hoisted on board, where a rope was slung round their necks and they were hauled forward. Seamen sweated and the deck steamed with fresh manure.

When the *Lady Julian* arrived in Sydney Cove a year later, there were 18 women aboard her who had been delivered from West Country gaols in cities closer to Plymouth than London. Conceivably, these 18 women out of the gaols of Exeter, Bristol, Gloucester and Taunton boarded at Plymouth, and Lieutenant Edgar knew nothing of them until he arrived in the Sound and found that orders had been issued over his head for their delivery. It was not uncommon for the Admiralty to make such arrangements without the knowledge of captains and agents, relying on their ingenuity to accommodate extra cargo foisted on them. The shipwrights of Plymouth Sound were used to making and mending to deal with last-minute changes to an Admiralty commission.

Once again, John Nicol set up his blacksmith's anvil on board to knock the irons from the new arrivals: a predictable, forlorn group of thieves and clumsy burglars. As in the Thames, relatives and sweethearts came aboard to take their leave of daughters, sisters, wives, mothers, possibly grandmothers, as one of the Taunton women was 63 years old. They passed over a few coins and pledged faith above the banging of hammers and the shouts of delivery men shoving them out of the way. Below, chests and boxes were pushed forward to make room for those of the arrivals, and the old girls squeezed up in the sleeping shelves to make room for the new. There were now somewhere between 225 and

240 women on board. Roughly 200 women and five infants were sleeping in the orlop; the rest of the women were sleeping, periodically or permanently, with the officers and crew.

The sailors' 'right' to a female mate was a piece of sexual piracy deeply enshrined in Honest Jack the Seaman's idea of his rights, and these relationships were not just a bit of roughhouse below deck to which the officers turned a blind eye; they were fully authorised and equipped. Every seaman and every officer on board the *Lady Julian* was entitled 'by law', as *The Times* reported in August, to oblige the woman of his choice to serve him as 'mate' for the duration of the voyage. The paper published a coy commentary that month: 'a ship is now laying [in Plymouth] which has 260 [*The Times* had yet another total] females on board, the youngest 11, the oldest 68 . . . the crew of the ship consists of 30 and 5 or 6 officers, each of whom is allowed to select a mate for the voyage. Government has ordered them baby cloaths for 60 – supposing the salubrity of the sea-air may, during the long voyage, produce babies to every honest woman.'

It was not only the forecastle that took advantage of what was on offer on the orlop; the custom of selecting a mate was also observed by the officers. One of the girls who came out of Exeter Gaol and probably boarded at Plymouth was 18-year-old Ann Mash, in prison since March 1788 for stealing wheat. Her stint on the sleeping shelves of the orlop was brief, for she had caught the eye of Surgeon Alley and was soon spirited away to his cubbyhole at the far end of the sickberth. Where the surgeon led, the men followed. 'As soon as they were at sea,' John Nicol remembered cheerfully, 'every man on board took a wife from among the convicts, they nothing loath.' The 'nothing loath' sits ill on the sensibilities of modern readers. One can only speculate on the attitude of the women towards the men on board – indeed, towards men as a species – and whether they believed it possible to have a relationship with any man which was not principally characterised by coercion. There are no records written by convict women to shed light on this. Sarah Whitelam may have felt affection towards her man – although even this is not certain – but whether this affection had developed by the time she was taken 'as wife' is unguessable.

Apart from the fact that it was impossible to say no, however, there were some reasons for a woman not just to accept, but to compete for, the position of sailor's mistress. Most important, there was protection. Every woman on board had by this time lived some part of her life competing for the necessaries of existence, literally fighting for her share of a plate of pork or a glass of gin. Most on board had come from extreme hardship and were, necessarily, selfish and cunning. Many were unaccustomed to the security of being regularly fed and clothed at someone else's expense. Some must have regarded the sailors coldly as a source of extra food, extra drink, extra privileges and some safety from the stealing, cheating and bullying going on at the bottom of the ship. Every woman who had spent time in gaol had been warped by a system in which you bribed the gaoler or starved; bribed the bullies or were mugged; and bribed the trusty or were raped. Many must automatically have seen sleeping with a sailor as a way of bribing him to look out for 'his' woman at the expense of the others.

Most of the women on board the *Lady Julian* were in their late teens or twenties. The sailors were the same age, the officers a little older – like John Nicol, in his mid-thirties, or Thomas Edgar, in his forties. On other ships where female convicts and males – both convicts and sailors – were segregated as a matter of policy (such as on the ships of the first fleet) riots had occurred whenever they put into port and the men got drunk, then attempted to raid the women's quarters. One of the first fleet lieutenants, Ralph Clark, wrote despairingly of the difficulties he had experienced in trying to prevent fraternisation – on his ship, the seamen 'brock throu the Bulk head and had connection with . . . those damn whores' before they had even got to Land's

End. Nor was this a one-way sport. 'The desire of the women to be with the men was so uncontrollable', wrote Surgeon-General White of the previous fleet, 'that neither shame . . . nor the fear of punishment could deter them from making their way through the bulkheads to the apartments assigned the seamen.' Sailors and male convicts risked heavy punishment if the women escaped their quarters by night and crept into the men's to visit someone who had caught their eye on deck. This did not stop it happening. Ralph Clark's men 'brock throu' once again just south of Cabo Verde. The men were flogged and the women put in irons, although had it been Clark's decision 'I should have flogged the whores as well'. Brutal though the *Lady Julian*'s rough-and-ready cohabitation sounds, it was not an unreasonable way to guard against the consequences of sexual frustration among young, single men and women living in close proximity. The difficulties experienced by officers of the first fleet echoed those of generations of officers before them on the Indian and American routes. Captains, officers, crew and passengers aboard most transportation ships accepted cohabitation during the voyage as normal and inevitable.

The sailors were also of a class and sort which was familiar to the women on board, coming, as they did, from areas where seamen just like these lived, partied, drank and formed their friendships and romantic partnerships. Seamen, dockworkers and ships' coopers were the natural partners of women from Limehouse and Shoreditch. Records of the *Lady Julian*'s voyage are few, but they do not indicate brutality towards the women. In contrast to the legends that have grown up around the convict ships to New South Wales, the voyage of the *Lady Julian* was a humane one, and for women coming from the brutalities of gaol, preceded by the brutalities of the streets, and heading for hard labour in Sydney Cove, it was an interlude of tranquillity and care. Cohabitation and easy communication between women and sailors were among the reasons the women on the *Lady*

Julian enjoyed different treatment from that on some other convict ships.

As the tide turned and the Sound began gradually to drain on 29 July 1789, the *Lady Julian* sailed out of Cawsand Bay under topsails. She bulged with temporary excrescences: cattle pens, poultry boxes, shacks erected in the waist for storage and accommodation. The guns of the grand battery on the Mount Edgecumbe estate slid slowly past to port and the sound of workmen's hammers from the landing place below echoed across. Their Majesties were expected daily and there was much to do. The entire landing place was to be covered in soft red baize to welcome the royal feet as they stepped from their barge; a triumphal arch had still to be constructed for them to walk under and a posse of 24 small flowergirls, in white with blue sashes, had yet to be taught to curtsy. This was the women's last clear sight of England. Fewer than 30 would ever return. That same week, the first refugees from revolutionary France began to arrive, among them Lord Mazarin, who fell to his knees on the beaches of Kent and declared 'God bless this land of liberty!'

A couple of hours out from the Sound, the *Lady Julian* cleared Rame Head and headed west towards the open waters of the Atlantic. Keeping a good offing from the rocks of the Cornish coast, the easterlies took her round Ushant, from where a course was laid for the north-westernmost corner of Spain. When the Spanish coast was sighted, she would head off due south for the Canary Islands.

The first few days out were busy ones for Nicol, responsible to Lieutenant Edgar for the storage and distribution of provisions. His stores were kept forward of the women's quarters on the orlop – a labyrinth of chests, trunks, barrels of biscuit, gunpowder, sacks of flour, oats, malt and, stacked against the bulkhead dividing the stores from the convicts' sleeping shelves, scores of wooden boxes containing bottles of liquor. For most of the two days it took to leave the Cornish coast behind, John Nicol was busy below decks, checking his casks.

For the first several hours of activity, all women were confined to the orlop, well out of the seamen's way. Leaving and entering port are the busiest times for a crew: between these two moments of frenetic activity, as long as nothing untoward happens, life on board a well-run ship sailing at the right season is uneventful – trimming the sails, cleaning, disinfecting, cooking, and making repairs. But the first moments of her voyage, from when she leaves port until her course and sails are set, are terrifying to the uninitiated. The noise can induce panic in those who cannot attribute each sound to an ordered activity. Sails flap deafeningly until the wind begins to fill them, ropes crack, urgent commands are shouted incomprehensibly, men run from one side of the ship to another. When the sails were set and the ship in good order, her motion settled and crashes and shouts on deck became fewer. The orlop hatches were removed. Some of the women would already have been suffering their first bout of seasickness and hung over the side to vomit into the slaty water or gaze at the Cornish headlands. Then they left Cornwall behind; from now on, it was parts beyond the seas.

Some sailors may have remained faithful to the first mates they chose among the women, others not. Probably there was a short period of chopping and changing before 30 or so women settled into coupledom and the rest remained cloistered on the orlop. Too much licence would cause fights, among the women as much as the men, and the formation of stable couples on board would reduce the spread of disease. If seamen and convicts were allowed uncontrolled access to each other, the pox would go round both forecastle and orlop like a bushfire. Eighteenth-century ships were chronically and routinely undermanned; if even one man from a watch was out of action in the sickberth, his watch-mates were put under a severe strain.

A muster would have been drawn up for the *Lady Julian*, with details of every man taken on. It no longer exists, or has not been found, so we know only the names of those seamen mentioned in other records, principally the baptisms in Sydney Cove of babies conceived during the voyage out. Not all the women sleeping in the forecastle gave birth, however, and the names of sailors who did not father a baby are lost. We know for certain only the names of seven women taken 'as wife' by the seamen early on in the voyage. One was Sarah Whitelam, already pregnant by John Nicol before she left the River Thames. Another was Sarah Dorset, the girl who had been abandoned by her lover and was arrested for stealing a cloak in a London inn by the servant, William Powell, who shared a name with her forecastle husband, William Edward Powell, on the *Lady Julian*.

If the girls we know about were a typical sample of wifehood before the mast, they seem to have been chosen on the basis of youth. Youth meant not only prettiness but a lower risk of disease. Sarah Whitelam and Sarah Dorset were both 19 or 20. Margaret Wood, a professional burglar from London, was also 19. She had been sentenced to death at the age of seventeen, spent two years in gaol, was respited in April and now shared a hammock with Edward Burgis. The other 'wives' were even younger. Two Warwickshire girls, Mary Warren and Mary Barlow, were 18 when they became pregnant to Sam Braiden and Edward Scott respectively. Ann Bryant, from Maidstone, was just 16 when she was convicted in April 1789, went aboard the *Lady Julian* immediately after her trial and was taken as partner by seaman William Hughes. She seems to have been taken under the wing of the gentle Ratcliff prostitute Sophia Sarah Ann Brown, at 27 years of age almost old enough, by eighteenth-century standards, to have been her mother, but certainly playing the part of older sister during the voyage. The youngest wife was younger even than Ann Bryant. Jane Forbes was 12 when she was tried for picking pockets and convicted of stealing eight shillings; she was 14 when seaman William Carlo took her into his hammock. It sounds like cradle-snatching, and perhaps it was. However, we do not know anything of William Carlo other than he was old enough to go to sea and father a child. He may have been the same age as Jane Forbes – plenty of seamen were.

One older woman from Exeter also bore a baby on the voyage out. Elizabeth Griffin, 35, would give birth to a baby on Christmas Day 1789. However, as she conceived towards the end of March and most of the women from the provinces came aboard between April and July, she was almost certainly pregnant before joining the ship.

It may be that we know about the younger 'wives' only because they did not have the older women's knowledge of contraception and swiftly became pregnant. A sailor's woman might be checked over for him by the surgeon to make sure she was clean of the pox, but when it came to contraception it was unlikely anything except a few words of advice were on offer. The days of mass handouts of condoms to men in the service were far in the future. Pregnancy was, of course, a woman's problem, as was any other unfortunate consequence of sexual intercourse. Condoms existed but were more to guard men against venereal disease than women against conception. Known as 'English overcoats', they were generally designed for gentlemen of means and were sufficiently expensive to put them beyond the means of any except an obsessively hygienic seaman. They were made of animal membrane and available in three sizes from London dealers such as Mrs Phillips who, in 1776, 'hath lately had several orders for France, Spain, Portugal, Italy and other foreign places' and invited 'captains of ships, and gentlemen going abroad' to procure 'any quantity of the best goods on the shortest notice'. Clearly, England was leading the way in many fields of maritime exploration at the end of the eighteenth century.

There was naturally a body of knowledge among women about how to prevent pregnancy, and the advice of the orlop hold was more useful to the teenagers in the forecastle than any dispensed by Surgeon Alley. It was already known to physicians that sperm had some role in conception, hence the need for something to block its entry into the cervix. Nobody in Europe, physician or layman, would know about the fertilisation of eggs from the ovaries for another 50 years. However, if the women on the sleeping shelves of the *Lady Julian*'s orlop deck did not know the exact sequence of the events inside them, or its terminology, surely after years of cohabitation or life on the streets they knew their way around the menstrual cycle well enough to realise some moments were more risky than others.

The most common method of prevention was simple douching after sex, with water and vinegar, alcohol, salt, soda or some other disinfecting and scouring substance. Some women used a syringe for this; some crouched over a pot of boiling water and fumigated themselves on its steam; others soaked a sponge with the mixture and inserted it like a tampon to absorb the semen. Rudimentary caps were also used. These ranged from half a squeezed lemon to beeswax, melted and carefully shaped to fit. These items may not have been available on board ship, but the seamen who had sailed the South Seas might have known of the technique used by islanders: they inserted seaweed into the vagina as a barrier. They may even have known of the customs of the Marquesas Islands, where group sex was common – one woman, several men – and etiquette was that the last man in then sucked his own and everyone else's semen from the womb. About 12 women became pregnant on board the *Lady Julian*. Far more than this number had sex during the voyage, and, given that most of the women were of an age to be fertile, it seems that some method of prevention was being used. Seawater and vinegar douches were routine, if ineffective; the low rate of pregnancy can more probably be attributed to the common practices of withdrawal, anal sex and abstinence at risky moments.

Chapter Eight

Becoming in Turns Outrageous

By the time the *Lady Julian* left Plymouth Sound, she was familiar to most women on board – for many, she had been home for several months. They knew their way from the orlop to the 'tween deck to the forecastle. They were familiar with the galley and knew where the tradesmen and officers messed and slept. They had watched work being done to the hull and masts; they had seen vast areas of canvas laid out on the dockside and later knotted to the masts and spars; they had seen cables and shrouds attached and tested as the ship was rigged in Deptford. They were familiar with the feel of timbers beneath bare feet and the smell of her bilge. They knew what was meant by aft and forward and leeward and below, which was the mizzen and which the main, which was a halyard and which a sheet. But a sailing ship at sea is a different animal from a sailing ship in port – a foreign land, with laws and language incomprehensible to strangers.

Activity never ceased. The small world of the *Lady Julian* now ran on three eight-hour watches, their work dictated by shifts in the direction and force of wind and current which could occur at any hour in the 24-hour cycle. Constant prediction and detection of these changes were the task of the officers commanding the watches. At every hour of every watch, a senior officer was looking upwards at the sails, or forwards to the forecastle, commands were passing from mate to midshipman, midshipman to bosun, bosun's pipe to barefoot seamen streaming upwards and outwards to trim the sails. It was the number and position of sails up, far more than the rudder, which kept the ship on course. Upwards of 20 separate sails could be set and then adjusted, according to the direction and strength of the winds, and the choreography of the men among the masts was crucial to the ship's speed and the ease of her movement. One member of the watch stood lookout at the masthead; another two manned the wheel below, while a gang of others padded ceaselessly about the ship checking, splicing, coiling, patching, mending, greasing, painting – the whole unending business of 'making shipshape'.

The sailors themselves were different at sea. The women had known ordinary men, with ordinary skills. They suddenly became creatures of prehensile ability who would swarm 50 feet above deck up a rope and spend hours aloft protected only by a sense of balance. The young gentlemen and ship's boys were no longer spotty lads who blushed at the convicts' jibes. The carpenter, whom the women had seen in the Thames and the Sound engaged on tasks not so different from those of any onshore chippy, revealed his own arcane knowledge of the ship's body. He was her physician: it was his task to know where she was scarred and how well she had healed, where her weak points were and how much she could bear, the age and seasoning of her skins, the warps and wrinkles in her timbers and the level of water which washed around her belly. The most impressive transformation was that of Lieutenant Edgar from a kindly old sot with a flask in his garter to ship's navigator. It was he who would draw the *Lady Julian* by an invisible thread of calculations and sights through months of empty horizons and bring her into the mouth of a river he had never seen 13,000 miles away.

The *Lady Julian* herself was a different animal at sea. The parts of the ship moved differently, each in relation to the others.

The behaviour of walls and floors changed; even the separate timbers moved in a different way. Everyone had to learn how to stay in time with the heave of the deck away from and towards her and to flex the knee to lengthen and shorten a leg whose support was never constant. The women now learned how to approach the ladders from orlop to 'tween deck and from 'tween deck through the hatch by catching a movement which helped them up and waiting through the next, which could send them sprawling back. They discovered handholds they had never noticed to keep themselves upright when the deck tilted. They found where to get shelter from spray or sun, where to stand for air and light, where and when to vomit.

For many on board, the first experience of being at sea was this: vomiting copiously over the side of the sleeping shelf, or the deck if they could reach it. Seasickness kicked in for Sarah Whitelam in the steward's berth and half a dozen other women in the forecastle just as morning sickness receded. At least one quarter of the women sharing the men's quarters had been suffering the nausea and vertigo of early pregnancy as the ship moved down the Channel from the Thames to Portsmouth to Plymouth Sound. Little could be done to alleviate seasickness; many officers were also suffering during those first days at sea. Years in the service were no guarantee against vulnerability – Nelson was a famous vomiter. His solution was to forsake the bunks with which officers' accommodation was equipped and sleep in a hammock. This remained stable while the ship moved around it, whereas a bunk bucked and plunged with the ship. The hammock protected most ordinary seamen against seasickness: there was more vomiting over the side of bunks aft of the mast than there was over the side of hammocks before it – and there was most of all in the sleeping shelves at the bottom of the ship.

The movement of the ship may have made the women queasy, but in other ways conditions were more pleasant on the open sea than they had been in Cawsand Bay. The seawater through which they were moving was clean, whereas in Cawsand (and even more so in the Thames) they had sat in water soiled by their own refuse each day until the tides cleansed their berth. In the heat of July, Plymouth Sound had smelled like one vast privy. As they sailed towards Spain, they left their effluent in their wake and the air was clean – or cleanish. One stench-provoker they had not left behind in Plymouth was the ballast.

Ships of the vintage of the *Lady Julian* were ballasted with a noxious mix of sand and gravel. Boards partitioned the hull like the sections of a quilt and an even quantity of ballast was loaded into each section. It went in loose, not casked, making it tricky to remove and replace and impossible to clean. It then rattled and swished about the bilge for years, growing steadily more foul as it absorbed the waste of years of life on board. Dead rats, dead cats, compost from mounds of vegetable peelings, faeces, urine, rotting fabric and decomposing sick all lay below the boards. The smell of an old bilge was notorious; on one of the first fleet transports, bilge gas seeping out not only blackened the wooden wall panels of the cabins on the lowest deck but tarnished the officers' gilt buttons. Even with the bilges shut, the stink of the ballast pervaded the ship, strongest at the lowest level where the women slept. The only place where the air was completely free of the smell was the windward quarter of the quarterdeck, and this small space, by unwritten law, was sacred to the captain.

Apart from its uncleanable bilge, the ship was as clean as salt water, gunpowder, holystones (soft sandstone), whitewash, vinegar and dozens of women on hands and knees scrubbing the decks could make it. It was believed that foulness trapped in the air contributed to or caused typhus and scurvy, the two diseases most common to crowded prisons and ships, and that sweet-smelling and free-flowing air would keep these at bay. 'I would recommend', wrote the respected physician Dr Lind, 'putting a red-hot loggerhead [a heated poker] in a bucket of tar, which should be moved about, so that all the ship may be filled with this wholesome antiseptic vapour.' Whenever conditions allowed it at sea or in port, the air between decks was rigorously 'cleansed' with this and other methods. Braziers burned aromatic herbs, when available, or the men boiled up cauldrons of pitch below deck. Another method of dispersing foul air was to explode small quantities of gunpowder between decks. Its acrid smoke was, like the vapour of tar, believed to dispel any 'myasma' from polluted breath and perspiration.

During the daytime, toilet arrangements at sea were clean and efficient. The 'heads' was an open platform with holes cut in it, lashed to the aftmost section of the bowsprit. This was the lavatory, through which sailors and women urinated or defecated directly into the sea below, rinsing off from a bucket of salt water. It was cleaner and easier than today's method of the pump lavatory. The women of the *Lady Julian* also enjoyed the advantage of not wearing any knickers: they just hitched a petticoat, squatted, rinsed and staggered back to their seat in the forecastle.

By night, when 200 women were shut into the orlop hold, it was all rather less hygienic. The orlop was equipped with 'easing-chairs' or commodes. The most prized berths were furthest from these and closest to the hatches, which gave some ventilation. The majority of women had now been living together in an all-female environment for months, even years, and their menstrual cycles would have started to synchronise. One week each month, the distinctive odour of menstrual blood was added to the smell of the easing-chairs. Wads of folded fabric were used as sanitary towels, pinned to the bottom of stays or held up by a piece of cord around the waist. They absorbed not only blood but salt water from spray and chafed the thighs and groin. If there was a rush of blood too great to be absorbed, it ran into the women's clothes, and remained there until next laundry day. The passage from Plymouth Sound to Santa Cruz de Tenerife in the Canary Islands was roughly the length of one menstrual cycle. With fresh water a precious commodity at sea, the women had a choice of boiling their pads in salt water with the other laundry, which would render them irritating in the extreme to the flesh, or packing them away for washing when they got to Santa Cruz and more fresh water was available. If they chose the second course, the smell of 200 dirty sanitary napkins stuffed under mattresses in the orlop hold must have almost beaten the ballast.

Despite the smell of old sand, urine and menstrual blood, the orlop deck of the *Lady Julian* was a cleaner and more comfortable place in which to sleep than many women had endured before coming on board. There were cockroaches, lice, fleas and rats – but what tenement, let alone gaol cell, did not have these? What the tenements and gaol cells had lacked was the discipline and rigorous hygiene enforced by good officers at sea. This ensured that their quarters were clean and their bedding dry, as long as weather conditions permitted. The cleaning and airing of clothes and hammocks which protected long-haul seamen from rheumatism and fever was imposed from the top, notoriously to grumbles from the seamen themselves. Orders were bellowed down the waist for hammocks to be brought out and aired, the men complained they had been out and aired yesterday and were bellowed at to get them out and aired again. Extreme captains lined up both men and officers and inspected their linen. Edgar's old brother-officer William Bligh, who took paternalism a little too far but was nevertheless a sound Cook-trained officer, wrote testily that 'simply to give [the seamen] orders that they are to keep themselves clean and dry as circumstances will allow is of little avail, they must be watched like Children'. The women in the orlop hold were treated with the same benign strictness. Edgar and Surgeon Alley were responsible for seeing that at least twice a week the bottom boards of their sleeping shelves were brought on deck and scrubbed with salt water, that the sides of the orlop hold were scraped and the floorboards swept. As a direct result, they lived in greater comfort during the first stage of their voyage to Sydney Cove than in the gaols and tenements they had just left behind.

The endless cleaning, scrubbing, scenting and airing served the second purpose of keeping the women occupied. The *Lady Julian* was now a ship at sea, but she was also a gaol and, just as the ship ran to unwritten laws on deck, so did the gaol below. The majority of the women were faceless and harmless – a docile mass that curled into the sleeping shelves at the bottom of the ship by night and sat in groups about the deck by day – but some were troublemakers. Fighting among women convicts was as vicious and frequent as among men. 'If ever there was a hell afloat, it must have been in the shape of a female convict ship – quarrelling, fighting, thieving, destroying in private each other's property from a mere spirit of devilishness', reported the surgeon of a later ship. Scarcely an officer sailed on a female transport but did not somewhere report in exasperation, like Lieutenant Clark, that 'the damned whores the moment they got below fel a fighting amongst one a nother'.

The codes of Newgate were alive and well on the bottom deck after lights out. 'Among such a Number that has been Convicted for Different Depredations on the public it is hardly to be thought when reduced to the lowest Ebb of poverty but they will Rob one another . . .' wrote a shocked middle-class observer, but this is exactly what convicts on all transports did. Each woman kept very few personal possessions in her shelf, as all trunks had been stowed away when they first went on board. But those few personal effects they had – a blanket, a drinking cup, a spoon, trinkets, a few coins, a bottle of liquor – were as unsafe from each other on the *Lady Julian* as they had been in the lodging-houses of St Giles or the cells of Newgate. As in any concentration of people in a confined space, convicts in the orlop hold quickly developed their own rules and hierarchies. Gangs formed. Those who had committed vicious assaults in

Seven Dials or Cable Street for trinkets worth pence were not going to stop committing them on board ship. Some became bullies, and others became victims.

It was not theft alone that beset the weaker convicts in the transports, but the intimidation that led to it and covered it up. When the hatches were barred at dusk, the weaker were left at the mercy of the stronger below deck. A stolen item could not go far from its owner within the contained world of a ship at sea, but a victim who complained to the officers placed herself at great personal risk by night. A diary written by a convict who sailed in 1798 recounts what an informer could expect from the gang leaders below deck. He nearly had his tongue cut off. In the end, his tormentors contented themselves with sticking needles through it and then beating him senseless.

After the initial shock of being at sea, those among the women who were habitually abusive or troublesome found their feet and reverted to their old habits. Once more, the seamen could expect a running commentary on their mothers, physiques and sexual activities from an irritating few who were always the last up the hatch in the morning, the last down at night, the laziest with mops and holystones, the first to get into a fight. This group was led by a woman John Nicol remembered as Nance Ferrel, who may have been the 34-year-old Ann Flavell from Gloucester who appears in other documents but whose indictment and sentence have been lost; or the Bett Farrell who broke into a house in Smithfield to steal the washing. The men had found that the best method of dealing with Nance and her friends when they were disobedient or abusive was simply to send them below, where the movement and lack of air would soon have them retching and begging to come back up and be good. The crew was perplexed when Nance, then one after another of her little group became 'in turns outrageous, on purpose to be confined'.

It was during a routine overhaul of the casks stored forward of the bulkhead which closed off the women's quarters that Nicol discovered two of his casks had been broken into. One entire hogshead of bottles of port had been drunk, and the empty bottles neatly replaced. Another had been started, with the empty bottles concealed at the back and full ones brought forward. Exploring further, he found a box of candles gone and a hole in the bulkhead. The ladies had been holding drinking parties. Nicol placed everything back neatly in its place so as to alert no one and climbed the ladders to consult Edgar. The lieutenant had a punishment up his sleeve. Nicol went off giggling to prepare a barrel, and Edgar gave the order that next time Nance and the girls swore at the men they were to be ignored. Shortly afterwards, Nance herself appeared with a few followers. Choosing her man, she fired off a list of casual curses and waited. The sailor blinked and went about his tasks. The women moved on, Nance shifted up a gear in language and imagination and insulted the next man in line. He, too, continued coiling his rope. The women then turned to the petty officers, who smiled and passed on. Steaming past the midshipmen, Nance tore through the ranks until she had climbed the ladder to the quarterdeck – a piece of impudence for which a seaman would have been flogged – and was insulting Captain Aitken himself.

Lieutenant Edgar now beckoned to John Nicol, who was lurking behind the wheel. Nance was seized and an empty wooden barrel with holes in the top and sides forced over her head. For the seamen and officers, it was a great joke. They came running to mock. So did the women, although not too obviously as they did not want to find her standing over their bed with a darning needle during the night. At first, Nance made the best of it. She strutted up and down the quarterdeck, playing to her audience below, pretending not to care; she had someone light her a cigar and smoked it as she went; she danced a little minuet back and forth, feet and head moving like a turtle's; she cracked some jokes. But a wooden barrel is heavy and its whole weight rested on her shoulders and she could not sit: if she rested the barrel on the floor, her legs were forced into a painful crouch. Eventually, she begged to be released, promising good behaviour, and the jacket was removed.

Nance's good behaviour did not last long. 'There was no taming her by gentle means', Nicol wrote. Within a week she was cursing as roundly as before. This time, the officers were not as lenient. 'We were forced to tie her up like a man, and give her one dozen with the cat o'nine tails and assure her of a clawing every offence. This alone reduced her to any kind of order.' Brutality was never far away.

The *Lady Julian* sailed on, her decks once more quiet, towards the Canary archipelago. Two and a half weeks out from Plymouth Sound, she passed Madeira and changed course a couple of degrees to head due south for Tenerife. Sailing through the archipelago was a novel experience for the women – their first taste of high winds at sea. In fact, these were short-lived gusts of gale force rather than the true gales they would experience some months later in the Southern Ocean, but still exhilarating. Around the string of African islands, the north-east trade winds have the trick of dividing at the northern end, creating a huge eddy around the island, and reuniting at the southern tip. The winds suddenly accelerate to full gale force down the length of each coast before fading away to almost nothing at the southern end. The seas remain gentle. The *Lady Julian*, under full sail, forged along, and finally they sighted the low-lying northern coast of the island of Tenerife.

Santa Cruz de Tenerife is on the northern coast of the island, sheltered from the prevailing winds by a pronged headland. Well before the first sails were reduced, the women were sent below. They sweated on their sleeping shelves and listened to the noises on deck as the *Lady Julian* approached land. An 11-gun salute from the Castillo de San Juan woke the babies. There was a terrific flap and slither of canvas and a scream of hemp as the

A courtroom in the Old Bailey Sessions House: judge to the left, defendant to the right, jury between them and public galleries behind. (Guildhall Library, Corporation of London)

Newgate Gaol to the left, fronting onto the Old Bailey alleyway, with the Sessions House adjoining on the right. (Guildhall Library, Corporation of London)

The magistrate's court in Bow Street, near Covent Garden, where Ann Garland and Francis Bunting were taken in November, 1788. (Rowlandson and Pugin, Guildhall Library, Corporation of London, UK/Bridgeman Art Library)

The 'cooing seats' in St James's Park where Rachel Hoddy picked up Nimrod Blampin in June, 1788. (Guildhall Library, Corporation of London)

Alice Haynes
Free Pardon.

George R

Whereas Alice Haynes was at the Sessions holden at the Old Bailey in December 1787, tried & convicted of stealing a Card of black Lace, and was sentenced to be Transported for seven Years for the same. And whereas some favourable Circumstances have been humbly represented unto Us in her behalf inducing Us to extend Our Grace and Mercy unto her and to grant her Our free Pardon for her said Crime. Our Will and Pleasure therefore is, that You cause her the said Alice Haynes to be forthwith discharged out of Custody and that she be inserted for her said Crime in Our first and next general Pardon that shall come out for the poor Convicts in Newgate, without any Condition whatsoever. And for so doing this shall be your Warrant. Given at Our Court at St James's the 8th day of June 1789, In the Twenty Ninth Year of Our Reign.

To Our Trusty & Wellbeloved James Adair Esqr Recorder of Our City of London, the Sheriffs of Our said City and County of Middlesex, and all others whom it may concern

By His Majesty's Command.

W W Grenville

A free pardon for Alice Haynes, shoplifter, granted shortly before she was due to board the *Lady Julian*. (Public Record Office, HO13/7)

The chapel in Newgate Gaol where couples would call across to each other during services. (Rowlandson and Pugin, Stapleton Collection, UK/Bridgeman Art Library)

Felons being taken from Newgate Gaol to Blackfriars *en route* for the transport ships and prison hulks in the Thames. (Mary Evans Picture Library)

The city of São Sebastião, Rio de Janeiro, in 1787, where John Nicol Junior was born two years later. (Mitchell Library, State Library of New South Wales, Australia)

Cape Town, South Africa, in 1787, painted by a first fleet officer. (Mitchell Library, State Library of New South Wales, Australia)

A romantic view of the wreck of the *Grosvenor* merchantman off South Africa in 1782. (Worlds Edge Picture Library)

The camp at Sydney Cove (now Circular Quay) a few months after the arrival of the first fleet in 1788. (Mary Evans Picture Library)

A British view of Aboriginal women in Port Jackson, 1788. (William Bradley, Mitchell Library, State Library of New South Wales/Bridgeman Art Library)

The Governor's house in Sydney Cove as it looked when the *Lady Julian* arrived in 1790. (William Bradley, Mitchell Library, State Library of New South Wales/Bridgeman Art library)

Norfolk Island, 1788:
taking provisions off
the wreck of the
Sirius. (Barnaby's
Picture Library)

A portrait of John
Nicol, aged 67,
which appeared in the
first edition of his
memoirs in 1822.
(National Maritime
Museum, London)

mainsails came down to reduce the ship's speed through the water. Waves breaking against the hull gentled as she slid into more sheltered waters, then a sharp turn through 90 degrees as the ship brought her bow up into the wind threw them into a heap. Babies wailed over the echo of orders relayed by speaking trumpet from quarterdeck to waist, and lungpower from waist to forecastle. The massive anchor cable forward thundered out and they floated slowly backwards until a slight tug brought the ship to rest when the anchor bit. She settled to a steady quiver against the cable and there was silence, broken only by the slap of water against her side and the pad of the seamen's feet on deck. When the hatches were removed, the women came up the ladders for their first glimpse of foreign parts. They saw a dirty beach, a castle in the far corner of the bay, a ring of guns and fortifications; low white houses shimmering in the August heat, ragged mountains rising behind and a snow-covered peak just visible in the distance; a stone pier with windmills to one side and a port full of slave-ships.

Chapter Nine

Santa Cruz de Tenerife

B locks squealed and the captain's barque was lowered into the water. Captain Aitken and Lieutenant Edgar stuffed themselves into their best breeches, adjusted their tricorns and rowed off to represent His Majesty to the Spanish governor and request permission to land. It was a formality that would become familiar to the women at later ports of call. The seamen set to work bringing up the empty water casks, shoving the women out of the way to roll them along the deck and lower them over the side into the longboats.

A river flowed down into Santa Cruz from the mountains of the hinterland and supplied both the town and visiting shipping. The water was conveyed along a gently sloping aqueduct to a pier in the bay, supported over the gullies in the hills by posts stout enough to hold it through the winter floods. When the captain and agent returned from visiting Governor Branquefort, the longboats rowed off with their first load of empty casks to be filled from the pier tanks. The water brought on board in Plymouth Sound three weeks earlier was already brackish, and the fresh water was eagerly drunk; too eagerly, women rushed to the heads with 'the flux' (diarrhoea) as their systems readjusted. The water round the hull began to pollute the air.

That day or the next, there was an orgy of laundry on board. At sea, dirty linen was washed in salt water, which turned it clammy and stiff and caused rashes under the collar, in the armpits and, for the officers, around the groin. Women and crew were spared the rash by the looseness of skirts and the baggy, knee-length 'trowsers' worn by the seamen. Officers' breeches, on the other hand, fitted snugly around the crotch, where a saltwater rash itched like poison ivy. Now, fires were lit on deck, cauldrons of water boiled, heaps of dirty clothes dumped next to them and parties of women rolled up their sleeves and set to for the biggest laundry day since Plymouth.

With nothing in the way of detergent, the dirt was boiled and then beaten out of the linen. Stripped to the minimum required by decency, the women did the washing. The top deck trembled as rows of them, up and down the waist of the ship, thwacked its timbers with shirts, shifts, sheets, hammocks, trews and a vast pile of sanitary napkins. Rivulets of filthy water trickled down the sides. By evening, the rails and rigging of the ship were festooned with drying clothes, and laundry had turned to horseplay. Faint female shrieks floated across to other ships at anchor. Shadows were cast of capering figures throwing water at each other, and those crews in the port of Santa Cruz who had not heard the news that there was a ship full of English whores in port wondered what was going on.

Casks full, laundry done, the provisioning rounds began, and Lieutenant Edgar went ashore to place his orders. His priorities were greens and fresh meat. A well-established shambles on the waterfront took care of ships' fresh and salt-meat orders; bulk fruit and vegetables were procured from the orchards and market gardens of Oratava, a small town a few miles inland.

Officers applied to Captain Aitken for permission to sleep out of the ship, taking up lodgings on dry land for the duration of their stay in Santa Cruz. Not all could go at once, clearly; those who slept out of the ship here would forgo the privilege in Cape Town and vice versa. Those women taken 'as wife' by the officers perhaps came into one of the privileges which went with their

status and followed them to their beds ashore as they had
followed them into their berths afloat. Seamen were also allowed
ashore in small groups, accompanied always by an officer. British
sailors in the eighteenth century had something of the reputation
of British football fans in the twentieth and were known for
causing trouble where late-night bars served cheap liquor.
Officers spoke gravely of 'the Enormities which English seamen
are too apt to commit in foreign Ports', and local authorities
were anxious that each ship take responsibility for the behaviour
of its own men. In some ports, groups of ordinary seamen could
not go ashore without an escort from the local militia, but the
governor in Tenerife permitted them to be escorted by one of
their own officers. The officers of the *Lady Julian* were aware of
their responsibilities – not only would 'Enormities' damage the
name of the ship, her commanding officer and the British marine,
but if one of the men in their party was arrested and incarcerated,
the captain would face a fee of several dollars to get him out.
One part of this would be recovered from the man who had
caused the trouble and another from the officer who had allowed
him to do so.

Decisions as to which of the officers and which of the men
could be allowed ashore at any time were taken by Captain
Aitken, advised by the first mate, according to well-understood
regulations and order of precedence. Lieutenant Edgar had the
more difficult task of deciding which of the women could go
ashore, with whom and when. It comes as a shock to realise from
John Nicol's memoirs and journals left by later convicts that
some prisoners spent their time in ports not fettered in the hold,
as convict legend would have it, but strolling the streets and
getting in some shopping. A society pickpocket who sailed in
1792, George Barrington, was treated by the officers almost as
one of themselves, dining with them on board ship and accom-
panying them on day trips whenever they were in port. Women
on the *Lady Julian* presumably did the same. A handful were of

a similar status to Barrington – literate, amusing, presentable.

Mrs Barnsley was unquestionably the First Lady of the ship. It was Elizabeth Barnsley, highwayman's sister and shoplifter of distinction, who had requested Lieutenant Edgar to let her wear her own fine clothes in the Thames. He had had to refuse then, but as soon as the *Lady Julian* left Plymouth Sound, she reminded him of his promise to let her do so when they put to sea. Elizabeth Barnsley therefore lived in clothes acquired in Bond Street while her shipmates lived in brown serge. It is unlikely she slept in the hold; money would have found her a better bunk and a little privacy on the *Lady Julian* as it had done on the Master's Side of Newgate, perhaps in one of the huts built on to the waist of the ship. Surprisingly, she does not seem to have been unpopular – in fact, quite the opposite, as she had qualities that made her a leader among the convicts. She was 29 when the ship sailed – too old to be competing for the attention of the seamen (who were probably rather in awe of her anyway) – and thus steered clear of scraps over sailors' favours. She was intelligent and literate, a skill that alone attracted admiration. She would have been able to express the other women's requests and complaints to the officers and be listened to. Lastly, she was generous with her money.

In Tenerife, Mrs Barnsley decided she would treat her circle to a cask of Canary wine, which she would herself choose from one of the *bodegas* along the shore. Lieutenant Edgar was informed of her wishes. He had no reason to deny her, and it would not have been shrewd to antagonise a clever woman with a following below deck. Elizabeth Barnsley was rowed off to be escorted through the wine cellars of Santa Cruz, probably by an officer. She was, after all, a lady. She was also a thief and a liar and an officer escort would prevent embarrassing incidents.

Weary Watkin Tench, lieutenant with the first fleet to New South Wales, thought that 'there is little to please a traveller in Tenerife.' He damned the town with faint praise as 'neither irregular in its plan, nor despicable in its style of building' and was displeased by the 'importunity of the beggars and the immodesty of the lowest class of women'. Santa Cruz certainly lacked the glamour of the South American cities and the prosperity of the Dutch ones, and for men who had travelled the world perhaps there was little here that was not bigger, brighter, higher or hotter somewhere else. But for the women, Tenerife represented all that was foreign. George Barrington would describe the governor's palace as having 'the appearance more of an auberge than the palace of a Spanish grandee'. Forecastle wives like Sarah Whitelam, Mary Warren and Ann Bryant, who had spent their lives in English market towns, did not know what a Spanish grandee's palace looked like, nor that the governor's palace fell short of it. If you were 19 and came from Lincolnshire, Tenerife was the height of exoticism. It was the women's first experience of being surrounded by the sound of a language not their own. They had never seen a peak the height of the Pico de Teide, nor lived in a climate in which snow covered a mountaintop while a sultry heat hung over the beaches. They had never walked along streets overlooked by a painted Virgin, nor seen bougainvillea, palm trees, banana plants, grapes hanging from the vine and fresh dates, nor urchins with the brown skin of Spain instead of the pinched pallor of London. Women did not walk the streets in black drapes and a scarf over their head in provincial Lincolnshire; they did not cross themselves when they passed a church in Maidstone. The *Lady Julian* wives did not see the dull town that bored Lieutenant Tench; they saw dark skin, fruit, colour and the insistent presence of an alien Church in the nuns and friars who passed them on the streets, the statues in niches, the murals, the genuflections, the bells and the incense.

Not all had brought money with them from England to go shopping with Mrs Barnsley but some on board were willing to earn it on the way out. By now, word had gone out around the town that 230 fallen females were aboard the squat little ship flying a Red Ensign in the harbour. When small groups of them appeared in the streets, accompanied by boisterous British seamen, some islanders would cross themselves and let the shutters down; others spat and muttered, but the more charitable reacted with pity. Pity could mean cash. One of John Nicol's Santa Cruz anecdotes concerns a group of Jewish convicts led by a woman called Sarah Sabolah, probably an alias or family name of the Jewish thief Sarah Lyons, convicted the previous year of stuffing seven yards of handkerchief silk up her skirt in a London drapery.

Sarah Sabolah's Santa Cruz exploit must have been carried out with the knowledge of the officers or she and her friends would never have got a lift to the beach or acquired their props – a couple of bolts of cloth and some pieces of wood. She and her group were dropped at one end of the quay, robed themselves in borrowed black and shook the spume from the crucifixes they had knocked together in the orlop hold. Then they assumed suitable expressions and processed solemnly from one end of the main drag to the other. Even among a people as accustomed to lavish displays of penitence and piety as the Canary Catholics, the trudging line of barefoot English convicts, bowed beneath their crosses, caused a stir, and the inhabitants of Santa Cruz pressed coins and benedictions on the women. Sarah must have been a woman of some cunning to have come up with the scheme in the first place and may have sewn her share of their takings into her seams for a rainy day. Others probably drank the profits away before they left Tenerife.

Scamming the burghers of Santa Cruz was not the easiest way to make money. 'We allowed the people to come freely aboard; the seamen and captains of the visiting ships paid us many visits,' John Nicol remembered. There was nothing unusual in the shipboard commerce of sex, but usually it was the prostitutes who were rowed out to the men, not the men who were rowed out to the prostitutes. A splendidly simple explanation was offered by a historian in 1990: 'the women – mainly London prostitutes – turned the ship into a floating brothel.' It is difficult to believe, however, that the women mounted the quarterdeck, informed the captain they would be turning his ship into a bawdyhouse for the duration and then sat back to count their takings. Brothels neither at land nor sea are operated thus. Where there is a prostitute, there is a pimp – and who played this role in Santa Cruz? Once again, the rules that governed life in Ratcliff and Newgate emerged aboard the *Lady Julian* and the percentage which might have been taken by a pimp on dry land probably went into the sailors' chests.

We enter the realm of pure hypothesis when imagining negotiations between seaman and seaman's 'wife'. Who knows what deals were struck by a sailor who saw his pretty hammock-mate and her little friends in the orlop not only as recreation but also potential cash-cows? A bottle of wine, a length of embroidered ribbon, a trinket, a quarter-dollar . . .? Whatever deal he made, it seems to have been tolerated at the top. Lieutenant Edgar had a better idea than most of what awaited the women. He knew that any money made turning tricks in Santa Cruz would serve them well in Sydney Cove; allowing prostitution was an act of pity as much as negligence. So the seamen from the other ships in port and thrill-seekers from the shore rowed across to the ship full of whores and, throughout the *Lady Julian*'s stay in Santa Cruz, some of the shelves in her hold, the hammocks in her forecastle and the huts on her deck were turned over to commerce.

It must have been the seamen who advertised the ship's wares and made the assignations, making sure the promised party of half a dozen pox-free girls was waiting when the group of neighbouring seamen rowed over, perhaps collecting the money and dividing it among the girls when they rowed off again. However, the business community on board did not consist solely of men. It was by agreement and negotiation, not by male coercion – still less by a wave of female lust – that some women sold sex in Santa Cruz. The girls most in demand were not necessarily those best able to defend their own interests. In the network of request and negotiation which sprang up in Tenerife, female pimps must also have played their part. Theirs could have been a protective role – an advisory service by the more to the less experienced on how to make the most of the situation. But there was probably as much pressure exerted and as many deals struck in the orlop as in the forecastle. There was one bawd down on the shelves with no fewer than three of her former girls on board the ship with her: Elizabeth Sully had run Poll Randall, Mary Butler and Mary Bateman in Cable Street. She and other canny women would have been making their own deals with the forecastle in Santa Cruz.

The quarterdeck, too, was implicated in these transactions. Lieutenant Edgar and Captain Aitken clearly countenanced the sale of sex on board. Officers used prostitutes no less than seamen, and plenty came on board in Santa Cruz. When the officers of the *Lady Julian* passed discreet orders for the entertainment of visitors, the likeliest go-between from captain's cabin to orlop deck was his steward, John Nicol. It would have been John who reported back the orlop's estimate of cost and conducted negotiations between the two until agreement was reached. A forecast of the entertainment value of the women chosen would determine whether they were invited to join the officers for dinner first in the captain's cabin or simply received in some secluded spot. Aitken and Edgar probably did not receive the sort of cash for services that the men in the forecastle and the pimps in the orlop wanted, but no visiting officer would turn up without a box of fine cigars or a particularly good bottle of port for the captain's table.

The officers participated in the Santa Cruz pimping for reasons of prudence as well as interest, as much to keep charge of the situation as to profit by it. The only way a woman could escape the *Lady Julian* was to sell herself to a seaman from another ship in return for being smuggled away. A convict had attempted escape in Santa Cruz two years before by slipping over the bow and begging a Dutch East Indiaman to take him on board. The Dutch refused and he was retaken with Spanish assistance. Two women had already escaped Sydney Cove on the French ships of exploration which had nosed in a few days after the British arrived. The men with them had been turned down. Four women from the *Lady Julian* herself had gone over the side the night before she left the Thames, and Edgar could not afford the embarrassment of losing any more in Tenerife.

The most faithful of their customers, in John Nicol's memory, were the crews of two slavers on their way to or from The Gambia. The men on board could have been British, Spanish, American, Portuguese, French, Danish or Dutch, for all these nationalities were eager carriers of slaves from the African coast. Most visitors to Santa Cruz were interested in the produce brought down to the wharfside markets to supply shipping: blankets, oil, corn, wine, fruit, vegetables, 'milch goats', pumpkins, onions, figs in season, grapes. An encounter with the 'abandoned dock women of Tenerife' was also considered an essential diversion for the younger visitor, but the real money made from ships passing through the bay came from slaving. The silver dollars of the slavers who bought in stores at Santa Cruz on their way from the Americas to the African coast were the engine of the Canaries' economy.

Santa Cruz did not profit only from spin-offs of the trade, however: a slave market was held every Sunday outside the Castillo de San Juan, and officers ashore probably stopped by to watch. Slavery had been outlawed in Britain by a High Court judgement of 1772, by which any Negro bought as a slave elsewhere became a free person from the moment of setting foot in England. (The judgement did not extend to preventing English merchants from participating in the overseas slave trade.) Most of the city women on board the *Lady Julian* had already seen blacks before they were confronted with the chained Negroes on sale in Santa Cruz. London shoplifter Elizabeth Smith, alias Cave, had committed her crime with a Negro accomplice, named in court records only as 'Thomas, a Black Man'. A colony of Negroes manumitted under the 1772 judgement lived around the docks of most sea cities, along with Chinese seamen looking for a berth to Canton, lascars looking for a berth to Calcutta and other floating foreigners.

A humanitarian, usually Christian, objection to the slave trade was beginning to be heard in Britain; much of the public comment hostile to transportation was couched in terms borrowed from the criticism of slavery. Until France became the home of people power later that year, it was Britain that was considered, and considered itself, the champion of sturdy egalitarianism. Its citizens were notorious for the defence of their liberties, especially in contrast to the serfs across the Channel. *Male* British citizens, of course. Despite the constant John Bull rhetoric about liberty, Britain was the country where, in the words of Lawrence Stone, 'a married woman was the nearest approximation in a free society to a slave' and an unmarried one little better. Romantic convict history, the stuff of ballad and campfire verse, would draw on a supposed fellow feeling among the downtrodden – convicts, slaves, Aborigines. This is 'the flimsiest sentiment', to borrow a robust phrase from Robert Hughes. It is profoundly unlikely that any woman in Santa Cruz drew analogies between the situation of the African slaves on sale and her own situation on board the *Lady Julian*. Political comment was alien to the lives of these women; fear of the savage was not. They did not see brothers and sisters in suffering among the merchandise blinking in its fetters outside the Castillo de San Juan. They saw 'savages', 'blacks', 'Africans', semi-naked creatures with sores round their mouths, frightened and incomprehensible, ripe with an alien sweat. The men who traded them and took some of their profit aboard the *Lady Julian* were probably no more odious to the convicts than were the seamen in the forecastle of their own ship.

In the second week of September, watered, provisioned and cashed up, the *Lady Julian* left Santa Cruz and headed for the Dutch settlement of Cape Town at the southern tip of Africa. This was another well-worn international trade route. Cape Town was the principal stopoff before and after the Dutch Spice Islands and the British trading networks on the coast of India. It was intended to be a 10–12 week, 6,000-mile passage before the Trades with a brief watering-stop at Cabo Verde. They would not arrive for five and a half months.

The first brake on the voyage were the slave ships they had picked up in Santa Cruz. When the British ship set sail, the two crews of slavers decided to travel south in convoy, 'for the sake', said John Nicol, 'of the ladies'. Some of the women had now been sleeping with a slaver for much the same duration as a modern Canary holiday romance and attachments had been made. The three ships sailed together from Santa Cruz.

The route to São Tiago, Cabo Verde, took them west-south-west about 400 miles off the west African coast. For three days the peak of Tenerife was clearly visible behind them, its summit still snow-capped. Daily, it seems, cheerful slavers rowed across for rest and recreation on the orlop of the *Lady Julian*. Hours each day of wallowing, nose to the wind, slowed their passage considerably, but a week out, the man at the masthead spotted the islands of São Nicolas and Boa Vista on the starboard beam. The following day, the little convoy made São Tiago. Canvas flapped, hemp howled, the anchor bit the sand eight fathoms below. The women emerged into a fierce heat.

They had left the rule of the Spaniards behind. Porto Praya was a far smaller harbour than Santa Cruz, and the town far poorer, its inhabitants more peasants than merchants. The Kingdom of Portugal was in charge here, and the islands were 'exceedingly oppressed by the Portuguese soldiery, who exact an exorbitant toll from the countrymen who bring their commodities to market'. A Portuguese cartel controlled both price and supply of provisions to visiting ships. Whoever was selling, the *Lady Julian* had to buy for the voyage to Cape Town. Nicol had been made cautious by previous Cabo Verde experience: 'the Portuguese here are great rogues . . . I bought two fat sheep from one of them. The bargain was made and I was going to lead away my purchase, when he gave a whistle and my sheep scampered off to the fields . . .' New purchases were haltered as soon as dollars changed hands, reluctant bullocks tied to the painter of a cutter and swum out to the ship, bellowing. The decks of the *Lady Julian* once more steamed with dung. Watering arrangements were more primitive in Porto Praya than in go-ahead Santa Cruz. The closest well was about 1,200 yards up the beach, down which a rolling-way for casks had been constructed. At the bottom end, the casks had to be roped together and floated out to the ship. Among the convicts, the poorer women who had not been able to treat themselves to Canary wine at Santa Cruz found they could do business in Cabo Verde. The islanders willingly swapped food and wine for their clothes and trinkets. Bargains were struck on the beach at Porto Praya, where 'the Air is remarkable Hot and to Europeing very unwholesome', which would be bitterly regretted further south. They stayed only one day here, possibly to avoid the mooring fee exacted by the Portuguese 'Captain-Moor'. His shoddy palace stood some way out of town, and it generally took more than 24 hours, especially in the heat of summer, for a slovenly guard to amble over and collect the $4 fee. Porto Praya was their last, brief stop in the northern hemisphere.

The sea route from the Canaries to Cape Town bulges far out into the Atlantic Ocean, following the currents that swirl in an inverted 'S' between the islands and the Cape – clockwise to the north of the equator, anticlockwise to the south. Ships heading for the Cape sailed along the northern currents from the African islands as far as the coast of Brazil with a following wind, then turned and headed south-east with the wind on the port beam. The right season for this passage was autumn, when the seas were still kind and the trade winds were steady. If the trades blew well and constantly, it was a swift and pleasant voyage. The area of risk straddled the equatorial line, a 200-mile stretch of fitful ocean known as the doldrums, and it was here that the *Lady Julian* would sail into serious trouble a few weeks later.

For the first week out from Cabo Verde, the sailing was easy. With the trade winds blowing a consistent force 4–5 from the north-east, there was a minimum of work to be done trimming the sails, and the sailors aloft took advantage of the good weather to put in a few days on maintenance, checking the hemp ropes for chafe. Ships' companies often spent good-weather days preceding a rough passage cutting out and sewing a complete new set of sails. The *Lady Julian* would need one leaving Cape Town for the gales of the Southern Ocean. Skilled women may have helped the men on deck with this, or they may have been kept to picking oakum, the traditional prison task of untwisting condemned rope into lumps of hairy fluff, which was part of the mixture stuffed between the boards of a ship. These were pleasant days, with all the women and most of the men on deck, whittling, mending, knotting, painting, greasing the blocks and making all the small pieces of equipment which were necessary for the ship and kept them from being idle. With a deck full of women to be talked to, keeping the men busy was important for discipline.

There were enough unpleasant tasks to be done that the men were in little danger of going soft. Pumping was one. If Lieutenant Edgar followed the same rules of shipboard health as Captain Bligh in equatorial temperatures, the first mate had the men pumping water from one side of the ship to another for a sweaty hour or two each day to cool the air below deck. When pumping was finished, there was the utterly foul task of slushing down the mast. Some unfortunate was given a pot of old dripping from the galley and sent to the masthead, from where he worked his way down rubbing in the fat with his hands as he went. It preserved the wood and helped the tackle run up and down the mast more easily; it was also a usefully nasty task to hand out to a lazy seaman. His colleagues sat under the awnings which kept the fierce afternoon heat off the decks, their backs against sun-warmed blocks, spinning yarn or manufacturing ropebands and points, explaining their Tahitian tattoos and their American scars to the little groups of women around them.

It was equally unwise to leave the women idle with lovelorn slavers on either bow who could offer a getaway to a choice of continents. The women on female transports were kept as strictly to a daily routine as was practicable in the changing weather conditions through which they passed between London and Sydney Cove. At five o'clock, convict cooks were on deck to prepare breakfast. At sunrise, the hatches were opened, and tubs of salt water placed next to them. As women emerged from the orlop, they pegged their bedding out to air on the bulwarks and rigging, were given a bucket of water from the bathing tubs to wash, then formed messes for breakfast. During the day, they were kept in work parties for as long as the agent could find work to keep them busy.

On all transport ships, a 'trusty' from among the convicts was made mess-captain for each group of six or eight convicts. Female trusties were known as 'matrons'. It was they who collected the rations for their mess from the cook or John Nicol, supervised the airing of linen and the cleaning of crockery after meals, kept order as best they could in their mess and relayed any petitions or complaints to the agent. John Nicol does not mention who was given this responsibility on the *Lady Julian* but it was presumably the older women who had some clout below decks. Elizabeth Barnsley and Nelly Kerwin were prob-ably too grand for the job. Humbler but motherly women in their thirties and forties like Mary Anstey, Warwick shoplifter, coiner Catherine Heyland, the 46-year-old mother from Reading sailing to be reunited with her son, Mrs Elizabeth Dell, Susannah Hunt and Mrs Ann Peter Rock, all of whom went on to lead deeply respectable lives in the colony (bar a little bigamy) were probably those chosen by Edgar for this task.

Agent Edgar had some information on the previous lives of most women coming on board, particularly those out of Newgate, whose records were more easily available. He knew which women had worked in kitchens, which on farms, which had nursing or childcare skills, who could read, write, add up figures and weigh rations. Elizabeth Parry, taken on as cow-keeper in Islington, Mary Rose, farmer's daughter from Lincolnshire and Mary Lammerman, who had stolen milk from a Northumberland farm, would have milked the cows in the bow. Sarah Acton had stolen ten suckling pigs and kept them under the bed in her Smithgate lodgings; Sarah Gregory, from Hertfordshire, had stolen 'one live pig, one spade sow pig and two barrow pigs'. These two, with Sarah's little daughter, might now have been tending the hogs. If stealing sheep on Dartmoor indicates some knowledge of husbandry, Susannah Mortimore now slung her baby on her back and set about tending the sheep and milking the goats. Women like Sarah Whitelam from country gaols which released their prisoners during the summer months to help on local farms were cleaning out the poultry, collecting eggs and sluicing away the night's dung with buckets of sea water. Catherine Hounsam, kitchen-maid in Grosvenor Square, might have been peeling vegetables with some of the other ex-maidservants – Mary Hook, Rachel Turner, Mary Cowcher, alias Christmas, Ann Kemp, Martha Daniels, Mary Lewis – there were dozens of them. Forger Nelly Kerwin perhaps helped Lieutenant Edgar keep his ledgers up to date, under strict supervision, or took dictation for Captain Aitken's dispatches. Nursemaid Ann Howard may have helped Surgeon Alley bandaging cuts and applying leeches in the sickberth. Those who had no particular skills or were under punishment made up the day's cleaning party, swabbing and disinfecting below deck, holystoning above.

Cleaning, laundry, food preparation, tending the animals, water-throwing, hair-pulling, horseplay and drinking did not mop up all the female energy. The 20 best needlewomen on board had already been commandeered by Captain Aitken, who had spotted a business opportunity waiting in Sydney Cove and invested in a quantity of linen. With no raw material or equipment for weaving in the colony, no soap for laundering, no thread but gut and no needles, the captain had reckoned that clean linen shirts would be as much in demand as sex and liquor. Free labour from the convict women was available. Lieutenant Clark had had the women of the *Friendship* run him up trousers, gloves, nightcaps, even a new frock coat on the voyage out – whores they might be, but handy ones with a needle. Part of the storage space in the orlop hold of the *Lady Julian* had been quietly set aside for the captain's own little business venture. His bolts of linen were now brought up and his private labour force issued with needles and thread.

There was heavy shipping traffic in these waters, for they were following the trunk of the sea route south from Europe. This would soon divide: traders would go east towards the Cape and the Spice Islands beyond, and whalers would go west towards South Georgia and the Falklands. The *Lady Julian*'s course was also taking her across the southern axis of the 'golden triangle' connecting Europe, North America and the western coast of Africa. Southbound ships brought cheap cloth and arms from Europe to Africa. Westbound ships crammed their holds with slaves for North America and the Caribbean, and those sailing east from the New World took raw American materials back to Europe. The peeling forts and seedy boulevards 400 miles away on the western coast of Africa produced the human oil to service a vast trading and production machine – spices for the Dutch in

Batavia, sugar for the British in the Caribbean, cotton for the Americans in the deep south. It has been estimated that about six million Negroes had left western Africa as slaves already that century. Latterly, some of them had replaced the convict labour from Britain which American ex-colonists no longer wanted.

About 100 miles out from Porto Praya, the slave ships finally peeled off west towards the cluster of European settlements around the mouth of the River Gambia, 'to pick up their cargo of human misery'. The phrase was Nicol's – he had seen slaves at work in the sugar plantations of Granada, where the women would sell themselves for 'a bellyful of victuals', and had no illusions about the life that awaited the slavers' cargo. The *Lady Julian* sailed on alone.

Two hundred British convicts had landed on the Gambian coast back in 1782, part of an intended first fleet to Africa. All but 50 had perished. These were not pleasant thoughts: how many aboard reflected that a similar fate might have overtaken the colony they were sailing towards? The *Prince of Wales* had brought back news that the colonists were alive and managing, but that ship had left Sydney Cove in July 1788, over a year ago. A year was more than enough time for a thousand people, alone in an unknown land, to be wiped out by famine, drought, disease or hostility from natives. News had not yet got back to Britain, but another colonial experiment on the African coast, 600 miles further south, had also just gone disastrously wrong.

When the British-German army that had fought the American colonists came back to Europe in 1783, disorderly women and crippled veterans were only two of the groups of urban poor who began to colonise the streets. Many of the loyalists who had fought with the British forces either went to Nova Scotia, still safely British, or came back to Europe with the defeated army. The former American planter James Smith was among them; he was now aboard HMS *Guardian* as superintendent for the unborn plantations of Sydney Cove. Among the loyalists were Negroes,

who joined a black population resident in Britain already
estimated to be 14,000 strong. Many of these were former slaves
who had been brought back from colonies overseas and, becoming free under English law, had been turned off by their masters.
They had drifted to the cities, where they joined the destitute
and unemployed already there. Finding a colonial home for black
loyalists and freed slaves was a project which ran parallel to
finding one for convicted felons in the 1780s.

The same year that the eleven ships of the first fleet to Botany
Bay left England, a smaller fleet of two ships was leaving for the
proposed settlement of Freetown. Squeezed among the poor
blacks returning to what was imagined to be their homeland
were a bunch of 'Whites . . . chiefly men and women of an
abandoned character'. As with the New South Wales expedition,
no advance party had been sent to prepare the ground. The poor
blacks and abandoned whites sweated on board while the captain
went ashore and negotiated the purchase of 20 square miles
around the Sierra Leone River from King Jimi, the local chief.

About the time the *Lady Julian* left the African coast behind
in 1789, a rumour was going round the camp in Sydney Cove
among 'some of the most ignorant' that 'they are to be left by the
troops and the shipping to perish by themselves'. Perhaps the
'most ignorant' had a better grip on the recent history of penal
colonies than the officer who reported the rumour as what they
feared was exactly what had happened in Freetown three years
before. The ship to Sierra Leone had dropped her 411 passengers
and sailed back to England, leaving London skinners, second-
generation slaves from Virginia, housebreakers and disorderly
girls to fend for themselves on 20 square miles of malarial African
coastline. Eighteen months later, 130 were still alive. The inland
blacks had consistently raided and stolen from the land they had
sold the English captain, and Freetown had degenerated into an
African Lord of the Flies. Just after the *Lady Julian* left the
Thames in 1789, a British man-of-war set fire to a town a little

way down the coast from Freetown and ruled by King Jimi, who decided to attack the new river settlement as revenge on the British. His envoys gave Freetown three days' notice to evacuate before the camp was sacked. Its inhabitants dispersed in panic on to the islands, crazed with fear and fever, where they were waiting for rescue as the *Lady Julian* was heading off into the Atlantic.

Those on board fortunately knew nothing of the fate of the poor blacks and disorderly girls of Sierra Leone. The *Lady Julian* had now turned her back on the African coast and was heading more west than south. The fauna of the sea was changing as she went. There were sharks, pilot whales, sperm whales and bottle-nose dolphins around her, and the diet of those on board changed accordingly. With a tidy ship and little work aloft while the winds held, the seamen turned to fishing. Each mess had its own area and its own collection of lines, and the ship dragged fish gut over her sides from bow to stern. Whenever the silver wriggle was sighted, news went round the deck and men rushed to untie and recast their lines in the most promising area. When the women realised that by maritime custom whoever caught the fish also ate it, they started catching their own. The seamen's women were luckier – they got a share of whatever their men caught. The rest of the convicts set themselves to learning the skills of sea fishing, stealing equipment from wherever they could find it.

Mostly they caught bonitos, glorious large fish that thrashed about the deck until someone knocked their head against a block and they died, their flesh turning an astonishing range of colours as the breath left them. What they could not catch were the numerous dolphins and porpoises which played around the ship, because for this they needed a harpoon. Harpooning was technically the prerogative of the first mate aboard a merchant-man. On the *Lady Julian* it was the bosun who excelled with a harpoon. He stood on the quarterdeck with his harpoon braced for the throw, watched by women and crew, waiting for the shout from the lighter below which meant there was porpoise for supper.

As they neared South America, the waters were still thick with slavers and merchantmen, mainly the Portuguese *compradores* who ploughed between the continents, picking up slaves collected for them by the coastal chiefs in Africa and selling them on to plantation agents in Brazil. The lookout frequently sighted a friendly flag on the horizon, signals went up, the two ships veered towards each other and hove to. Captain Aitken passed the order for his barque to be made ready, put on his best hat and was rowed halfway towards the fellow captain rowing towards him. They would sit there, gently riding the waves while the seamen backed their oars, swapping news of who had been seen, in what latitude, of the weather immediately south and north, of seafaring gossip and warnings of increased harbour fees and changes in the personnel commanding foreign ports. If it turned out either ship were going on to an appropriate harbour, correspondence and messages were rowed over to be carried by the other.

Captain Aitken comes over as rather a lonely man. He figures hardly at all in John Nicol's account, although as officers' servant Nicol had daily contact with him, far more than the average seaman before the mast. He did not seem to attract the same affection as Lieutenant Edgar. A captain dined with the officers at least once weekly, but these were rather awkward occasions, with the young gentlemen too much in awe of the boss to crack the jokes they would have made in their own mess and the captain unable to unbend for fear of losing authority. The only real conversations he could have, perhaps, were with the captains of visiting ships, and he made the most of these.

One day a southern whaler was sighted sailing up from the Falklands. Signals were passed, perhaps the ships hove to and the captains met. A week or so later, the whaler sighted another Red Ensign, this time on an imposing man-of-war and hove to once again at 2°14' north.

The man-of-war was HMS *Guardian*. She had still been in Portsmouth harbour when the *Lady Julian* sailed for Plymouth Sound in mid-July and had not left Spithead until the second week of September, far later than the Admiralty had intended. Lieutenant Riou had been instructed to reach the colony as swiftly as possible. He had stopped briefly at Tenerife to take on wine, bypassed Cabo Verde and made it to just north of the equator in a little over three weeks. The *Lady Julian*, Lieutenant Riou now learned from the whaling captain, was ploughing south a few days ahead of him.

Chapter Ten

Crossing the Line

It is about two weeks' sailing in good winds from Cabo Verde to the equatorial line, the 0° and lifeless air which held a curious, semi-mythical place in the lore of the sea. The ceremonies of 'crossing the line' were a high moment in a voyage but could easily degenerate into grotesque and violent horseplay. The men who took control, and directed the humiliations inflicted on the young and the unpopular, were ordinary sailors. The officers took a back seat, although first mates, and even captains, were ready to step in if order was threatened or practical jokes became too dangerous. This was an uneasy occasion on a ship whose crew was not happy or which carried some seaman, officer or passenger to whom too many people had taken a dislike. Men had been keelhauled on the equator or dragged behind their ship for a mile at the end of a rope – not as punishment from the senior officers but as licensed high jinks among their messmates. On a transport ship that sailed in 1792, the cook was suspected of keeping back a part of the company's rations to sell later for private profit. He was nearly killed when his ship crossed the line. The seamen tied his hands, fastened him to a block and tackle, ran him 50 feet up to the main yardarm, let go the rope and cheered as he hurtled 50 feet back down into the sea – once, twice and a third time before the first mate stepped in and the man was released to retch and gasp on the deck. There could be a curious connivance between quarterdeck and forecastle when the captain was 'obliged' by the master of ceremonies to surrender his protection of a hated purser or an unpopular junior officer and hand him over to the mob in the bow.

Not all ceremonies were so rough. Giggling seamen aboard the *Lady Julian* now gathered in the forecastle, excluding the women, for these were masculine mysteries and half the fun would be making the ladies jump and squeal. A request emerged from the huddle and was carried to the bosun. The bosun fetched his harpoon, received permission from Captain Aitken to mount the quarterdeck and struck heroically until a fat porpoise was speared. Further errands were run to the galley for a large knife and to John Nicol for a piece of iron hoop.

Seamen disappearing into the forecastle looked sly and refused to say what was going on. The tropical dusk came suddenly and the women were sent below to interpret the noises filtering down the hatches and from behind the forecastle bulkhead. A dim rumble and a splash overhead were empty casks being rolled to the forecastle and filled with sea water. A creak of wood and another splash were seamen raising the boards and taking water from the bilges. More sploshing as this went into the casks; faint guffaws. Depending on who was to end up in which barrel, and the forecastle's opinion of his personality, the seamen were spitting, urinating or defecating into the casks.

The sound of preparations continued for some hours, then there was a patter of feet across the deck. Officers' voices bellowed and the women were thrown against a beam as the ship made a lurching quarter-circle turn into the wind, came to a halt and settled to a new motion with her sails loose. There were shouts down the orlop hatches to come on deck. The night was now truly dark, and the gleam of stars and yellow lanterns on the sea were disorientating after the black of the hold. They waited in groups, uneasy, then a gong boomed and a group of manic figures heaved themselves over the bow and on to the foredeck.

King Neptune and his Nereids had arrived, and the party could begin.

The lanterns behind the party of capering drunks who had vaulted up from the gratings cast inhuman shadows. King Neptune was wrapped in the skin of a porpoise, its snout towering above his head to twice the height of a man. His followers had tattooed their faces with red dye and wore trailing wigs of seaweed. They advanced towards the quarterdeck through the throng, causing pandemonium as they went. Women screamed and knocked each other over trying to escape the thrusts of Neptune's pitchfork and the lunges of his drunken nymphs. When the royal party stood facing the row of officers drawn up on the quarterdeck, Neptune's great book was produced and handed to the king by an acolyte. Neptune hammed it up, squinted and licked his fingers to turn the pages in a parody of his literate superiors, checking his lists to see whether there was any officer on board who had not yet crossed the Line. Virgin mariners were forfeit a double liquor ration and had to undergo initiation rites.

With everyone's attention on the quarterdeck, a commotion among one tangled group of women went unnoticed. One among them must have fallen over and been kicked in the stomach during the pushing and shoving which had followed Neptune's entrance over the bow. So had others – but this woman was pregnant. As Neptune demanded Captain Aitken's rum, she was being carried into the forecastle or down the ladders into the sickberth by her friends. They got her into a hammock or bunk, curled on to one side to fight the pain in her belly. To women experienced in childbirth, it was clear what was happening. Someone went for Surgeon Alley; someone else may have pushed through the crowded deck to find the father. Shouts and screams came down the hatch and a roar of approval as Captain Aitken passed over his bottles of flip (a mixture of rum and sugar) as payment for crossing Neptune's frontier. The lantern swayed as hundreds of feet rushed to the foredeck to watch Neptune's barber.

Those seamen who had never before crossed the Equator were having their hands tied behind their backs and being seated on the planks over the barrels. The Nereids soaped their faces with a mixture of tar, dripping, crud from between the boards and dung. Neptune's barber brandished the blunt iron hoop which served him as razor and went to work. The victims struggled, overbalanced and disappeared into the bilge water. Sailors climbed on to the rails, women pushed for a view. The boys in the barrels splashed about, unable to get a purchase with their feet against the slime of the bottom, swallowing great gulps of filth. Eventually, they were hauled out and when they had their breath back, it was round two: they were hurled over the rail to be washed clean at the end of a rope.

If Surgeon Alley had been found and came to attend the woman below, he could do little to stem the miscarriage. He probably let blood from her arm with leeches or an incision, this being a general-purpose first step for an overheated or malfunctioning body. It did not work. In any case, the older women knew better what to do for a woman losing her baby than a naval surgeon. The matrons and mothers were alerted, probably Elizabeth Barnsley, a mother of two or three infants and a known midwife; perhaps Nelly Kerwin, another mother who had herself suffered a miscarriage at seven months in April 1787; perhaps Susannah Hunt, the 40-year-old teacher from Ipswich. More lanterns were brought and hung from the beams. Hot water came. Younger friends and men were told to go. When it was clear they could not save the baby, their main task was to ensure that all the dead child's appendages left the mother's womb. Infusions were needed; ashore, they would have been hartshorn or camomile. On board it was China tea, probably with opium drops. Eventually, the foetus was heaved from the mother's body into the basin held beneath her by her midwives and her belly massaged to expel the afterbirth. When the last clot of blood had haemorrhaged from her, she was given laudanum to numb the pain and send her to sleep. The party still raged on deck.

It was time for the boys to 'confess their amours' to the king and, said John Nicol, the number confessed was 'astonishing'. It is unlikely no sailor on board had exceeded the official ration of one 'wife' per seaman. One by one they were brought before Neptune and interrogated while the women named hid among friends or retaliated. Bottles of Captain Aitken's rum went round, and there were bellows for more. When the last salty anecdotes had been obtained, the music began, and the dancing. Finally, in the forecastle for those who got that far, and, on deck for those who did not make it, bleary copulation among the empty bottles – until officers' voices and officers' boots forced them up, halyards squealed and they turned south. It was while their hangovers were still fresh, and the initiates still picking lumps of tar from their hair, that the ship struck the doldrums.

About 100 miles to either side of the equator, winds die and currents slap against each other. It was, and is, a notoriously likely spot for a vessel under sail to be becalmed. Lucky ships sailed these 200 miles in three days or less with the trades behind them. The less lucky took weeks. When the *Lady Julian* turned at the end of Neptune's party to fill her sails and sail south, her crew found that yesterday's white crests were now a lifeless, oily sea and the fresh winds that had blown her along since Cabo Verde had died. Sails hung like empty sacks and the ship floundered, wayless. The motion was unpleasant; a ship which cannot make way is a graceless beast and her shuddering under the aimless slap of crosscurrent waves induces more nausea than the rhythmic plunge of passage. The idle days of the trades were on hold until the crew could get the ship through the doldrums and pick them up the other side.

When wind is scarce, there is more work for the men among the sails – and for the officers commanding their adjustments – than when it is blowing strongly. Sailing through the doldrums means trimming sails every few minutes to catch the latest cat's-paw of wind, each blowing in a different direction from the last. The men at the sheets came off each watch tired and demoralised by the log readings – a mile an hour, even less. Lieutenant Clark, suffering in the same spot two years previously, had recorded fretfully one evening that they had 'gone 10 miles back again from where we was yesterday'.

On and below deck, the women suffered too. Heat was intense; humidity intolerable. Sir Joseph Banks had been caught in the doldrums one October many years before:

> The nearer we approached to the calms, still damper everything grew. This was perceivable to the human body and very much so, but more remarkably upon all kinds of furniture: everything made of iron rusted so fast that the knives in people's pockets became almost useless and the razors in cases not free. All kinds of leather became mouldy. Portfolios and trunks covered with black leather were almost white . . . mould adhered to almost anything . . .

Any movement among the bodies packed into the orlop by night, lying under awnings on deck by day, caused a debilitating sweat. They dehydrated, just as the rationing of water began. On the first fleet the ration was cut here to three pints per day per person, which the surgeon said was 'a quantity scarcely sufficient to supply that waste of animal spirits the body must necessarily undergo, in the torrid zone, from a constant and violent perspiration, and a diet consisting of salt provisions'. The *Lady Julian* convicts did not reach the dangerous levels of dehydration that those on worse-run transports suffered. On a 1798 gaol ship, the men were confined for up to 23 hours per day below deck, and corruption and intimidation were such that the convicts responsible for distributing water to their messes hoarded and sold it instead. Casked water fetched two shillings a pint;

rainwater from the tropical showers which leaked down the hatches was sold for ninepence a quart. Aboard the *Lady Julian*, women were allowed free access to the deck during the day and had a more conscientious agent and surgeon to watch for abuses.

The stench that plagued the ship in harbour caught up with her again. Becalmed, a pool of effluent from the heads and the galley spread around her. This became home to a long, green train of plant life which trapped sewage and scraps of food in its fronds. Men lowered the ship's boats to hack away what they could of it, but could not reach it all. Thunderous tropical showers briefly cleaned the deck but the relief they brought steamed away in minutes.

There were various theories about how to make way when becalmed. Some seamen thought watering the sails to make the canvas heavy would allow them to hold more wind. Others held that knocking a wedge into the foot of the masts to stop them moving in their shoes had a better effect. But the only proven way to get a ship through windless waters – and away from its own cesspool – was to tow it. Thus, watch after watch, the ship's boats went down and the men towed the ship across a glassy sea. The doldrums meant exhausting work for the men and unending nights of discomfort. It was in the doldrums that Surgeon Alley diagnosed his first case of scurvy and the *Lady Julian* sprang her first serious leak.

Surgeon Alley had been in the service since 1783 and had seen plenty of cases of the sailors' diseases: scurvy, the pox and rheumatism. He was also familiar with the less serious but equally common *mals de mer*: nausea and the constipation caused by a salt diet and lack of fresh greens. It was the job of the surgeon on a transport ship to visit the convicts in the orlop hold when they were seasick, to ensure good hygiene in their sleeping areas and to supervise their exercise and diet. So far, there had been routine treatment of minor injuries, attempts to allay seasickness, checks for pox and any sign of lingering gaol fever which would require quarantine. Alley's duties had been light, but in mid-October he became a very busy man.

'The Scurvy', wrote Lieutenant Edgar's old colleague William Bligh, 'is realy a disgrace to a ship where it is at all comon, provided they have it in their power to be supplied with Dryed Malt, Sour Krout [pickled cabbage] and Portable Soup [small cakes of soup powder].' That his cargo should get scurvy was an embarrassment to Edgar, pupil of Captain Cook. During all three of Cook's voyages of discovery, the captain and his surgeons had been charged to perform and record dietary and other experiments on the seamen to test theories about the prevention and cure of scurvy. During his first and second voyages, which both lasted three years, he attained astonishing success in keeping his men free of scurvy: not one died of the disease on either voyage. However, too many different vegetables, essences, preserves and dried foods were experimented with to draw firm conclusions as to which had been responsible for keeping the disease at bay. Among them were 'Sour Krout', mustard, vinegar, essence of malt, 'Inspissated [reduced] Oranges and Lemon Juices', 'Portable Soup', sugar, molasses, carrot marmalade and soda water. Captain Cook had insisted that every man take his ration of these, whether he like it or not – and frequently he did not – and that they be varied whenever possible by fresh fruit and greens locally available wherever they put in. The captain knew that somewhere in this cocktail lay part of the secret of keeping a crew healthy, but he himself believed that diet was not the most important factor in beating the scurvy. In his opinion living conditions were the key to a healthy ship. With 'plenty of fresh water and a close attention to cleanliness,' he concluded, 'a ship's company will be seldom afflicted with scurvy, though they should not be provided with any of the antiscorbutics before mentioned'. The system of three watches, not two, he believed essential; also the purification of air below deck. For Captain Cook, keeping the men clean, dry and living in sweet-smelling air was more important than feeding them lime juice.

We can presume that Lieutenant Edgar adopted many of the revered captain's methods of keeping a crew happy and healthy – as did Captain Bligh, although with disastrous results. We do not know Surgeon Alley's thoughts on scurvy and, as there were so many different theories flying around in the 1770s and 1780s, he may have had different ideas from the lieutenant. It is probable that a variety of cures were attempted on the women of the *Lady Julian* in the hope that one of them would work.

The two most famous writers on scurvy, Dr Mead and Dr Lind, believed the disease was caused by the trapping beneath the skin of foul matter which then burst out as the black pustules which disfigured the bodies of sufferers. This waste matter, they thought, would normally have been expelled as faeces or sweat but, as these natural cleansing mechanisms were clogged by a damp climate, inactivity or an unhappy state of mind, expulsion had to be induced artificially. Retention of waste could be reduced by bleeding, by eating raw onions to induce sweat, by purging with a salt-water laxative or by eating fruit, whose acid, Dr Lind thought, would help break down the trapped matter and allow it to disperse. Some doctors believed that other types of acid, particularly 'elixir vitriol' (a dilution of sulphuric acid) and hydrochloric acid added to the sea-water purge were just as helpful in clearing waste from the bowels.

Cabbage had been provided by the Admiralty, preserved between layers of salt. This was now soused in vinegar and served as sauerkraut. It was not an attractive meal. Cook had found that his seamen would not eat it until he had it dressed and served to the officers with orders to express delight, noting wryly, 'the moment they see their superiors set a value upon it, it becomes the finest stuff in the world'. Portable soup was drunk. This had been made near the slaughterhouses of Deptford from cattle offal, boiled, flavoured with salt and vegetables and evaporated down to hard cakes for storage on board ship. It was usually served as a sort of crude minestrone, with dried peas or any available fresh vegetables boiled up in it. Anything up to four pints of sweet-wort – 'without doubt one of the best antiscorbutic sea-medicines yet found out' – was served to the sick each day when water supplies allowed. This was an infusion made by pouring boiling water over dried, powdered barley, leaving it in vast tubs in the galley for four or five hours to steep, and straining it to get rid of bits of husk. There were probably also rations of 'rob of lemon' or 'rob of orange' – a reduction of citrus juice – or wine and vinegar, also believed to have antiscorbutic properties, before noon dinner each day.

Despite all the varied cures being practised in the sickberth as the *Lady Julian* floundered in the doldrums, a severe outbreak of scurvy had taken hold of convicts and crew. Fresh greens from Cabo Verde were running out, and the ship still rolled in its own waste. One metabolism after another succumbed to a deficiency in vitamin C: 'the smallest appearance on the flesh in a day or two spread broader than your hand and soon made its way to the very bone.' Livid blotches erupted over the bodies of frightened women. Crops of pimples exploded round their mouths, their teeth loosened and their gums turned to fungus.

Temperatures by night were now so high that sleep was impossible. Below deck, melting tar dripped from the seams above the women's sleeping shelves and burned their faces and forearms. Even on deck the heat was uncomfortable. Pitch bubbled between planks. The seamen's feet could withstand anything, and the officers had their boots; the women wrapped scraps of tarpaulin around their feet to protect them from the burning boards. Even the seamen, whose backs were tanned to leather, wore a shirt if their work took them into direct sun in these waters. The glare off the sea was intolerable. The women's appetite left them; the deck was strewn with knots of fainting convicts.

Incessant rains fall across the equator at this season, with frequent violent thunderstorms. The *Lady Julian* should, like Arthur Phillip's fleet, have left England in May, but she had been delayed waiting for the assembly of a fleet which in the end was commissioned too late to join her. She began to suffer the consequences in the doldrums. As Surgeon Alley worked in the sickroom, the carpenter, carpenter's mate and any other man skilled with tools were working to plug the leaks which calms, rains and depredations of the sea life feeding off her hull had caused.

Many running repairs could be made to a ship while she was under canvas, but a leak far below the waterline was inaccessible. The men pumped as well as they could in the heat below deck. The ship's boats went over the side to scrape off plants and animals and expose any leaks above the waterline. Fires were lit on an already unbearably hot deck, cauldrons of pitch boiled up and lowered to the men in the boats to caulk those leaks they could get at. If the ship sprang a bad leak below the waterline, they stopped it by fothering her, binding her hull with an old sail coated with oakum and dung to create a waterproof second skin over the wood.

By October, 60 women were on the sick list; the galley was low on fresh water and fresh greens; the ship was leaking badly and, although fothered ships had sailed thousands of miles before reaching a harbour where they could be beached, no captain would do this unnecessarily. Even when the winds picked up again south of the doldrums, there was at least 2,000-miles' passage to be worked to Cape Town – a good three-weeks' sailing in sweltering temperatures. Lieutenant Edgar, Surgeon Alley, Captain Aitken and the first mate began emergency consultations in the chartroom. Not only might the extra miles to the Cape prove fatal for some of the women in the sickberth, but the Dutch authorities would not even let them into the harbour if they suspected disease on board. The obvious place to make for was the sprawling, decadent city of Rio de Janeiro, where the first fleet to New South Wales had put in two years previously. Instead of making another ocean crossing back towards the tip of southern Africa, they would hug the Brazilian coast, put into the Portuguese port to recover, and make the ocean passage from further south when numbers on the sick list had fallen and the worst leaks had been tackled. Aitken's planned voyage to Cape Town would have to be interrupted.

News that the ship would be back in port earlier than expected must have come as a relief to everyone aboard – the scurvy-sufferers, the heat-stricken and most of all the women now in the last months of their pregnancy. From one hour to the next in mid-October, the winds freshened and the *Lady Julian* picked up speed on a broad reach south-east. Her motion was easy, her decks level. A couple of days later the masthead sighted the white blur of Recife spreading up a hill, and the men aloft hauled the sails in to allow the ship to reach gently away from the coast on the currents that now swirled her anticlockwise back out into the Atlantic. It would be only ten-days' sailing with good winds on the beam to take them to the Tropic of Capricorn, where they would tack and head inland for the harbour of São Sebastião, Rio de Janeiro. They were ten days of anticipation. The stifling, airless weather of the equator was gradually replaced by fresher breezes. The crew, with a steady wind from the south-east, no longer spent the wearying hours aloft that had been necessary in the doldrums.

For the women due shortly to give birth, these were weeks of apprehension. They were all first-time mothers, the eldest 19 or 20 and the youngest 14 or 15. They were nervous about the physical ordeal of childbirth and because no one could tell them exactly what conditions they could expect for their confinement. At least they now knew the name of the continent off which their babies would be born – but that was the extent of their knowledge of this Portuguese Catholic port for which they were heading. So far they had been in the care of Surgeon Alley (himself an expectant father by 18-year-old Ann Mash), their more experienced fellow convicts and their seamen partners. Sarah Whitelam was now seven and a half months pregnant, scarcely able to waddle up the ladder from John

Nicol's mess to her seat beneath an awning on the deck.

John Nicol records not a word about the progress of her pregnancy. His attitude may have been coloured by the fact that his own mother had died giving birth to a younger brother when he himself was still an infant. Death in childbirth was far commoner then than now – just another hazard of being born a daughter of Eve – but the circumstances of his mother's death may have left some scars on John. When it was obvious that Sarah would have to give birth on board ship, or at best in a foreign port, one can only speculate on his thoughts on her chances and on the part he had played in getting her into this situation. Mary Rose had refused to have anything to do with the seamen, and it was she who was looking after Sarah until dusk each day, when Sarah went back to John's mess and Mary returned to her shelf in the orlop.

John Nicol's work kept him away from Sarah during much of the day, but his duties did not include standing watches. He could spend his evenings and nights in her company, except when shouted for to attend an officer. He was the most constant and entertaining of sailor lovers – a rough Othello to his temporary Desdemona. Sarah had had little experience of foreigners – in provincial Lincolnshire, black servants and lascar seamen were scarce. She had certainly never left England; it is unlikely she had ever left her county of birth before she was shackled to the coach which took her south to London. It was from John Nicol that she gained her knowledge of how the world fitted together, whence came the tea she had served her mistress in the parlour, the tobacco her master had smoked after dinner, the cotton shift she wore beneath her brown serge skirt.

It was John who explained to Sarah, Mary Rose and their group of friends sheltering from the sun beneath the awnings why it was that the American colonists had rebelled and what had happened over there in the New World during the wars. He told them about the great lakes dividing the rebel Americans

155

from the loyal Canadians and the vast rivers up which the fur-trappers disappeared for months on end each winter. He recounted his adventures fighting off American privateers in the Caribbean, cutlass in his hand and prize money on his mind and the glory of overpowering an American vessel off St Kitts and sailing her into harbour. He told them of the miseries he had seen among the slaves there. He remembered how British seamen would intervene to save slaves from brutal punishments in the West Indies and how gentle South Sea Islanders would do the same thing for British seamen caught breaking ship in Tahiti. He described the horrors of being ice-locked in Newfoundland and surrounded by hostile Indians. He told them of eating turtle off Cape Horn, snakes in French Canada and coconuts in Grenada and emphasised the invariable superiority of the British seaman over seamen of any other race. What neither he nor any other man on board could tell the women about was New South Wales, for none of them had ever been there.

In the privacy of his mess, perhaps, he told Sarah Whitelam about his childhood in Scotland and the death of his mother; of the loneliness of his father, bringing up five boys by himself; of the death of two of the brothers in childhood, and the disappearance of the other two – the youngest to America, from where nobody had since had news of him, and the eldest as a lieutenant in the West Indies, where he died of his wounds fighting the French. He told her about his plans to settle down, how he had nearly done so before this voyage but had been tempted back to sea by the prospect of seeing New South Wales. He promised he would not desert her but would return to the colony to marry her and take her back to Scotland as soon as her sentence expired.

In his memoirs, John Nicol says that had there been a clergyman on board the *Lady Julian* he would have married Sarah Whitelam. From the rest of his story, it cannot be doubted that his love and concern for Sarah were sincere – which makes one wonder why he did not get Captain Aitken to perform the marriage service instead. Either John did not ask him or Captain Aitken refused. There would be good reasons for Captain Aitken to turn down a request, if one were made. He could not afford to lose his steward and cooper on the return voyage, which would happen if Nicol stayed in New South Wales with his new wife. Jobbing seamen looking for their next berth did not yet hang round the new port of Sydney Cove, as they did in better-established harbours, and Nicol could not be replaced. Apart from this, Captain Aitken was probably not entirely clear on the legal implications of such a union. Was a seaman, or any other man for that matter, allowed to marry a woman in bondage to the British government? Sarah was government property and Captain Aitken could no more transfer her to the private ownership of a husband than he could transfer the rest of the stores aboard the *Lady Julian* to whatever merchant made him an offer for them.

Marriage might have been out of the question but sex was not. Pregnancy, of course, was the natural result of the cohabitation the agent and surgeon of the *Lady Julian* allowed, perhaps encouraged, among the crew and in which the surgeon actively participated. At the start of the next century, commissions appointed to investigate allegations of maltreatment on the New South Wales passage were informed by one sea officer after another that the taking of 'wives' aboard ship and on arrival was common practice – had been for decades, whether the destination was America, the East Indies or New South Wales. A gap would open between the practical men of sanguine views like Governor Phillip, who had suggested a whores' ghetto in Sydney Cove, and Lieutenant Edgar, with his easy acceptance of shipboard concubinage, on the one hand, and, on the other, reformers who complained of moral pollution. The practical men who ran the transportation ships and organised the Sydney Cove chain gangs thought moral pollution an acceptable price to pay for good order (especially if they only half-believed in the concept anyway). To their mind, the bleeding hearts in the English shires did not understand conditions on the ground.

A modern view may incline more towards that of the bleeding hearts than the practical men – less because of the moral pollution of unlicensed sex than because of the degradation the system forced on many females. But modern critics are as far removed in time from the world of seamen, convicts and marines in the 1790s as contemporary critics were in class and circumstance, and it could be that the practical men knew best.

Within a decade, another transport ship carrying female felons would leave London to make the passage across the Atlantic Ocean and on to New South Wales. She never made it past the coast of South America. The *Lady Shore* was a far less happy ship than the *Lady Julian*. When she reached the waters through which the *Lady Julian* was now passing peacefully, her crew mutinied and put the officers over the side in a small boat. The men then took the ship into Montevideo but their plan backfired: they discovered they were at war with Spain only when the Spaniards seized their ship as a prize and distributed the convict women as maidservants among the Spanish ladies of the city. Attempts at mutiny were not uncommon. They could be caused by a desire to get at the cargo, the provocation of short rations, an over-ferocious discipline, or the ambition to get to the New World, where honey flowed and all men were rich.

One woman on board the *Lady Julian* had had first-hand experience of mutiny. Mary Kimes, alias Potten, was now aged 29. Her known criminal record began in 1783 when she committed a felony somewhere in Bristol for which she was sentenced to seven years' transportation to America. In March 1784, she was loaded into the Bristol gaol wagons and taken to Portsmouth, where she embarked on the *Mercury* with 200 other convicted felons bound for the plantations. The ship was only one day out from Portsmouth harbour when the convicts and a part of the crew mutinied, took control and put in at Torbay, from where most of them escaped. Mary Kimes disappeared into the sinks of

Bristol until June the same year, when she was discovered and once more taken up by the peace officers. Two years went by before the government in London decided it might as well pardon her as keep her in gaol. As she had 'betaken herself to an industrious and honest course of life', she was returned by the Bristol authorities to her home parish in London as a free woman towards the end of 1786. Her burst of honesty, or prosperity, did not last. In 1787, she stole 30 yards of linen worth 30 shillings from the drapery of James Gibson in West Street, St Giles. The trial was cursory. This time she was sentenced to death. She was one of the 22 women who had been conditionally pardoned in thanksgiving for George III's recovery from insanity that spring and, six years after mutiny had saved her from America, she was on her way to Sydney Cove.

Another transport ship leaving England in 1792 would experience the threat of mutiny in Santa Cruz de Tenerife. A plan was made down in the orlop hold to rush the quarterdeck, seize the arms chest and make for America, where, the ringleaders promised the other convicts, 'Congress would give every man a tract of land for free'. Most of the orlop hold remained unconvinced, and when the leaders made a break for the arms chest, few followed. The 'Americans' were summarily hanged from the yardarm. And it was not only aboard transport ships that seamen could make trouble: as the *Lady Julian* neared Rio de Janeiro, Captain Bligh was recovering in Dutch Batavia after 41 days in a small boat following mutiny aboard the *Bounty*.

The creation of human relationships between males and females, and between officers and men, was prudent management. These were not the only relationships that had developed aboard the *Lady Julian*. By now, the connections which bound together this little township bouncing sturdily on towards Rio de Janeiro were many and complex. There were the clientage systems, run by the matrons or orlop gang-leaders who would convey requests and complaints to the officers and had some

power to grant or withhold favours. There were simple friendships, some of which had begun in the streets or gaols of England,
some of which were initiated on board ship. There were relationships between the generations. With the youngest female on board
aged 11 and the oldest 68, the convicts easily spanned three
generations. Although a handful of women had been allowed to
bring their babies with them, many on board had had to leave
older children behind. Elizabeth Barnsley had left at least two, as
had Nelly Kerwin; Catherine Wilmot had left four. They were
the natural candidates to take the younger teenagers and children
under their wing. The crimes committed by the 13- and 14-year-
olds on board disguise their ages: assault by Poll Randall and
Mary Butler, prostitution by Mary Bateman and Jane Forbes,
and what narrowly escaped being manslaughter by 11-year-old
Mary Wade and her 14-year-old friend Jane Whiting. Old enough
to commit violent crime, they were also young enough to miss
their mothers and grandmothers and seek out replacements
among the older women around them.

It was not only on the orlop hold that grieving mothers and
lonely children formed relationships: there were seamen on board
young enough to be the sons of some of the *Lady Julian* convicts.
The most junior officers, midshipmen, were commonly sent to
sea at the age of 12 or 13, often in ships commanded by relatives;
Lieutenant Riou of the *Guardian* had entered the navy at the age
of 12. During the early years of a midshipman's commission, the
ship was school and its officers and crew were family. Ships'
boys, his equivalent before the mast, were of a similar age.
However manly a face a midshipman or ship's boy might assume
on deck, a young boy away from home for the first time missed
his mother and his sisters, and surrogate mother–son and sister–
brother relationships must have been among the curious mix
which brewed in the *Lady Julian* as officers, crew and convicts
spent one month after another in close proximity.

Chapter Eleven

The Birth of John Nicol Junior

HMS *Guardian* had been only a few days north of the *Lady Julian* where she wallowed in the doldrums and had followed in the wake of the female transport towards Recife. But while the *Lady Julian* continued south, the *Guardian* swung back into the Atlantic and made direct for Cape Town. There was no scurvy aboard the man-of-war, which carried only 25 convicts and was making good time towards Sydney Cove. On 24 November, she arrived in Table Bay, Cape Town, expecting to see the *Lady Julian* at anchor there. There was no sign or news of her. 'I conclude', wrote Lieutenant Riou in a letter to Sir Joseph Banks, 'that she is gone to Rio.'

Far more worrying than the non-appearance of the *Lady Julian* and his former sailing-master, Lieutenant Edgar, was the news Riou now received from the Dutch colonial authorities about affairs in Sydney Cove. In November 1787, Commodore Phillip's fleet had sailed from Cape Town for New South Wales. At the beginning of 1789 his flagship, HMS *Sirius*, had reappeared in the Dutch harbour to buy emergency supplies for a starving colony. The colonists had almost run out of the dry goods supplied by the Admiralty 13,000 miles away in London and had had little success in growing crops. Already, the colony was in deep trouble. Captain John Hunter loaded up the *Sirius* on Admiralty credit and headed back across the Southern Ocean to relieve the camp and garrison. When this news was passed on to Lieutenant Riou, he decided no time could be wasted in getting the last supplies aboard the *Guardian* for Sydney Cove, and leaving as soon as possible. Consequently, HMS *Guardian* stayed only two and a half weeks at the Cape, the time necessary to take on livestock for the settlement. She set off to the south-west on 11 December 1789.

Five days after the *Guardian*'s departure, a Dutch brig arrived from Batavia bearing an illustrious British passenger. He was Riou's other former sailing-master, William Bligh, lately of HMS *Bounty*. Captain Bligh had last been in Cape Town in May of the previous year. Then, he had been proud and undisputed captain of his ship, with a prestigious commission. He had mentioned the possibility of dropping in on 'our friends in Botany Bay' en route for the South Sea Islands, but nothing came of this idea. Instead, he sailed direct for Tahiti with a shipful of happy sailors looking forward to love in the surf. What happened on board his ship and in the small boat in which he and a group of men loyal to him spent 41 days at sea is another story. He was to return finally to England in January of the following year, thus missing both Lieutenant Riou and Lieutenant Edgar in Cape Town.

November and December 1789 were significant months all round for the future of the settlement at Sydney Cove. In the River Thames, the three transports which originally had been intended to sail in convoy with the *Lady Julian* were finally ready to leave, carrying 928 male and 78 female convicts. Ann Wheeler, partner of Elizabeth Barnsley, had recovered from gaol fever and boarded the *Neptune* on 10 November. The same ship would also carry Lieutenant John Shapcote, the boundlessly corrupt agent who was the *Neptune*'s equivalent of kindly Lieutenant Edgar. A few weeks later, the hulks in Portsmouth disgorged over 100 male convicts, including Elizabeth Barnsley's husband, Thomas. He, too, sailed aboard the *Neptune*, while Sarah Gregory's husband, also Thomas, went aboard the *Surprize* with

Thomas Higgins, William Pimlott and James Saney. The experiences these convicts were to suffer on what became known as the 'coffin ships' were among the worst of any voyage during the decades in which felons were transported to New South Wales.

By the end of November 1789, connections between Britain and New South Wales were strung out across the globe. The *Neptune*, *Scarborough* and *Surprize* were heading south towards the Canaries. HMS *Guardian* had overtaken the *Lady Julian* in the Atlantic Ocean and was in Cape Town. Colonists in Sydney Cove, Rose Hill and Norfolk Island were planting their second round of crops. And on the first day of the month, the *Lady Julian* had finally tacked her way into the harbour of Rio de Janeiro, Brazil.

Brazil was the proudest overseas possession of the Kingdom of Portugal, and Rio de Janeiro was its capital. Portuguese navigators had been the first of the European explorers to open up the trade routes with Africa, South America and the islands of the Indies, but since their early days of glory they had withdrawn all over the globe before newer powers on the imperial scene. First Spain, then the Netherlands, then upstart Britain and France ousted them from settlements in three continents. In Brazil, however, they had hung on doughtily, and Rio in 1789 was still sending back New World profits to her masters in Lisbon. The masthead on the *Lady Julian* sighted Cabo Frio on 31 October and turned to sail west-by-north along the Brazilian coast. She was in sight of the Sugar Loaf Mountain to the left of the harbour of São Sebastião, Rio de Janeiro, by the following nightfall and anchored two miles out from the town. The next day she moved over the bar at the harbour mouth, with forts on either side, and waited for the guard-boats to nose out and ask her business. Turtles crowded round her hull. She did not have to ride the gentle waves of the middle harbour for long before the slave-rowed launches arrived carrying representatives of His Excellency the Viceroy of the Brazils, son of the king of Portugal, to enquire the ship's business. They were not the first on the scene: small boys in home-made boats had raced each other from the shore as soon as sail was sighted, and their urchin oarsmen had already swarmed up the side of the ship. The biggest ones stood in the boats, slicing up fruit with a machete, the middle ones balanced on the side and passed up the wares, and the little ones hung off the rails and shrouds holding up pine-apples, hands of sweet bananas, oranges, lemons and limes, shouting each other down in shrill Portuguese and pushing each other in. They made a lucky strike with the *Lady Julian*.

An abundance of tropical fruit was not the only surprise in these little boats for the women. The children who rowed them were of a range of colours and features they had never seen. The seamen had seen and maybe even sired children of mixed race on their travels, but they were unknown on the streets of Britain. In Rio, cheerful miscegenation had been the rule for generations, accepted at all levels of society and even by the Catholic Church. It was a singular city. Unions with native women had character-ised the early days of most European colonies, but when these matured and colonists began to hanker after respectability, native wives would usually be replaced by European ones and relation-ships between the races would harden to bigotry. This change of attitude did not occur, or occurred only at a very high level, in Rio de Janeiro, and the result was a population of exhilarating variety. Among the little boys dripping on the deck with their lemons, there were skins of every colour, from ebony black to sallow Portuguese white, and noses, hair and eyes of every racial type. Convict infants in tattered serge and ship's boys in tattered broadcloth stared at lithe, brown children with black hair and scraps of cotton round their loins.

Meanwhile, Captain Aitken and Lieutenant Edgar sweated in the tight breeches and frock coats required to uphold George III's dignity when his officers faced a foreigner, and went ashore. Much ceremony was observed. Formalities could take two days or more to complete, but British sailors were welcome in Rio de

Janeiro, especially any British on their way to see Commodore Phillip in Sydney Cove. Arthur Phillip had at one time served in the Royal Portuguese Navy, when Britain was briefly at peace and commissions hard to come by, and was esteemed by the Portuguese authorities. He and his senior officers had been offered every aid and courtesy when the first fleet spent a fortnight in Rio two years previously, and the viceregal court was anxious to hear whether his adventure in New South Wales had been successful. Although the name of Aitken did not invoke the same respect as the name of Phillip, the captain of the *Lady Julian* was assured of all assistance. This was just as well, for he not only had 60 in need of medical attention, but at least six about to give birth.

With the tide rising, the *Lady Julian* now made ready to enter the inner harbour of São Sebastião. Once again, the women went below to clear the deck for operations; once again, an 11-gun salute made the babies cry and the timbers shiver around their heads. The ship anchored either just inside the Ilha das Cobras or opposite the Benedictine friary and, back on deck, the women had their first close-up view of a Portuguese colonial capital. What they saw was an estuary dotted with lush little islands, a harbour encircled by fortifications, guard-boats rowed by Negro slaves passing among the ships, and a hot, glittering city spread up the hill before them 'surrounded by high mountains, of the most romantic form the imagination can fashion to itself any idea of'. If they had thought Santa Cruz the last word in gaudy Catholicism, it had nothing on Rio de Janeiro. There were churches everywhere, and almost nightly ceremonies to one saint or other. The harbour seemed continually full of the reflection of devotees' candles and the infuriating tinkle of convent bells. This exotic scene would become familiar to the women, for the *Lady Julian* was to remain in the harbour of São Sebastião for the next seven weeks.

From a long description of Rio de Janeiro in the journal of

Surgeon-General White of the first fleet to New South Wales, it sounds remarkably like that other Portuguese colonial capital, Panjim in Goa, which has changed less in two centuries than the Brazilian one. One wide avenue, known to the English as 'Strait Street', swept from the viceroy's palace through the town to the Mosteiro de São Bento, the grand Benedictine convent at the other end, and was the city's main socialising and shopping street. It was crowded with sedan chairs carried by slaves, chaises pulled by mules 'found to answer better than horses, being more indefatigable and surer-footed; consequently better calculated to ascend their steep hills and mountains'; the captain's guard on horseback, trotting slaves on errands. Sedan chairs were particularly awkward as the obese of Rio preferred to move crabwise – one sidestepping slave mounted the pavement, another stayed in the street and the sedan chair lurched along between them. Smaller streets ran parallel to or bisected Strait Street, just wide enough to allow two carriages to pass each other, flanked by high pavements so narrow that pedestrians had to walk in single file. Ground floors were shops; the upper floors, closed in by lattice-work balconies, were family residences. Female shadows behind the fretwork looked down. Every street was watched over by a Virgin in her niche. Churches were everywhere – falling down, going up, in the process of restoration, each with its own faithful congregation, its own patron saint and its own claim to miracles. The cathedral of São Sebastião, in what is now Praça xv de November, was half-finished (it is still not quite completed) with an arresting image of the patron saint of the city on its façade; further up was Santa Cruz dos Militares, then the Igreja da Ordem Terceira do Monte do Carma, in the first stage of construction, the Igreja da Nossa Senhora de Candelaria and finally the Benedictines. Visitors on the streets at dusk would frequently find themselves caught up in a public procession, led by some mendicant friar with a lantern in his hand, to raise funds for a church roof.

Several of the officers who had not had shore leave in Santa Cruz now left the ship to take lodgings in the town and, when the usual tasks of watering and making shipshape were completed, groups of seamen were also allowed off the ship for rest and recreation. The Portuguese of Rio were stricter than the Spanish of Santa Cruz, and the sailors of the *Lady Julian* were tagged wherever they went by a mournful Portuguese officer trailing his sword along the cobbles. Private Easty of the marines had gone ashore here two years earlier and wrote in his diary that the Brazilian Portuguese 'are a very strickt Sort of People the Solders have the whole Command of the Place thay have a great many Troops to the amount 6 or 7 Thousand men'. Rio was a city dominated by the military and the strict rules that governed its honour. 'Although the dreadful custom of private stabbing is at an end', polite male society in Rio de Janeiro still dressed for vendetta. Gentlemen bristled with frightful swords. Boys as young as six strapped them on before they left the house and wore them with hauteur.

The military had more reason to be 'strickt' when the *Lady Julian* passed by in 1789 than they had when the first fleet to New South Wales was there in 1787. This was a decade of revolution for more than one New World colony and Old World coloniser. North America had won her revolution against the taxes, trade restrictions and prohibitions on manufacture imposed from Europe. In Brazil, a group of creoles – the term used by both Spanish and Portuguese to denote those of European blood but colonial birth – had decided to do the same, inspired by Thomas Jefferson. The 1789 *Inconfidencia Mineira*, or Miners' Conspiracy, united poets, priests, landowners, merchants and army officers under the leadership of 'Tiradentes', a part-time dentist and lieutenant in the Brazilian army by the name of Joaquim José da Silva Xavier. Before the conspirators had had time to act, their plans were betrayed. Lieutenant da Silva had been hanged and quartered in the square later named

Plaça Tiradentes a few months before the arrival of the *Lady Julian*. His head had been impaled on a pole and his limbs sent to be exhibited in the mining towns which had supported him. It was a death ritual as terrifying as those in which Margaret Sullivan and Christian Murphy had died. The other leaders were sent into exile to the Portuguese equivalents of Sydney Cove in Angola and Mozambique. Rebellion had been crushed, but Rio de Janeiro was an uneasy city at the end of 1789 and the officers who accompanied the men of the *Lady Julian* were on edge, mistrusting both the creoles they ruled and the army they served. Nor had the civilian population recovered from the brief thrill of insurrection earlier that year, or its brutal end. The British officers, cadging invitations from contacts in the military or the colonial administration to midnight receptions, probably heard more about this than the seamen. The attempted revolution in Brazil, like the successful one in Washington, was an affair fomented in private salons, not public bars.

The Portuguese in Brazil would have been more reluctant to allow even well-behaved convicts ashore, especially in the tense conditions of 1789, than their compatriots at Cabo Verde or the Spanish at Tenerife. Edgar and Aitken themselves may have decided it was not safe. However, a privileged convict who sailed in 1792 went ashore here, to stock up on little necessaries and encash bills at British merchants' offices in the city, so it is possible that Elizabeth Barnsley, Nelly Kerwin and the other moneyed convicts of the *Lady Julian* also did so, accompanied by both a British and a Portuguese officer for safety. Chief among their purchases were the country's 'excellent tobacco' and 'aquadente spirit, [which] by proper management and being kept till it is of a proper age, becomes tolerable rum'; tolerable, and very, very cheap.

The female felons of England would have been conspicuous on the streets of Rio. Any Portuguese ladies of good family who left their house on foot did so under impenetrable mantillas.

Those not swathed in black lace were women of the port, or slaves. Private Easty had made some study of these two years before: 'the natives of this place are of a Dark Clompecton much Like the Gipsies of England Likewise Great meany of the Coast of Gueany neagoes . . . thay ware no aparell Exept a Clout Jest around ther Privits the negos weman ware a Short kind of bed gownd wich jest Cover their Brists and Shoulders and a Short Peticaoc wich Come About half way down their thies thay ware no kind of Shirts or Shifts So that thare Bellies is naked . . .' Portuguese Brazil was the single biggest slave purchaser of the eighteenth century. The streets were full of city slaves, and the markets sold goods produced by plantation slaves on latifundias that stretched from Pernambuco to São Paulo: coffee, sugar, tobacco, rice, cotton, indigo, pimiento. For Surgeon Alley, or Mrs Barnsley, or whoever was buying in supplies for the confinement of the mothers-to-be on the *Lady Julian*, the supplies available from the Rio druggists were of particular interest. There were many apothecaries' shops in the little streets behind the main boulevard and Surgeon-General White had found their products excellent and fresh.

John Nicol remembered 'I here [in Rio] served out 20 suits of childbed linen', implying that 20 mothers gave birth, but this was in memoirs written when he was an old man and which are inaccurate in other details. A document much closer to the date of the babies' birth was a letter sent home by another father-to-be, Surgeon Alley, in which he gives a total of births and deaths as far as Cape Town, from where his letter was sent. This states that five died and seven were born, but his tally of five seems only to take account of deaths among those who embarked in England, not stillborn babies or infants who survived only days in Rio. A minimum of nine women gave birth in November or December, so clearly he did not take account of at least two dead babies. Nor did he mention in his letter home that one of the surviving babies was his.

169

It is improbable that every baby born between the River Thames and Sydney Cove survived. Infant mortality rates in conventional hospitals were high. They may have been higher still on board the *Lady Julian* – or not; sickberths on well-run ships with a competent surgeon or midwife could be safer than city hospitals. Robert Bland, the 'Man-Midwife' in the Westminster General Dispensary, kept records of births there in the 1780s. He compiled a table of 1,897 babies delivered in one year and his figures were grim: 1 in 270 mothers died in childbirth, usually because of an 'unnatural Labour' in which the baby presented in a difficult position. More frightening still, 1 in 241 babies born at Bland's hospital that year had been 'deficient or monstrous'. In these categories, he included babies with webbed fingers, harelips, 'dropsical heads' and distorted spines, one missing part of its palate and two missing 'a considerable part of the cranium'. Bland also delivered a pair of Siamese twins, described as a baby with two heads. Hazards did not end with confinement. Two of his new mothers had been 'seized with mania but recovered in about three months'. Many others had delivered a baby safely but died soon afterwards. One in 16 lost their children within two months and one in seven within two years. This was the lottery Sarah Whitelam, Ann Bryant, Jane Forbes, Mary Barlow, Elizabeth Griffin, Mary Warren, Margaret Wood, Ann Mash and Sarah Dorset would play in Rio de Janeiro or out on the ocean beyond if their babies did not come in time.

John Nicol's only comment on the circumstances in which his son was born was that 'the ladies fitted up a kind of tent for themselves' on deck. It was late spring in Rio. Temperatures were rising, and by Christmas they would be approaching the fierce heights that the *Lady Julian* had just escaped in the doldrums, and the hills enclosing the city of São Sebastião would keep the heat in and the air out. Despite its richness and ornament, it was, wrote an officer of the previous fleet, 'an unhealthy spot, excluded from refreshing sea and land breezes'. A tent would be needed.

In John Nicol's memory it was Mrs Barnsley who played the part of chief midwife, and apparently played it so successfully that she continued to practise after arrival in Sydney Cove. Someone forceful must have taken charge to ensure that the awning was rigged and moved through the hours of sun to keep the deck in shade; that lavatory buckets were regularly emptied and cleaned; that flies and mosquitoes were fanned away; that the women beneath the awning had adequate bedding and clean linen, fresh greens to relieve constipation, herb teas against backache, barley water against cystitis, and pillows on which to place swollen ankles; that sheepish seamen who did not feel like fetching more fresh water and fruit in that heat were reminded of their responsibilities.

Spring was becoming summer, the sun rose higher and temperatures with it; humidity thickened. Repairs continued to the hull, masts, spars, sails, yards and shrouds, which had all taken a battering in the tropical storms of the equator or fallen prey to the teredo beetle which fed off the ship's timbers. Soon, work could be done only in the first hours of the morning or after the sun began to lose its strength in the late afternoon. Between these hours, little stirred in the harbour or the city of Rio de Janeiro. The noon light was so dazzling on the water that it hurt the eyes. When the heat lessened at dusk, the streets filled with blacks and Indians. Female slaves appeared from the doors of the houses with bundles of laundry on their heads, to be washed at the stone fountains which stood in every street. Friars, priests, sisters passed among them, and the whole street-borne population dipped and rose as it passed the niched statues which drew an automatic genuflection from free and bond alike. When dusk became night, the slaves stopped their chores and knelt in long rows down the street, chanting their vespers.

Again, the tar started to melt and drip from between the ship's timbers. Again, women ran to the heads with the flux from drinking too much fresh water and gorging themselves on too much fresh fruit. Again, the smell of the ship's waste soured the air until the next tide washed it clean. There was fitful silence in the midday hours, broken by the sighs and scratchings of a deckful of women curled beneath old sails brought up from the hold to be made into shelters. Occasionally, small children scrambled over the rail, lifted a canvas flap and peered in at the foreigners dozing underneath. The women whose babies were shortly due were allotted their own patch of deck and their own awning. Each was attended by a best friend or group of friends. It seems Sophia Sarah Ann Brown was with Ann Bryant, Mary Rose with Sarah Whitelam, Mary Barlow and Mary Warren perhaps with the other girls of their age from Warwick, Margaret Wood and little Jane Forbes with former cellmates or surrogate mothers.

Sarah Whitelam was in the eighth month of her pregnancy. Since leaving London she had gained anywhere between one and a half and two stone in weight. Her belly was now fully extended, and she had had to give up her convict serge, with its seams designed for the chaste. She or Mary Rose had probably sewed a drawstring cotton skirt of some type for her pregnancy. She could no longer wear stays, so her breasts, swollen with milk, were unsupported and movement was painful. It was difficult to find a position in which to lie or sit which did not leave some part of her body aching. She and the other heavily pregnant women moved from their backs to their sides on mattresses on the deck, drawing up first one leg then the other. They were sleepy from the heat and the weight of their bodies, waking occasionally from a doze to put a cushion between their knees, turn a pillow for coolness or answer some question from Mrs Barnsley. Frequently they would rise carefully, turning to one side, swinging the shoulders round, pushing themselves up to kneel and then staggering up to go and use the bucket.

The fathers – indeed all the seamen and officers except Surgeon Alley and perhaps Lieutenant Edgar – probably steered well clear of the maternity tent. Although male doctors had been progressively and controversially taking over the profession of midwifery in England, most men still considered childbirth to be strictly a female business. The pregnant women had probably moved out of the seamen's quarters and into huts or tents on the deck as soon as the ship reached the quiet waters of São Sebastião. The life of the ship moved around them. The birth of half a dozen convict babies was, after all, of little importance to most on board. The chores of cleanliness and food preparation still went on; so did the continual small jobs required to keep the ship neat and watertight. There were 220 women aboard not giving birth and 25 men not about to become fathers who also had to be tended and kept occupied. The agent, cook and steward still had to go ashore and make their deals for fresh greens, meat, coffee, sugar and rum. The officers still wanted to make their day trips and shopping expeditions ashore. Seedlings for the Sydney plantations still had to be tracked down, haggled over and brought on board. Someone still had to feed the chickens, muck out the hogs and water the plants.

The babies waiting to be born in Rio de Janeiro would be born into circumstances of great singularity, to a convict mother impregnated by – a seaman lover? an unwilling gaoler? a camp guard? a man such as she would have had such a baby by had she stayed in London, Warwick or Exeter? John Nicol and his *Lady Julian* colleagues had had no part in the decisions by which these women were being sent into exile. They were the mercenaries of their trade, merchant seamen who signed on for the most advantageous terms on offer. If it was by their labour that the women were physically transferred from one country to another, they were only obeying orders, and if one took 'as wife' a 14-year-old girl, he was only doing what someone else would have done if he had not. Is this how the pregnant women saw the fathers of their babies? Analogies with camp guards who condoned or at least did not condemn the practices in twentieth-century gaol camps are dodgy; any analogy which assumes a twentieth-century view of morality and personal choice in an eighteenth-century mind is unreliable. Whatever the relationship between their parents, the ship babies of Rio were born into limbo. Their mothers had been exiled from one state. They were on their way to another not quite two years old, whose identity was still in question: not yet a nation, not quite a colony, not quite a gaol. Even the name of the territory to which their mothers would take them was uncertain. Would they be English? British? New South Welsh? New Hollanders? Antipodeans? Fundamental questions hovered over the extended bellies on board the *Lady Julian* from which six lost little ship-born creoles would shortly emerge.

The birth of their babies was the principal experience of Rio de Janeiro for the women who bore them, but for others it was a sideshow to more important events. The maternity tent was not the only corner of activity. Under canvas to one side of the ship's waist, the nine-month cycle of reproduction was about to end, but in huts, hammocks and berths elsewhere, it was just beginning. John Nicol remembers nothing of Sarah's labour but does remember that in Rio once again 'the ladies had a constant run of visitors'. Wheeling and dealing between forecastle, orlop, visiting seamen and curious inhabitants of the port got under way in Rio with the same dispatch and efficiency as in Santa Cruz de Tenerife, with the same tacit acceptance from the quarterdeck. The liquor-soaked sponge-on-a-string and candle-wax caps came out from beneath the orlop hold mattresses to be dusted off and inserted.

The pregnant doze of half a dozen swollen women under their tatty sail was interrupted in late November or early December when Sarah Whitelam went into labour. She was a first-time mother, young, as far as we know reasonably healthy. From the breaking of her waters to birth may have taken as little as four hours. The little maternity ward on one corner of the deck swung into action. 'She has frequent warm and cold fits, with urgent desire to make water & co. and is exceedingly restless as every situation appears unsupportable and uncomfortable to her,' as Dr Bland wrote in his midwifery manuals. In the first stage of labour, contractions came every five minutes or so. Someone checked the dilation of the cervix and soon 'the Shews', the membranes of the uterus, ruptured and her waters broke. Shortly afterwards, her bowels emptied. Mary Rose and Elizabeth Barnsley mopped, cleaned, changed, reassured. At 8–10-centimetre dilation, Sarah was in transition from the first stage of labour to the second, her contractions sharp and irregular, her breathing harsh. She ran with sweat; she may have had the hiccups, belching fits or vomiting that commonly accompany this phase. Her midwives gave her infusions of camomile, hartshorn or whatever herbs Mrs Barnsley had been able to find ashore.

It was not yet the custom to lie down to give birth, and Sarah probably walked around during much of her labour. The upright position encouraged the baby to press downwards and outwards. The shackles and buckles which held women in place during later labours had not been thought of, and there were no forceps on the *Lady Julian* to require a woman to be on her back for access. Any support required came from a chair or, commonly, a birthing stool. This was a seat in the shape of a horseshoe, with the gap to the front, low enough that a woman squatted rather than sat on it, wide enough to provide handgrips and support for her lower back. Whether the ladies of England had provided any of these along with their suits of childbed linen goes unrecorded. If they had not, it was well within the ability of John Nicol or the ship's carpenter to make some, perhaps on a request from Mrs Barnsley conveyed through the surgeon, perhaps on an order from Mrs Barnsley direct.

Squatting on a birthing stool, or kneeling on the deck, Sarah pushed and minutes, hours, a day, two days later, John Nicol

Junior emerged, wrinkled and slimy, with a great gush of liquid behind him. Someone checked the baby to remove the cord from around his neck and any membrane from across his face then turned him slightly downwards so mucus drained from him. Someone else placed a birthing stool beneath Sarah's buttocks in readiness for the placenta and another rush of blood to slip out. After some time had passed, they tied and cut the umbilical cord and placed the baby boy at Sarah's breast.

Perhaps activity stopped, and the ship held its breath when one woman then another in the maternity tent went into labour and gave birth. Perhaps everything carried on as normal except in that one corner where the violent business of bringing life into the world ground on and a group of frightened teenagers bled on to the deck. Some of the seamen may have been shaken, others may have shrugged their shoulders, reflected that having babies was what women had always done, always would and thought no more about it. Not even John Nicol, whose tenderness for Sarah he expressed so vividly, remembered anything of his son's birth.

'After four weeks,' wrote Dr Bland, Westminster midwife, new mothers 'can go abroad and should . . . at first, take an airing in a carriage for two or three days, then walk a little when the weather is favourable and defer going to church until they feel themselves in the natural state of good health'. For the new mothers of the *Lady Julian*, the first months of motherhood took a different course. At the end of December, they left São Sebastião and headed for the city at the Cape of Good Hope from which the Portuguese had been ousted by the Dutch East India Company, who would themselves shortly be ousted by the British.

Chapter Twelve

The Wreck of the *Guardian*

Lieutenant Riou on HMS *Guardian* had arrived at Cape Town, been given the news of Captain John Hunter's emergency provisioning trip from Sydney Cove earlier that year, loaded up with extra stores and set off for New South Wales while the *Lady Julian* was in Rio de Janeiro. He had left the Cape on 11 December and sailed more south than east, a course that took him dangerously close to the Antarctic regions Captain Cook had circumnavigated in his second voyage of exploration. Among Riou's many problems was conserving fresh water for the mares, stallions, ewes, rams, goats, rabbits, poultry and the pair of exotic Mauritius deer he had taken on at Cape Town. The *Guardian* masthead sighted icebergs three leagues off on 22 December. They were at 42°15', unusually far north for ice. On Christmas Eve, at 43°40' south, another huge ice mass was sighted and the decision taken to try to scoop some chips out of the sea in order to melt them for the cattle. Two boats were hoisted out to go ice-gathering. The operation was dangerous as iceberg waters hold lethal traps. By the time the longboats had returned with their chunks, fog had closed in around the ship and visibility was down to three-quarters of a mile. Extra lookouts were posted but, struggling to find a passage into safer waters, no one saw the ice-mountain on the ship's starboard beam until it was too late and the ship was impaled. When she tore free, her rudder was left in the ice and water was streaming into her hull. Guns, cargo, fodder were all thrown overboard, the ship was fothered with one, then two layers of canvas, but the water inside her continued to rise. Forty-eight hours of frantic activity followed; men pumped for their lives but one by one gave up the fight and drank themselves into oblivion on stolen liquor. On Boxing Day, Lieutenant Riou permitted any who wished to abandon ship. The boats went out and most of the seamen went with them. All but 15 of those in the boats would perish at sea, in these lonely waters where few ships sailed. The 15 survivors had the astonishing good luck to be found by a French merchantman blown off course from Mauritius who brought them back into the Cape on 18 January.

Riou stayed with his ship along with the 60 people for whom there was no room in the boats. A temporary rudder was rigged. His log of 28 December reads: 'steering was my first object, fothering if it was only to keep her up a day or two, and by standing to the northward a chance of the *Lady Julian* passing or some other ship.' When the 15 surviving men and their French rescuers arrived in Cape Town three weeks later, it was assumed that the *Guardian* had gone down, one more victim of the Southern Ocean. Dispatches were sent to the Admiralty, personal letters to Riou's mother with the news of her son's death, others to Prime Minister Pitt with news of his cousin's. In the Southern Ocean, the *Lady Julian* did not appear, for she was still on her way from Rio to the Cape; no other ship appeared either, and hopes turned to finding some desert island instead. No island loomed; they were saved on 22 February when whalers were spotted who led them in to the Dutch harbour of False Bay at the Cape of Good Hope on 21 February, 'covered in dirt and rags and with long beards, looking like men from another world'. Riou's was an outstanding achievement, the equivalent in seamanship and charisma of Captain Bligh's a few months before.

The officers of the *Lady Julian* knew nothing of the mutiny on the *Bounty* or the shipwreck of the *Guardian* when their lookout sighted land on 28 February. They had made what was, for the *Lady Julian*, a reasonably fast passage: 50 uneventful days' sailing east from Rio to the African Cape. Within a couple of hours of the lookout's call, the astonishing flat-topped mass of Table Mountain was visible to those on deck. A little later they saw the Devil's Peak and the Lion's Head, then the creases and folds of the hills running down from the mountains, and finally the churches and low houses of the town cradled in the amphitheatre between mountains and sea. By evening, they were at anchor in Table Bay, about a mile and a half south-west of Cape Town, the Tavern of the Seas.

The huge bay was full of shipping. Dutch merchantmen put in here between Antwerp and Batavia, Portuguese between Lisbon and Bengal, French between Madras, Mauritius and Bordeaux, British between Calcutta and London. There were also Americans, whalers or private merchants dealing with any colonist who did not mind breaking a European monopoly. The Americans even had their eyes on trade and emigration to Botany Bay. They had contacted Phillip's officers through a third party to sound out British feeling on the matter when his fleet was here in 1787. The one ship the men of the *Lady Julian* had not expected to see in the bay was HMS *Guardian*.

When Dutch Company officials came out to greet the *Lady Julian* at the mouth of the harbour, they brought with them news of the shocking recent events. The guesthouses of the Cape currently hosted survivors from two British ships, one overtaken by mutineers in the South Pacific, the other holed by the ice in the Antarctic. Lieutenant Edgar and Captain Aitken hurried to complete the formalities at the house of Governor van Graaf and then to track down Lieutenant Riou at his lodgings. From him they heard the dramatic story of the *Guardian*'s misadventure first-hand. Edgar also offered a slightly sheepish explanation of the *Lady Julian*'s exceptionally long voyage. 'Constant calms about the equator,' he told his ex-junior; 'the female convicts much afflicted with Scurvy; the transport was very leaky.'

Agent Edgar next paid his compliments to John Fryer, master of the *Bounty*, who had remained in the Cape when Captain Bligh sailed for England in January. Master Fryer and those of the *Bounty*'s company who were fit were helping Riou with the salvage operation on the *Guardian*. Some could not: the surgeon's assistant from the *Bounty* was confined, and it was feared he had lost his mind as a consequence of the thirst and fear of his 41 days in a small boat at sea. The misadventure of the *Bounty* and the fate of her captain, a man personally known to both Riou and Edgar, was a tale of there-but-for-the-grace-of-God fascination for his brother-officers, but it was the wrecking of the *Guardian* whose consequences had more immediate effect on Edgar's plans. The colony at Sydney Cove had been in distress when Captain Hunter had left Cape Town a year ago; if harvests had continued poor and no stores had since been received or sent for, how much greater distress were the colonists in now? It was imperative that the *Lady Julian* should take on as many extra stores as she could find room for and leave for New South Wales as soon as possible. There would be no leisurely seven-week stay at the Cape as there had been at Rio.

Lieutenant Riou had been in the Dutch settlement for only a week. The stores that had not gone overboard to lighten the *Guardian* among the icebergs were still aboard the listing ship at her berth in the harbour while he sought warehouse space to rent in town. It was decided that whatever stores could be transshipped from the *Guardian* would be carried to Sydney Cove aboard the *Lady Julian*. What would once again hold her up were the leaks she had sprung during her passage from Rio. Before any new stores could be taken on, her holds would have to be emptied of any stores already in them and her decks cleared for repairs.

Nobody had better recent experience of plugging leaks than Lieutenant Riou and the carpenter of the *Guardian*, whose services were now lent to Edgar. The *Lady Julian* was piloted up the harbour and brought in to be thoroughly overhauled before she took on the rough waters of the Southern Ocean between Africa and New South Wales. Work was in progress for at least three weeks. Careening – the operation of beaching a ship to expose one side of her hull to repair it – required as much of her cargo as possible be taken ashore. The women were about to land at their fourth foreign city and their third continent. Casks and barrels were hauled on deck, lowered over the side, rowed or rafted to land and rolled up the beach to safety. With up to 1,000 casks in storage, this was a hot and tiring job.

The Cape Town authorities were famously nervous of unconventional cargoes. When Commodore Phillip's fleet had put in two years before en route to Botany Bay, they had posted extra sentries along the beach and doubled the guard in the city. When the women slept out of the beached ship, on their orlop mattresses or beneath shelters rigged from deck-awnings, they, too, may have been guarded by Dutch militiamen on loan to the accident-prone English, or may simply have been on parole. Where, after all, could they escape to if they crept up the beach at midnight and made for the town? There were only mountains and deserts beyond.

The ship emptied, careening could start. All sails were unbent and rowed ashore. The topmasts were detached, lowered and stacked on the beach. Cables were attached to cleats on the seaward beam of the ship, rowed ashore and taken once round trees. Teams of men then hauled the ship on to one side, exposing the leaks on the other. Getting the ship into a position where these were accessible could easily take two or three days, then they had to repair her hull. Fortunately, they were not without friends in Cape Town: the rump of two other British crews could lend a brawny shoulder and heave on the ropes. The beach became a temporary camp, workshop and forge as carpenters and blacksmiths set up their equipment. Sails and spare canvas were spread across the sand, examined for mildew and bleached bone-dry in the sun. One fire boiled cauldrons of pitch for the men working on the hull, another cooked the food prepared by the cook, his mate and their team of convicts to feed the women on the sand, the working parties and the officers.

While the ship was careened under the supervision of the first mate, Lieutenant Edgar got on as fast as he was able with provisioning. What was left of the *Guardian* crew, supplemented by any man from the *Bounty* not incapacitated by fever or insanity, was stocktaking aboard the wreck and rowing off whatever the *Lady Julian* could not carry to be kept in the immensely expensive warehouses Riou had now found in town. Among the stores the *Guardian* had been taking to Sydney Cove were plants, some British, some African. The plant cabin that Sir Joseph Banks had chalked out on her quarterdeck in Deptford was gone and the 93 pots he had placed inside it had been jettisoned in southern waters. These had to be replaced. On hand in Cape Town was the English botanist Francis Masson, also part of Banks's international plant-gathering network. Like James Smith and George Austin, the two gardening super-intendents selected by Sir Joseph for Sydney Cove, Francis Masson had been sent from Kew in 1772 at his instigation. From there, he had conducted botanical expeditions into the interior, sending whatever he could back to Kew and making pleas to be allowed to go home.

Much of the livestock that Riou had bought in Cape Town for the Sydney Cove farms had also been lost in the wreck. Some had gone overboard. Smaller animals had been trampled and crushed when the cattle panicked or drowned when the water washed over the hutches. Riou had managed to save his flock of 22 sheep and two Cape stallions, and it was decided that these would be transshipped to the *Lady Julian*, along with 75 barrels of flour, 100 gallons of wine and some Admiralty dispatches for Commodore Phillip. Edgar also inherited passengers from his former midshipman. Five of the seven superintendents had survived the wreck and all 25 gardening convicts had remained on board and helped bring the *Guardian* safely back to the Cape. Riou had promised these men, 'so meritorious, before and after the disaster', that he would petition for their pardon in recognition of the part they played. It was arranged that the 25 convicts would remain in Cape Town and sail on the *Neptune*, *Scarborough* or *Surprize*, expected within weeks, but that the superintendents would sail with Lieutenant Edgar. When she was pronounced as fit as she could be made by the carpenters, the *Lady Julian* was righted, reloaded and returned to her berth in the harbour. Work for the carpenters did not stop, however, for now they had to devise new accommodation to house the six humans, two stallions and flock of sheep that would join the ship for the last leg of the voyage. At the end of March, John Thomas Doidge came aboard, as did flax-dresser Andrew Hume, Philip Devine and Hessian ex-mercenary Philip Schaffer with his ten-year-old daughter, Elisabeth, the first genuine 'young lady' on board. They were probably accommodated in huts put up in the waist of the ship at Cape Town. Miss Elisabeth may have shared a hut with her father or Mrs Barnsley or some of the officers may have been turfed out of their mess to hand it over to her.

These discussions, works and removal of stores took the whole of March to accomplish. If any of the women went ashore during this time, they went with an officer clinging like weed to their sleeve. The Dutch were more chary than the Spanish or Portuguese of foreign ships' companies, especially of these gangs of convicts the British had started sending south. Officers certainly went into lodgings ashore, as in any other foreign port. The house favoured by Commodore Phillip and his officers in 1787 belonged to a Mrs de Witt, whose husband seems also to have been one of the merchants involved in supplying foreign shipping; it was a happy arrangement for all. The seamen may also have gone ashore. Well-to-do and trusted convicts on later ships went with them and presumably the well-to-do and trusted of the *Lady Julian* had the same opportunities.

The landing place stood at the eastern end of the town. None of the foreshore, which is now office blocks, gardens and municipal statuary, had yet been reclaimed from the sea. The first building the newly disembarked walked past was the massive pentagonal Castle of Good Hope, which was also a store and quarters for bachelor officers of the Dutch East India Company. A newer fort defended the western part of the town. In a different way, Cape Town was as foreign as Rio and Santa Cruz – Teutonic and Protestant rather than Latin and Catholic but equally strange to Londoners and Bristolians. After their weeks in Rio, the ladies had become accustomed to streets full of trotting slaves and bright light, but in Cape Town there were new ethnic and penal variations. Each European colony had its own take on the status and treatment of slaves. Each preferred a different nationality in the house or the fields. There were Negroes and creoles among the Cape Town slaves but also Malaysians brought from Dutch possessions further east to work as soft-footed house-servants. Too soft-footed; according to urban myth in 1780s Cape Town, Malaysian slaves 'frequently assassinate their masters and mistresses' and every Malay was required to carry a lantern after dark. Creoles were admired and expensive; the Negroes of Mozambique and Madagascar were liked best as they were 'affectionate and faithful', along with Hottentots from the interior, who were, sadly, almost impossible to get hold of. There was more of a desertion problem among the Cape Town slaves than among those at Rio. A popular day trip for visiting officers was an excursion into the tableland from where an apparently inaccessible ledge would be pointed out by a local guide as the home of gangs of runaway Negroes. At dusk, their fires could be seen far above, and dark tales were told of depredations made by night on kitchen gardens.

Equally popular, but considerably more strenuous, was a trip to the top of Table Mountain. This could be 'a sultry and fatiguing expedition', but the view from the top was universally held to be one of the world's finest. The extreme neatness and regularity of the town became apparent from the mountain, and the exact 90-degree angles at which its streets intersected each other were pointed out to visitors. It is hard to find a contemporary journal which does not describe the Cape as clean, regular and well ordered. There was no vulgar Catholic excess here, but pristine, flat-roofed white houses such as survive in Bo-Kaap, only two storeys high as a precaution against the strong winds of the summer, and a few decently imposing buildings for official Company business. The governor's house was one of these, and the Company gardens in which it stood, part functional, part ornamental, were superb (although Watkin Tench was predictably sniffy about the little zoo the gardens housed: 'It is poorly furnished both with animals and birds: a tyger, a zebra, some fine ostriches, a cassowary and the lovely crown-fowl'). The Dutch churches were soberly Lutheran and Calvinist, and the Dutch ladies walked bare-faced and forthright. On the surface this was a more orderly society than that of Rio, but for all its calm and efficiency there were glimpses of a justice shocking in its severity. The execution place was very close to the spot where arriving ships watered, just above the fort. It contained not only a gibbet but a pole for impalements, wheels, and six crosses for breaking criminals. Body parts from the executions performed here were suspended at street corners around the town.

Centuries of European miners, planters and latifundias had subdued vast tracts of the older colonies in coastal South America, but outside the Dutch enclaves on the African continent the land and its people reverted abruptly to their natural state. Tales of cannibalism and black ritual emerged from the bush, some true, some less true, but all passed on with relish. According to a 1798 convict, who never left the ship during his weeks in Cape Town harbour, the savagery of the bush also enveloped the city: 'Elephant.

185

Rhincerosses. Some with One Horn others two, Lyons, Tygers, Wolves in aboundance that infest the towns. Hynas Jackalls Wild dogs. & Cats. Swines. Zabra. Otters. Baboons Monkeys of a Silver Colour. Camelleopards also the great-Horned Animal resembling the Horse Ox & the Antelope, there is Serpent Scorpions Lizards. Locusts. Mosquitos that are venomous . . .'

Even more chilling than the wildlife were the natives. The true and terrifying story of the *Grosvenor* merchantman was back in the Cape Town news when the *Lady Julian* arrived in March 1790. The *Grosvenor* had gone aground on the coast of 'Caffraria' eight years earlier, and those of her crew and passengers who survived the wreck, including several women, had been 'detained among the Caffres, the most savage set of brutes on earth'. Governor van Graaf and Colonel Gordon, a charming Dutchman of Scottish extraction who commanded the Company troops, had made several attempts to find and rescue them, but they were eventually presumed eaten or enslaved. Then fresh news was received from the interior. When Captain Bligh stopped at the Cape on his way to Tahiti, he received an update from Colonel Gordon. 'In his travels into the Caffre country, he had met with a native who described to him, that there was a white woman among his countrymen, who had a child, that she frequently embraced the child, and cried most violently.' The colonel gave this man letters written in English, Dutch and French, instructing him to have the woman make some mark on one to prove her existence and bring it back. He never returned and the story subsided, but when the *Lady Julian* arrived the following year another sighting had just been reported. Preparation of expeditions into the bush to track down the survivors of the *Grosvenor* was a hot topic during the weeks the *Lady Julian* spent at the Cape. It was little reassurance to those on board who feared that savages awaited them along a coast further east.

During their month in Table Bay, the season changed. Late summer became autumn. Every ship entering the harbour now struck her yards and topmasts as a precaution against the violence of a south-east wind that could drive ships completely out of the bay. Delays in Britain and the weeks spent at Rio meant the *Lady Julian* would be crossing the Southern Ocean dangerously late in the season. The ideal time to make this passage was spring, when Commodore Phillip had taken his fleet east two years before. The *Lady Julian* had been in Table Bay less than two weeks when the first casualties were claimed by autumnal gales. On 12 March, eight seamen and the bosun of the *Guardian* came over the side with the news that a fishing vessel was in distress at the mouth of the harbour. A launch was immediately lowered and the eight *Guardian* men, with the bosun at the tiller, made for the spot where the vessel had been seen. They were just in time to hold her with a small anchor and cable taken from the *Lady Julian* and stop her short no more than three cable lengths from the surf, where 'had she come on shore, She must have been dashed to pieces without a probability of saving the Lives of the Crew'.

Cape Town was the place where reality bit, even for the most nonchalant. The Southern Ocean was a dangerous sea, and the winds that had begun to howl through the rigging in the shelter of Table Bay warned of a rough passage. The *Guardian* had been wrecked in this ocean three months since and half her company drowned; the *Grosvenor* had been bashed against the African coast by frightful waves, and the fate of her survivors brought a shudder. And if the *Lady Julian* survived the passage, realisation now crept through the orlop that there was nothing left between them and Sydney Cove, no more delays, no foreign ports, no friendly slave-ships. On 31 March, the *Lady Julian* left Table Bay with the 'Cattle rather uneasy'. She sailed into hazy weather and gales from the south-east.

Chapter Thirteen

Cape Town to Sydney Cove

The day after the *Lady Julian* left the Cape, a reduced food allowance was announced in Sydney Cove: 'to every person in the settlement without distinction: 4 pounds of flour, 2½ pounds of salt pork, and 1½ pounds of rice, per week.' It was the beginning of a disastrous month. The Cove had been empty of shipping for three weeks since the colony's two remaining ships, the *Supply* and the *Sirius*, sailed to Norfolk Island with 65 marines, 5 marine wives, 116 male and 67 female convicts and 27 of their infants. The advance party of 23 people who had sailed to Norfolk in February 1788 had sent back promising reports to Governor Phillip – so promising that he decided to relieve the public store in Sydney Cove by sending up as many mouths as he thought the island could support.

The conclusions reached by Edgar, Aitken and Riou in Cape Town as to the colonists' prospects were substantially correct. The mainland harvest of summer 1788–9 had been poor, and a meagre yield was further reduced when the stores in Sydney Cove were overrun by rats in February. The colony lived in hunger, and civil unrest lurked beneath the food shortages. The same month as the rats invaded, six marines were discovered stealing food from the public store. Governor Phillip immediately imposed the maximum penalty *pour encourager les autres* and they were hanged outside the store. Bad feeling already festered

188

between the civil government and the marine corps, which considered its rights to include a privileged food ration, and its duties to exclude manual labour, horticulture and the supervision of convicts. A note of rage creeps into Phillip's otherwise sane and balanced dispatches when he mentions the marines. Now the food crisis sharpened the tension between these two crucial colonial elements. When hope faded of a store ship from England, two more emergency victualling expeditions were planned, the first to China, the second to Batavia. The *Sirius* was to drop off its passengers at Norfolk Island and sail on to China for food. The *Supply* would return to Sydney Cove with some of the marines due for relief from Norfolk duty then turn and follow the *Sirius* north.

Events on Norfolk Island changed these plans. Norfolk was a fearsome place to make a landing. A fierce onshore wind in March made it impossible for the ships to land on the south coast at Sydney Bay, the main settlement on the island. They sailed round to Cascade Bay on the northern shore, where conditions were marginally better. It took five days for the men and women on the two ships to get ashore, along a lifeline shuddering in surf which broke over their heads. They could go ashore only at low tide, in small groups. The lighters had to manoeuvre themselves stern, first towards a rocky promontory which was cut off when the tide rose. On the sixth day, the ships attempted to turn away from the beach and sail for the safety of deeper waters, but the *Sirius* was caught in currents, blown on the Cascade reefs and wrecked within minutes. She was impaled on the coral as the *Guardian* had been on the ice, with her bilges bleeding into the sea. The *Supply* sailed south alone on 24 March, bearing dreadful news for the garrison in Sydney Cove and leaving over 400 people marooned on Norfolk Island.

She arrived between the headlands on 5 April. The news that the *Sirius* was lost shook the colony. There was now only one ship to connect Sydney Cove with the civilised world. Should anything happen to the *Supply*, sailing valiantly between the three settlements or undertaking another dash to buy supplies from the Dutch, the colonists would be utterly isolated. Two years had already passed with no sign that anyone in London remembered the promises of further supplies 'within the year'. They had been thrown increasingly on their own resources and by a stroke of atrocious luck had lost one of the most important.

By May, work was almost at a standstill. The official hours for convict labour were cut back to end at one o'clock. Men and women on the rations issued by the public store in Sydney Cove could not be expected to work longer hours. About 90 per cent of their diet now consisted of wriggling rice infested with weevil. The peas were finished. The plots of land sown with lettuce and corn on Garden and Clark Island and dotted about the settlement under an increasingly corrupt armed guard would not be ready to harvest for weeks, and a spate of desperate night thefts was reducing the already dismal acreage of plants left to ripen. Despite the evacuation of 280 mouths to Norfolk Island, the townships of Sydney Cove and Rose Hill still struggled to feed themselves. Scurvy had taken the camp; Phillip himself was suffering badly. Venereal disease had spread. Everyone was malnourished. For two weeks the governor weighed the risk of losing the colony's only remaining ship by sending it on another provisioning run against the risk of starvation before the promised ships from England came in. Perhaps his faith had been dented in two years of waiting for a signal from the men at the South Head that a Red Ensign was sailing in. On 18 April, the *Supply* left Sydney Cove for Batavia to buy food.

The same week in which the *Supply* sailed from Sydney Cove, the *Neptune*, the *Surprize* and the *Scarborough* were leaving Cape Town. They had arrived in the African harbour within days of the *Lady Julian*'s departure, been greeted by Lieutenant Riou and learned of the disaster that had befallen the *Guardian*. Agent Shapcote of the *Neptune* was less accommodating than

Agent Edgar when it came to carrying on the stores saved from the wreck. Riou commented sourly that he did not want to lose storage space in the three ships allotted to the liquor and other items in short supply in Sydney Cove which he would sell on his own account. It took veiled threats before Shapcote agreed, and the three ships took on beef and pork and, wrote Riou, 'had not a misunderstanding existed between Lieutenant Shapcote and myself . . . I could have sent many articles which would not have taken up much stowage in the ships under his direction that would have been very acceptable to His Majesty's colony in New South Wales'. They also took on the 25 gardening convicts. There was far more room for them in these ships than on the crowded little *Lady Julian*: 46 convicts had already died on the *Neptune*, 8 on the *Surprize* and 15 on the *Scarborough*. More would be heaved over the side in the Southern Ocean.

There was now more shipping heading for New South Wales than at any time since December 1787. The *Lady Julian* was three weeks out from the Cape, nearing Kergueten. The *Neptune*, *Surprize* and *Scarborough* were a couple of weeks behind her and catching up. A second store ship, the *Justinian*, of which Edgar knew nothing but which had left England after the three transports, had stopped at neither Rio nor Cape Town. She was now sailing a couple of degrees north on a course that would bring her to the headlands of Port Jackson within a day of the *Lady Julian*. Despite delays in putting the intended convoy together in Britain, the *Lady Julian* had taken so long to cross the world that by the time she got into the Southern Ocean the rest of the fleet had almost caught up with her.

As these five ships sailed east, the *Supply* was sailing north between Norfolk Island and the coast of New South Wales on her way to buy flour in Batavia. On the island, the population had suddenly increased from 50 to almost 500 when the *Supply* and *Sirius* offloaded passengers and then the company of the wrecked *Sirius* herself was also forced to stay behind. Among the newcomers was Major Ross of the marines, sent to relieve the previous lieutenant-governor of Norfolk Island. Ross immediately imposed martial law and introduced capital punishment for the theft of food, but even this deterrent could not prevent thievery and starvation. The Norfolk Islanders were saved by the discovery of the muttonbird, a fat, innocent creature which lived in great colonies of burrows on Mount Pitt, in the centre of the island. Muttonbirds had never before been hunted, and when they flew back to their nesting sites at dusk each day they had no collective memory of death to protect them from the cosh. The colonists drove paths through the trees held together by thick strands of vine to get to Mount Pitt. They went out daily through April and May to wait for the birds to return to their burrows, club them, grab them by the legs and bash their heads against stones, poke baited hooks down the burrows and raid their nests for eggs. The muttonbird kept the islanders going through the desperate winter of 1789, the howling south-easterlies of July and August, and the 'evils, three in number, viz Blights, Grubs and Paroquets' which destroyed their first crops. By August, French beans, lettuce, cabbage and potatoes were coming up to relieve the island's reliance on Mount Pitt. They were grown in small, fenced plots tended by at least two people, one of whom spent their time picking off the grubs and the other scaring away the parrots. More gardens were being cut from the woodland and the gardeners learning how to harness the fertility of the soil. To the flesh of the muttonbird was gradually added home-grown salad stuff, but not before the bird had been hunted to extinction.

The *Lady Julian* was now sailing through seas 'mountains high'. During autumn and winter in the Southern Ocean, the wind averages a force 5–6; spray continually soaks the deck, the bowsprit goes under completely and temperatures drop to freezing. A full gale will blow once every two weeks on average and last anywhere between eight and 48 hours. Elisabeth Schaffer, her father and the other superintendents, wrecked here four months ago in summer, were now returning in winter conditions towards the scene of their terror. Their experiences, the even more recent wreck of the fishing vessel off Cape Town and the fate of the *Grosvenor* were fresh in the mind, and the horror story traditionally told to the nervous in these waters now started its rounds. Over a century before, two Dutch merchantmen had put out from the Cape into angry seas and had been taken by a storm. One survived and struggled back to the Cape; the other went down with all hands. When the surviving ship left the Cape a second time, the nervous crew saw the ghost of the *Flying Dutchman* bearing down on her out of the mist with dead men in the rigging, dead officers on her decks and a terrible silence among her sails. The story spread among sailors of all nationalities and thereafter one of the watch aboard any ship sailing at dusk south of the Cape would see a ghastly galleon 'standing for [the onlookers] under a press of sail as though she would run them down'.

When a gale rose, the sufferings were intense aboard the *Lady Julian*. Water entered a ropy old ship like the *Lady Julian* from all sides. She shipped water straight down the hawser-holes and on to every deck. When waves driven by a screaming wind engulfed the topdeck, a river of sea water crashed down the orlop hatches. It hung in spray on the air, it crept in from beneath. Old tar leaked like the devil in heavy seas. The ship groaned at each forward plunge and more salt water worked its way in through stretching seams and shrinking timbers. Men at the pumps fought the water round the clock in rough weather, but sometimes the sea forced itself into the ship's belly faster than the men could force it out. The eeriest sound in a Southern Ocean gale is not the scream of wind or the groan of overstretched canvas but the rumble of the wave imprisoned in the ship herself, rolling like an underground stream around her bilge. It ebbs and flows from bow to stern, thunderous as it passes, then fading away and returning.

On other transport ships, convicts on the orlop deck were washed completely out of their beds and on to the floor in these seas. Many of the women on board the better-run *Lady Julian* who had not already done so would now have left the orlop and gone to sleep wherever they could find space on the 'tween deck above. Their time on the weatherdeck was curtailed, their bedding and clothes remained wet and they coughed on the spray that penetrated every level of the ship. Those who had bartered their clothes for wine in Cabo Verde shivered and begged the surgeon for extra blankets. When too much water was shipped, the galley stove could not be lit and no one got hot food. Extra rations of grog were ordered for the men brushing ice from the yards aloft and for the women in miserable huddles below, so the glow of alcohol could boost cold pease and biscuit made soggy from spray. The cold was intense. Sailing through in December 1787, Lieutenant Clark noted 'what must it be in winter if it is now so cold in the middle of Summer', and never took off his greatcoat nor wore less than two pairs of stockings. The men on watch during fierce weather worked in extreme cold. Seamen in the rigging could not wear gloves, for this would interfere with their work. They were continually subject to frostbite and friction from the ropes. Blood froze as it left the cuts on their hands, nails were torn out by the roots from frozen fingers and icicles hung from the rigging.

Fore and aft hatches were battened down all day and all night when the weather was wild. This lessened the water washing into the orlop and 'tween decks but did nothing for their air quality. Easing-chairs overflowed and it was a brave woman who would stagger up the steps to empty her bucket into a force 9 gale and a deck streaming with water.

Somewhere between the Cape and New South Wales, 'man overboard' was called on the *Lady Julian*. The carpenter was caught by a wave and went over the side. Most likely he was trying to mend a spar or yard brought down by the winds. He may, like the second mate of a 1787 transport who also went overboard here, have been trying to urinate from the heads, or, like a rash convict, have been trying to hang linen to dry from the bowsprit. There was no chance he would be picked up – the captain would not risk the ship's being overwhelmed by waves over the beam, and he was anyway lost from sight in seconds in these wild waters. The ship's company was already one down with a man left sick at Rio; now they had also to maintain her without the help of the carpenter.

For Lieutenant Edgar, as navigator, this was the most challenging leg of the journey. There can have been no other man on board the *Lady Julian* who had sailed this passage before, as the only possible second-timer would have been one of Phillip's seamen and the crew were taken on before the first of Phillip's ships returned. When Lieutenant Edgar had sailed to New Zealand with Captain Cook in 1776, he had covered a large part of the route he was now navigating on the *Lady Julian*: from the Cape of Good Hope to the south of Van Diemen's Land (now Tasmania). There the routes to Sydney Cove and New Zealand would diverge, the *Lady Julian* turning to the north where the *Discovery* had continued to the east. It was still thought that Van Diemen's Land was a part of New South Wales; it was not until 1798 that a Lincolnshire man, Matthew Flinders, would circumnavigate the island, to praise from Sir Joseph Banks, always a fan of enterprising lads. The charts Edgar was using on board the *Lady Julian* in 1790 were those drawn from the surveys made by Captain Cook 20 years earlier, when he mapped the coast of 'New Holland' from the position of present-day Melbourne east and north as far as the Torres Straits. Since Captain Cook had handed in his charts to the Admiralty, only 11 British ships had used them. Those 11 were the first fleet to New South Wales. Nobody had had reason to sail the vast, bare, lonely passage from Africa to New South Wales before the British set up their colony in Sydney Cove.

There was fresh blood on board the *Lady Julian* during this passage. The presence of Miss Elisabeth Schaffer, who had just survived the wreck of the *Guardian*, would have put several noses out of joint. She was only two years younger than the youngest of the Rio mothers but of a different class. Although not quite old enough for the attentions of any gallant officer – and anyway chaperoned by her father – some concession had to be made to convention in her presence. Activities behind doors and below hatches remained unchanged, but a little more discretion was practised to shield her from the behaviour which, after so many months in this little self-contained world, had become the norm.

Elisabeth Schaffer's periodic presence in the captain's cabin may have put the dampers on the social schedule hitherto enjoyed but, given the conditions into which the ship was now sailing, this would anyway have been curtailed. The women were less visible than they had been in warmer waters. They came on deck in smaller groups and for shorter periods. Most of their meals were taken below. Nevertheless, in this two-month passage, Superintendent Devine discovered Margaret Smith and Superintendent Doidge discovered Charlotte Simpson, alias Hall. If they did not consummate the relationship on board, they certainly did so swiftly after arrival, as both couples had babies a little more than nine months after arrival in Sydney Cove and remained together for some years. Margaret Smith, a 23- or 24-year-old from Liverpool, does not seem to have had any existing connections in the colony. Twenty-one-year-old Charlotte Simpson, alias Hall, had committed her crime with the George Simpson who was taken off the *Ceres* hulk in Portsmouth in November 1789 and was currently on the *Surprize*, a couple of weeks' sailing behind Charlotte. The order of Charlotte's surnames suggests they were not spouses or *de facto* partners. If they were, she had weighed up the benefits of maintaining an existing liaison with a convict against those of initiating one with a superintendent and chosen accordingly.

Six weeks out from Cape Town, the man at the masthead sighted Tasman's Head, the southernmost point of Van Diemen's Land. According to Edgar's charts, they had another 14 to 18 days' sailing before they came to Port Jackson. They swept past the coast of Van Diemen's Land, with a wind on their beam which pushed them in towards the shore with the ship at 45 degrees to the waves. Some of Cook's men had described a narrow escape from giants on this coastline 15 years before. They went ashore here on the never-ending search for fresh greens. A gong sounded in the woods while they were picking their wild celery and then they stumbled across steps cut over seven yards apart. They deduced from this that the natives of these parts were giants, and fled for their ship in Adventure Bay. It was a scary story and it added to the horrors of the hold on the *Lady Julian*. The coast of the unfriendly giants was behind them by nightfall. The following day they veered northwards, now sailing with the wind hard behind them, reduced canvas and a level deck.

Two weeks' sailing further north, the colony in Sydney Cove continued to stagger through its second winter, its colonists cold and apathetic. Scurvy was still common. So was dysentery, and in May smallpox was diagnosed. No one knew where it had come from. It entered the camp at the end of April and on 2 May the first victim died. Throughout the month, the sickness struck indiscriminately at convicts, marines and officers in the Sydney Cove camp. Several died, already weakened by malnutrition, but there were fewer victims within the camp than without. The worst affected were the Aborigines, who died in scores. Small boats put out daily from the Cove to land on the beaches in the river, collect their bodies and take them over to the north shore for burial. The sight and smell was gruesome; dingoes invaded the beaches after dark and fed from the recent dead. It was the colony's lowest moment yet.

The second of June 1790 was wild and stormy, with low

197

cloud and a strong wind from the south. It was 17 months since the arrival of Governor Phillip and his fleet and five since the passing of the year within which they had been assured of relief. The lookout at the South Head had been manned since the earliest days by three marines. It was not an envied post. They were cut off from Sydney Cove by half a dozen headlands, and it was rumoured that their hut had been built in an Aboriginal graveyard whose ghosts were offended at the intrusion. The men maintained a fire outside their hut night and day for warmth; its flames also kept the ghosts away. The flagpost at the lookout could be seen from Dawes Point, and every day a few marines and convicts would walk down there, more from habit than hope, to gaze south towards the headlands where no flag ever hung, until 2 June, when the signal went up that a sail had been sighted.

It was far too soon for the *Supply* to have returned from Batavia – unless she had been wounded on her voyage north and was stumbling back, like the *Guardian* to Cape Town, with holes in her hull and half her company lost. Up at the lookout, the men did not lift their eyes from where they had briefly seen a sail far out to sea, but no ship re-emerged from the spray. Night fell with no further sighting, and the next day the colony gathered at Dawes Point. When the flag was eventually run up again, there was pandemonium in the camp. People ran from Dawes Point through the huts shouting the news, burst into tears, embraced. Lieutenant Tench recalled the moment with uncharacteristic emotion in his journal:

> . . . my next door neighbour, a brother-officer, was with me; but we could not speak; we wrung each other by the hand, with eyes and heart overflowing. We raced for the harbour, begged to be among the governor's party, pushed through wind and rain and at last we read the word 'London' on her stern.

It is seven miles from the headlands at the entrance to Port Jackson upriver to Sydney Cove, and it took some hours for the first boats to appear bearing hysterical officers drenched with spray. They were in time to see the *Lady Julian* sail into peril. The heads are about three-quarters of a mile apart, a good enough gap in decent weather but not when both wind and tide carry a ship on to the North Head. The *Lady Julian* very nearly came to grief here, caught by the strong southerly behind her and the last of the tide, blown perilously near the rocks of the North Head. Her crew, hauling on the sheets to bring her round and tack off into the wind, were losing the battle. Only the set of the tide stopped her drift to the rocks and allowed her crew to bring her round and into Spring Cove, in the lee of the North Head. It was a heart-stopping finale to her voyage across the world.

The men were still coming down from the rigging when Watkin Tench and a handful of Sydney Cove officers came swarming over the sides of the ship like the urchins of Rio, slapping the seamen on the back, shaking hands with the officers, all speaking at once. They knew nothing of the upheavals in France, nor the terrible illness and recovery of His Majesty, nor the wreck of the *Guardian*: 'news burst upon us like meridian splendour on a blind man,' wrote Tench. They stayed until dark.

The night of 3 June was the first in two months that the women had not slept through heavy seas, but they were exhausted and apprehensive and few can have slept well. Rumour and supposition raged. The officers who had rowed out to meet them had been dressed in tatters, with holes in their boots and skinny limbs, faces pockmarked and drawn by hunger. The women had taken a distant second place in their enquiries as to the number of flour barrels and cattle on board. Perhaps already the news that they were a disappointment rather than a relief had gone round the orlop. They could not see the camp from their anchorage at Spring Cove but the harbour of Port Jackson was unwelcoming in the worst of the June weather. A mass of low, dripping green lay across the headlands; the coves were deserted. For any who had heard the sailors' tales of South Sea Islands and expected palm belts and smiling natives in canoes, Port Jackson in June was a rude shock. Dark had come suddenly, at about six o'clock. Lieutenant Tench and his comrades had gone back to their huts in Sydney Cove. Anyone on deck would notice flickering pinpoints of light from fires on the beaches where the unknown savages of Botany Bay were coming out to watch them.

The fourth of June was another blustery day; the *Lady Julian* would not be able to move upriver. The usual morning rituals of eating, cleaning and airing were observed amid tension and uncertainty. The distant firing of small arms from upriver shocked the company before they realised the camp was honouring His Majesty's birthday. Mid-morning, longboats started to appear from Sydney Cove with convict men aboard, sent to unload the first provisions. Hunger was too immediate to wait for the *Lady Julian* to come alongside the wharf in Sydney Cove which had been built to receive a mighty store ship.

The workers who now came aboard were not officers who gazed past the women and asked after the cows, but convicts like themselves. Two Maidstone men, John Jeffries and Robert Abel, were among them and, with ten Maidstone women on board, unloading must have come second to the exchange of news: who was dead, who still alive, who in prison, who had had babies, with whom, which partners left behind had struck up new relationships in England, which partners sent overseas had done the same here. And Sydney Cove? The Indians, the hard labour in plantations, the overseers? Any lingering expectation that a new America had been planted in the Sydney soil was finally dispelled. The colony was newly excited because a whole four fields of corn were predicted from the Rose Hill harvest later that year and the potatoes were promising on Garden Island. It was not the bounty of Virginia.

As to the 'Indians', if Robert Abel and John Jeffries believed the rumours current in the camp, their answers were scary. A few had been tamed; two orphaned children actually lived in the camp and one fellow was a frequent guest at the house of the governor. His hospitality to this black was viewed with suspicion. The rest were savages, with a bone through the nose and white clay markings on the face, animals' teeth and lobster claws glued into their hair with gum, vicious and accurate with their spears, dangerous to any white settler in the bush. Twelve men had already gone missing, thought speared; one convict who had lost himself in the sinister hinterland of Sydney Cove came back with reports of a human body burning in a native bonfire.

The reunion was brief, because the men had orders to obey, and tainted when John Nicol discovered that records of the sugar landed on the Sydney wharves did not match those of the sugar disembarked in Spring Cove. He would have to give evidence against them.

It was not until 6 June that the wind abated sufficiently for the *Lady Julian* to be towed upriver. They passed Clark Island. Its lettuce and bean plots had been sown by Lieutenant Clark – or, rather, convicts lent him for the work – before he was posted up to Norfolk Island and had to leave his greens to the public store. Rounding Bennelong Point, where the Opera House now stands, the women had their first view of Sydney Cove. Jubilant officers had reported in more optimistic times that Port Jackson could hold 100 ships of the line, supplied from the wharves of Sydney Cove, but in June 1790 the wharves were unbuilt and the harbour empty. The *Supply* was on its way to Batavia; the *Sirius* was wrecked on the coral of Norfolk Island. The *Lady Julian* was the only ship there.

She moored in a narrow bay between two muddy headlands dotted here and there with huts sodden from recent rain. At the head of the harbour the water narrowed to a silvery snake flowing beneath a trestle bridge. To one side stood a bunkhouse. This was the barracks, from which more skinny men with holes in their uniforms watched them and cheered. Next to it, strategically placed, was the thatched barn that served as the public store. On their right was a hospital, a cookhouse and more tatty soldiers guarding more tatty cabbage patches. Further back were little rows of wet huts, the rushes on their roofs sagging beneath the weight of rain. Rivulets of dirty red water ran between them down to discoloured pools in the waters of the Cove.

On the other side of the bridge, at the top of a slight slope, was the only decent-looking house in the place: two storeys, double-fronted, an attempt at a porch but with an eccentric kitchen garden running from the front steps to the water's edge, patrolled by barefoot sentinels with muskets over their shoulders. Could this truly be the residence of the governor? More sad huts spread between his gardens, the river and the shoreline. At the water's edge, gaunt men and women stood among the rocks to see the *Lady Julian* warped in. Relentless rain on water drowned any noise from the shore. They had arrived.

Chapter Fourteen

A Cargo So Unnecessary

espite the scurvy the far side of Rio and the cold and wet since Cape Town, most of the women aboard the *Lady Julian* were healthier when they arrived in Sydney Cove than they had been when they left England. Their diet had on the whole been decent and their alcohol intake restricted. Fresh air and clean linen had improved skin, hair and breath. On 4 or 5 June, with the ship still stormbound in Spring Cove, they had brought their trunks up from the hold where John Nicol had stowed them in the Thames and shaken out their best dresses. They had given each other whatever haircuts they could manage, cleaned their nails and teeth, plucked, squeezed, tweezed and sluiced.

Fear of savages was one expectation of New South Wales, but not the only one. The expectations of the wiser women were informed less by lurid tales of *pots aux missionaires* than by a century's experience of convict and indentured labour in America and the Indies. This was played by tough rules but had been far from uniformly negative. Women had returned from America, and returned richer. There had been opportunities in that New World, and there would be opportunities in this one. There had also been rough rituals, one of which notoriously followed the arrival of fresh female blood in the older colonies. This would now presumably be carried over to the new one. The captain would make his arrangements with dealers on the docks, and women would be put up for sale, sometimes at open auction, standing on bales of newly landed cloth on the quayside, sometimes by the agreement of gentlemen behind closed doors. Surely this was what the kinder matrons were preparing the little ones for as they dressed themselves to look their best sailing into Sydney Cove?

Too little information is available on Captain Aitken's past to tell us if he had previously been involved in the transportation of convicts or slaves. His appointment to the *Lady Julian* implies relevant experience. He may, like Lieutenant Edgar, have sailed in the South Pacific or the Southern Ocean in the 1770s, or he may have worked in some connected branch of maritime trade. Given his rank, he was certainly old enough to have been sailing before the American wars cut off the plantations; he could have been making delivery runs to the Indies well into the 1780s. Certainly, he had demonstrated familiarity with the traditions of the transportation industry: he had used the labour of convicts for private gain; he had accepted the cohabitation of convicts and seamen, and he had connived at the sale of sex in their ports of call. In Sydney Cove, Captain Aitken also observed another ritual of his profession – the sale for private profit of articles he had bought on speculation in England or on the voyage out. He had his fresh linen shirts, sewn by the convicts, he had a private supply of wine and liquor, and he had either held back from government supplies or had bought on his own account a large quantity of sugar.

Within two years, the American model of distributing incoming females was well established in Sydney Cove. A marine arriving in 1792 on another female transport saw his ship overrun by male colonists thrusting each other out of the way in order to claim their prize. 'The women', he wrote, 'were no less objects of desire than the animals.' This arrival ritual would continue for a further 30 years, until changing ideas of decency put a stop to it.

But the *Lady Julian* arrived at a unique moment in the colony's history, and the apprehensive women in their best dresses who came up from the hold when their ship was warped into Sydney Cove on 6 June were only one of two cargoes aboard.

Governor Phillip had petitioned for more skilled men, more food and more women to remedy the imbalance of the sexes. London seemed to have answered his petitions in the wrong order. The colony had been expecting a store ship, with a few skilled men aboard to take charge of the building and agricultural projects. What it got in June 1790 was 222 females with their brats to be housed and fed. True, it brought the immediate relief that England had not forgotten them but 'it was not a little mortifying to find', wrote the normally gallant Judge Advocate Collins, '. . . a cargo so unnecessary and so unprofitable as 222 females, instead of a cargo of provisions'. Of all the receptions the women of the *Lady Julian* had hoped or feared, it was surely not this one.

The distribution of women took second place to the distribution of stores in Sydney Cove and Rose Hill, then achieving a swift turnaround and sending the *Lady Julian* up to Norfolk Island to relieve the settlers there. It took five days to get all the provisions off her decks and out of her hold. Cask after cask went down the wooden wharf at the foot of the governor's garden, into carts that convict gangs in yokes hauled round the head of the cove and into the store, where they were kept under armed guard. Sheep, cattle and stallions were swum ashore through the rain and given into the charge of convict herdsmen. Recent experience of hunger showed in the colonists' reverence for food. All remaining hay and fodder were taken off the ship to save the settlement's own supplies. Surgical materials, remnants of linen, spoons, pots, plates, needles, patched blankets, reels of twine, oil, vinegar, wine, flour and every last wet piece of biscuit which the seamen would not eat between Sydney Cove and China was handed ashore, itemised and stowed away in the store by the creek. When the final sums were done at the end of the week, it was calculated that the colony could increase its weekly ration from four to five and a half pounds of flour per week (male ration) for three months. The relief the *Lady Julian* had brought would make almost no difference at all.

There were no salutes from weatherworn batteries to mark the *Lady Julian*'s entry into this colonial port, nor candlelit Government House dinners. The colony had run out of candles and anyone invited to dine with Governor Phillip was expected to bring his own bread. Edgar's reception was a barrage of questions: how far behind were the other ships of the second fleet? What supplies might be expected from them? Was a relief corps of marines on board? How many women, men, super-intendents, convicts skilled in building and farming? Edgar knew only that the transport vessels were still in Deptford in mid-September 1789, when the *Guardian* left. The mystery of the sail sighted the day before the *Lady Julian* arrived was discussed. The only conclusions they could draw were that another stray European explorer had passed by – or that one of the transports had made a rapid passage before the gales and another shipload of convicts would shortly arrive with more mouths to feed and bodies to shelter. Consensus was quickly reached that Sydney Cove could not support the *Lady Julian* women. They would have to go to Norfolk Island. The only ship available to carry them over was the one they had arrived in, but the *Lady Julian* would once again require substantial repairs to her hull. In the meantime, the women would be accommodated in the camp.

They finally came ashore on Friday 11 June, jumping down to the wharf with their bundles on their heads, watched by the marines at the barracks, the storemen and oarsmen unloading and stacking supplies, and any of the colony not out with the brick and timber gangs. Those women who had no sentimental attachment on board cast no backward glances. For others, this was the first separation. The *Lady Julian* was warped out of

Sydney Cove and taken across the river to the north shore to be careened. On one side of the river were John Nicol, Edward Powell and the other new fathers; on the other, their wives and babies in the huts and tents of Sydney Cove. They would now depend for communication on the marines, who rowed to the north shore each day with greens and potatoes for the seamen, on meetings at divine service each Sunday and on the wangling of errands to take the men across the river. Perhaps for John Nicol and Sarah Whitelam, Edward Powell and Sarah Dorset, the reality of the faith they had sworn was just becoming apparent. From the moment they left the ship, the women no longer belonged to the *Lady Julian*; they belonged to the colonial government of Sydney Cove. With the *Lady Julian* at the north shore, her women would be absorbed into the huts and tents of the settlement.

Throughout Friday, women squelched up paths between the rocks to the convict huts, red mud oozing between their toes and clinging to the hems of their skirts. They brought their bedding with them, for there were no spare blankets in the colony, nor even enough to go round the people already there. They may also have taken crockery and cooking-pots off the ship, on official loan or quietly hidden when no one was looking, as there were so few of these in Sydney Cove that each hut ate in shifts. Some women were accommodated temporarily in the hospital, a low, brick building which occupied the plot bounded by present-day Argyle and George Streets. Others squeezed into the huts made from a Sydney wattle and daub: fronds of the cabbage tree worked into a pine frame and fixed with mud and lime, white-washed with clay, standing in uneven lines which would later become Cumberland and Gloucester Streets. Their rush roofs were disfigured by the bushes piled on top to keep out the cold. Those last off the ship and those who had no connections in the colony probably curled like the spokes of a wheel into the giant roots of the trees later named Moreton Bay figs or on ledges sheltered by overhangs in the rock faces behind what is now Gloucester Walk. By six in the afternoon, it was dark. Surrounded by hungry strangers who had been wearing the same clothes for over a year, they did not let go of their bundles and boxes.

When the convicts of the first fleet to New South Wales disembarked in January 1787, the sexual frustrations of the voyage were worked off in an orgy among the rocks, carried on with the usual half-knowledge, half-collusion, half-condemnation of those in charge. The marines had requested – and been given by the officers – 'rum to make merry with the women upon landing'. Perhaps Governor Phillip thought he might pick out the inhabitants of his whores' ghetto as soon as possible. No officer's diary records a similar party on 11 June, but a few marines surely went knocking at a few doors where lanterns were lit and voices raised into the small hours, and men from the labour gangs in camps inland, forbidden to enter Sydney Cove after dark, surely did so to greet the new arrivals from home.

The women had been squeezed into the hospital and the two existing women's districts. The smaller of these stood to the west of the governor's house; the other was way down the eastern arm of the Cove towards Dawes Point, far from any intervention by officers. Many newcomers were friends or acquaintances of women already in the colony, and their arrival was celebrated: Bristol with Bristol, Ratcliff with Ratcliff, Seven Dials with Seven Dials. Most had liquor, bought at Rio and the Cape. In huts a few yards away, there were men – unmarried marines and convicts nearing the end of their sentence – who knew their governor was more anxious to keep them in the camp than they were to stay. The borrowing of bedding, cooking-pots, food and lantern oil for new hutmates meant any person making trips back and forth among the huts had a ready excuse for breaking the curfew. Judge Advocate Collins may have thought the women useless mouths, but he returned each day to the convict embraces of Nancy Yates. Those who did not enjoy the same privileged access to a female saw possibilities in the cargo of the *Lady Julian* which Collins could afford to disdain.

Whatever unrecorded licence prevailed on Friday night, during the weekend the women were firmly reintroduced to the tired old world of expiation – first the rod, then the Bible. On Saturday, Robert Abel and John Jeffries were marched to the whipping tree at the head of the creek and given 200 lashes each, in public, for their theft of sugar from the *Lady Julian*. On Sunday, all women were assembled by the tree which had become the spot for divine service, there being no building in the camp large enough to hold its congregation, and heard a sermon from the Reverend Richard Johnson, which, he recorded with satisfaction, brought home to them so sharply their new situation that several were moved to tears. That Sunday, the first of the *Lady Julian* ship babies were baptised. The pagan waters of Sydney creek burbled Christian into the Reverend's hands and Edward Dorset Powell was sprinkled and handed back. It was the first Sunday in a month of baptisms, burials and holy matrimony.

Richard Johnson had come out with the first fleet and was an old hand at baptising illegitimate babies and blessing unusual unions. What he could not do, however, was legitimise the *Lady Julian* couplings. For some of the seamen, parting from mistress and baby was just part of the seafaring life, but John Nicol wanted to marry Sarah Whitelam and, finally, here was a reverend, authorised by God and George III to pronounce them man and wife. Nicol begged to be allowed to stay in New South Wales, to work as a free man until Sarah's sentence expired and then bring her home. Skilled and experienced workers were desperately needed there; men like Nicol were what Governor Phillip had had in mind when he petitioned for artificers and superintendents. Agent Edgar and Surgeon Alley were both staying. Their contract was with the Admiralty only; they had not signed on for the East India Company tea-run. One of the seamen was also to remain in Sydney Cove. This was Sam

Braiden, forecastle husband of Mary Warren and Rio father of baby Sam, more probably because he was sick or injured than because of an attachment to Mary. He did not marry her, he showed no interest in becoming a settler and he left the colony alone a year later.

Captain Aitken would not release John from his contract. The ship was already three men down, with one sick in Rio, the carpenter lost overboard in the Southern Ocean and now Sam Braiden ashore in Sydney Cove. If Nicol were allowed to stay, how many other men would want the same? Certainly, Edward Powell, to stay with Sarah Dorset – and they would then be five down on a 36-man ship, sailing a winter passage to Canton. The captain's East India tea contract was conditional on his arriving there by 15 January 1791 and on the *Lady Julian*'s being in a fit state to take on the cargo. Undermanned, and without cooper or carpenter, he stood to lose a lucrative commission.

By the end of June, Captain Aitken was not the only force to prevent seamen jumping ship and becoming colonists to stay with their wives. The 'useless mouths' had been a sore disappointment on 3 June, but by the time the first of the *Lady Julian* wharf brides signed her cross on 28 June, the potential of her shipmates had been reassessed. On 20 June, another sail had been sighted by the lookout at the South Head, and on 21 June, the store ship *Justinian* was warped into Sydney Cove. Her arrival saved the colony.

The *Justinian* had not even been commissioned when the *Lady Julian* left the Thames a year earlier. She had made a remarkable five-month dash from London, bypassing both Rio and Cape Town, and had run into adventures just at the entrance to the colony. The gales that had kept the *Lady Julian* in Spring Cove had sent the *Justinian* hurtling up the coast of New South Wales and nearly driven her on to the rocks around Black Head (now Port Stephens). Had she gone down, the New South Wales colony might have gone down with her, one more colonial experiment ending in dry bones on a beach. The *Justinian's* arrival tipped the balance from probable starvation to probable survival. The stores on board would keep the colony going for some months – and by then the rest of the second fleet would have arrived, the *Supply* would have returned with grain from Batavia and the sullen Australian soil might have started to yield. The women of the *Lady Julian* could now be assessed not as unnecessary consumers of food but as providers of the services London had sent them over to deliver: sexual comfort and a breeding bank.

The colony had only one week of relief between the blessed arrival of the *Justinian*, the joy of taking off the stores she had brought, and the horrors that came up from the holds of the next three ships in. At the end of the month, a signal went up at the South Head that a sail had been sighted. This time there was no mystery. It could only belong to the *Neptune*, the *Scarborough* or the *Surprize*, with cellmates, lovers, pimps, receivers and husbands among the convicts aboard. Again, the colonists of Sydney Cove headed for Dawes Point to gaze downriver. Elizabeth Barnsley would be reunited with a husband she had last lived with in 1785. If Ann Wheeler had survived the gaol fever, she might also be on board. Sarah Carter awaited the arrival of William Pimlott; Elizabeth Saney would see her brother James; Charlotte Simpson, alias Hall, would have to tell George Simpson of her arrangement with Superintendent Doidge; Sarah Young did not know if her husband, whom she had left petitioning Lord Sydney to join her, was among the convicts at the far end of the river. They had a night to prepare themselves. Like the *Lady Julian*, the new arrivals lodged in a cove at the mouth of the harbour overnight and were warped upriver the following day to join the *Justinian* in Sydney Cove. It would become clear later in the week that their crews spent much of the night bringing on deck the bodies of the convicts who had died in the hold since Cape Town and throwing them over the side. For days, bodies washed up on the beaches around Sydney Cove, bloodless hands still fettered.

At the beginning of the month, the waters of the Cove had been deserted. By the end, they lapped at the hulls of five large merchantmen riding to anchor. Men rowed back and forth, water casks floated across, there were shouts, the splash of oars and the smell of boiling pitch – all the cheerful activity of an international port of call. The optimistic picture in the river was deceptive because on land the scene was one of horror. Of 1,017 convicts who had embarked on the *Neptune*, *Scarborough* and *Surprize*, 759 survived; 273 were buried at sea or thrown over the side in Spring Cove, and 486 of the survivors were now unloaded too sick to feed or care for themselves. More would die during their first days in the colony. The convicts of the first fleet, with all their sufferings in an inhospitable and infertile country, had been treated with fairness and stern humanity by Arthur Phillip. The convicts of the *Lady Julian* had lost only five of their comrades on the voyage out, none of them due to neglect. When the first boats put out from the transport vessels just in with the first heaps of stinking, dying humans in irons, the colonists in Sydney Cove stood unbelieving at the water's edge. 'What a difference between us and them', a *Lady Julian* convict wrote home; 'God bless our good Agent.'

Dying men and women were heaved from the decks like bales of cotton, one on top of another, into the boats below. The lighters rowed to wading distance of the shore and the oarsmen stood, levered the convicts over the side and went back for more. A few drowned in the shallow waters of their destination. Those who could crawl ashore collapsed there in mewing heaps. The governor's fury galvanised rescue teams. People plunged in to pull their comrades up the shore. Blacksmiths knocked off fetters on the beach, but many could not walk on muscles atrophied from months in shackles. The healthy carried the sick on their backs and in their arms through the rocks to the hospital. The lighters ploughed back and forth, dumping more of the helpless on to the shoreline from where they were ferried to makeshift tents. It seemed to go on for hours – boatload after lousy boatload of men and women blinking at the light, so filthy, drawn and disfigured that even lovers and brothers were unrecognisable.

Women from the *Lady Julian* pushed across the beach, turning over bodies and demanding information from people who could not answer them. Forty-six-year-old Elizabeth Dell from Reading was searching for her son John, who had sailed as a marine aboard the *Surprize* to stay with his mother and brother, transported on the first fleet. Elizabeth Barnsley, Sarah Gregory and Sarah Young were looking for their husbands, Sarah Carter was trying to find William Pimlott, Grace Maddox was searching for her accomplice, Thomas Higgins. Elizabeth Saney and the Fidoe family sought James. No one could help – the convicts themselves did not know who had come out of the holds alive and who had gone over the side in a sack. It would be days before it became clear who had survived and who had not. Elizabeth Saney's elder brother was among those who never made it to Sydney Cove.

The 80 beds of the camp hospital had been swamped and its dispensary drained by the smallpox in May. At the beginning of June it had had to house some of the women just off the *Lady Julian*. It could not cope with the casualties of the *Neptune*, the *Scarborough* and the *Surprize*. One of the three ships had on board a prefabricated timber frame designed in Deptford as a 'portable hospital'. When the scale of sickness aboard became clear, disembarkation was halted until this was put up on the Argyle Street plot. Most of the *Lady Julian* women had their first employment here, tending the sick. Bonfires burned at a careful distance from thatched huts, fed by serge rags stiff with human filth. Fleas leaped in the flames. The naked sick were wrapped in blankets until clothes could be made for them. Bales of cloth brought by the *Neptune* were issued to *Lady Julian* seamstresses to run up a wardrobe for 800 convicts. Men were sent into the bush, guarded by marines against unfriendly blacks, to replenish supplies of myrtle against the dysentery which swept the camp.

Reverend Johnson was stretched. On 2 July he buried four men; the following day he buried another four, then two, then five. On 6 July, five men and one woman went into the sod. The woman was 26-year-old Ann Hardiman, who had pawned Nimrod Blampin's clothes along Fleet Street two years before, after he had been robbed and left naked by Rachel Hoddy. The cause of her death was unrecorded: it could have been infection from the lingering smallpox of May, or typhus brought by the newest arrivals, or dysentery, fever, childbirth – the list of possibilities is long.

Within the chaos caused by the arrival of over 400 sick, some of the *Lady Julian* women were quietly sorting out their futures. Word had crept out that most were to be sent to Norfolk Island, a colony even more isolated than the one in which they had just arrived. Those who stayed on the mainland would be the ones who had someone to plead their cause for them – an employer or patron, a husband whose work or prospects kept him in Sydney, a marine whose officers would look sympathetically on a request to maintain a mistress. Thomas Barnsley was now reunited with his wife Elizabeth. The Reverend Johnson had been complaining for months of overwork. If a literate, plausible assistant presented himself and his capable wife at a moment like this, when graveyard duty was on the rise and more ship babies had just arrived requiring salvation, such an aide would have been gratefully employed. It seems Thomas swiftly found his feet as clerk to the Reverend Johnson and Elizabeth became the colony's midwife. The Barnsleys had arrived.

A network of persuasion and protection, favours granted and withheld, had bound the women and the ship's company of the *Lady Julian*. This was beginning to dissolve and another to emerge between the women and the men of the colony. Some had been taken, or had taken themselves, off the availability list. Jane Forbes, Sarah Whitelam, Sarah Dorset, Elizabeth Griffin, Ann Bryant and Margaret Wood were all nursing babies. Mary Flannegan was pregnant, so were Hannah Teesdale Gee, Susannah Mortimore and Elizabeth Gale, all to *Lady Julian* seamen. Charlotte Simpson and Margaret Smith were living with two of the superintendents who came aboard in Cape Town. Ann Mash was with Surgeon Alley. Mary Warren may or may not have continued her liaison with seaman Sam Braiden. But in a colony 'in great want of women', bigamy, imminent childbirth and the maintenance of other men's sea-born offspring did not have the same impact on a woman's marriage prospects as they might have back home.

There is little evidence among the emerging relationships to reveal how they were initiated, by whom organised, by whom approved. The men in charge had a utilitarian view of camp women, if one often tinged with compassion: basically, they were an undifferentiated mass of mouths and wombs. The people attached to these fundamental body parts would be moved from place to place according to what the first required and the second offered; it was unnecessary to know them as individuals to determine their colonial future as a group. They had been brought over from England to sleep with the camp guards and bear children to male settlers, and this is largely what they did.

In one case there is clear evidence of an arranged marriage. John Nicol was quite sure that the story of Mary Rose had had a happy ending in Sydney Cove. According to him, after the departure of the *Lady Julian*, her relations had discovered the fate of their lost and ruined Mary. 'By their exertions, the whole scene of the landlady's villainy was exposed' and she stood in the pillory at Lincoln for her perjury. 'Upon our arrival,' he continued, 'we found a pardon lying at Port Jackson and a chest of excellent clothes sent by the magistrates for her use in the voyage home.' In John's memory, Mary spent the rest of her time in

Sydney living in the governor's house, restored to her status of lady, a gentle heroine with her wrongs righted. Some version of this story had presumably gone round the camp. It is true that Governor Phillip took a personal interest in Mary Rose's case. Probably a rare summons from the convict huts to the big house and the rumour that Mary Rose had important connections at home contributed to the story of her pardon; perhaps the magistrates who had had a whip-round for pocket money in Lincoln sent out some articles for her on one of the later transports. Among the letters brought for Phillip aboard the last three ships of the second fleet was one from Sir Joseph Banks, requesting he keep an eye on her. Phillip assured him he had fixed Mary up with 'one of the best men in the colony'. This was John Trace, a Devon man who seems to have had some agricultural knowledge and was therefore a colonist to woo. With two years of his sentence left to serve, he was a promising future emancipist and over 20 years older than the bride the governor had picked out for him.

Evidence for Mary Rose's arrangements survives because she had an important patron. It is possible to infer from the background and occupations of the men who married the wharf brides of June and July that men whom the governor wanted to keep in the colony were granted favours from among the cargo of the *Lady Julian*. Of the 24 women who were married by the end of September, some married convicts who had risen to a position of some responsibility in the colony and others married men with agricultural knowledge. The first of the wharf brides, Mary Williams, married William Whiting on 28 June. Whiting was store-keeper, one of the first men to get a look at the women while the stores were being taken off the ship and, given his employment in the most important public institution, a man esteemed by the governor. Elizabeth Ayres married John Cuss two weeks later. He was 22 years older than her and a trusty. Isabella Manson married literate Cornishman John Rowe, like

John Trace a man with agricultural knowledge and little time left
to serve of his sentence. The next round of weddings saw the
colony's chief game-killer, Patrick Burn, married to Mary
Newton. However, the granting of favours to men is not the only
possible inference; another, equally likely, is that the *Lady Julian*
women were setting up the most advantageous unions for
themselves. Elizabeth Ayres, Isabella Manson, Mary Williams,
Elizabeth Cook and Mary Newton may have married their men
because they had made a swift assessment of who would succeed
and who would not. The vows taken under the marriage tree in
June and July were a considered gamble. The privileges of
marriage worked both ways; if a woman had judged her man
correctly and he turned out to be a humane keeper and steady
provider, her life in the colony would be more comfortable than
if she remained single.

To see them only as a lump contingent of comfort women
handed out to the men denies them any individuality. Throughout the rest of the year in Sydney Cove, a picture emerged of
women silently pairing up with colonists and reproducing; silent,
because no woman's voice speaks from the records. But there
are too many glimpses of individual decisions, the stamp of
personality emerges too often in records of marriage, baptism
and land grants, and there are too many stories which circum-
vented – perhaps subverted – any orderly plan for social
engineering to believe the women were simple building-blocks
in the colonial edifice. Officialdom clearly entered the private
life of Mary Rose and may have entered those of the wharf
brides signed up to approved men. However, if the women for
whom scraps of information still exist are typical of the rest,
there was a vital stream of personal choice flowing beneath the
formation of breeding pairs in the colony.

What emerges clearly is that many of the men and women
signing up for life together in New South Wales had either known
each other in England or had some English connection in

common. Everything else was alien. People sought the comfort of familiarity and attempted to re-create something of their former lives in this unfriendly country. Within the structure of a penal colony where so much of a convict's life was public property, the women and men in the huts and the labour gangs clung to their personal history.

On 30 July, two *Lady Julian* women stood beneath the marriage tree with two men who had arrived on the *Scarborough*. Mary Winsfield had been convicted in April 1788 of stealing three pairs of shoes from a house in Whitechapel and selling them on in Rosemary Lane market. Her new husband, John Young, was a market dealer who had been convicted the following month of stealing 23 pairs of shoes in Cable Street, 200 yards away from Rosemary Lane. Their witness was Mary Davis, who had snatched three pairs of leather shoes from a shop in east London. Next in line were Mary Winspear's 19-year-old shipmate Esther Thornton and her bridegroom William Sherberd, in his previous life a Whitechapel shoemaker and dealer in secondhand clothes in Rosemary Lane market. You could take the convicts out of Rosemary Lane, it seems, but you could not take Rosemary Lane out of the convicts.

The following week, Mary Kimes, alias Potten, married William Ayres, West Country highwayman. Here was a couple whose connections extended even further back than those of the Rosemary Lane gang. Six years earlier they had both embarked on the American-bound *Mercury* which had gone no further than Devon. William was one of 77 ex-*Mercury* convicts now in Sydney Cove. His partner in highway robbery was also in the colony, Patrick Burn, now game-killer and husband of shoplifter Mary Newton. Connections which might have been tenuous back in England were revived in the tiny colony.

By the time the *Lady Julian* left Sydney Cove at the end of July, five of her women were married; four more would marry the day after she left. The rest were still bunking up in the huts of the female districts, working in the hospital, sewing clothes, waiting to hear who would stay in Sydney Cove, who would go to Rose Hill, who to Norfolk Island. The *Lady Julian* had been patched up on the north shore to get her first to Norfolk and then Canton. Now she came back across the river for her last few days in the colony and the seamen and their wives were reunited. When John Nicol had signed up for the voyage at the end of 1788, he had done so to see New South Wales; once there, he scarcely left the huts of Sydney Cove. 'Any moments I could spare, I gave them to Sarah,' he recalled, misty-eyed at a distance of 30 years. 'The days flew on eagles' wings. We dreaded the hour of separation.' It seems the wives were permitted to return on board for the last few nights in port and that the men were allowed ashore by day. The officers may have thought this would defuse the situation, but it did not. There were couples on the *Lady Julian* who had been living together for over a year, some of whom had become parents; temporary sexual partners had become lovers. If Aitken's intention back in London had been to keep his men contented by letting them sleep with convicts, the strategy backfired when the women had to be left in Sydney Cove.

There were two ways in which these couples could stay together: either the men jumped ship or the women stowed away. Requests that the men be allowed to stay in Sydney Cove threatened to become demands. Captain Aitken had had the story of the *Bounty* first-hand from Master Fryer only three months ago at the Cape. Fryer's men had turned mutineer to stay with their women in Tahiti and, as far as anyone knew by July 1790, had done what they set out to do. The exploits of the *Bounty*'s company were known to men as well as officers. Wild plans were made during the *Lady Julian*'s last days in Sydney Cove to steal the women away and hide them in the ship until they were too far north to turn back. There seemed no possibility of the women getting back to England by themselves. Both Sarah

Whitelam and Sarah Dorset had been sentenced to seven years, like most of the *Lady Julian* women, but, as one of their shipmates wrote dolefully home that month, 'I do not think I will ever get away from this place'. Not only were the practical difficulties of earning the price of a passage home almost insuperable for single women, but the letters from Sydney's office which listed the term of transportation for each woman had been left behind. 'I do not suppose the women will give us any trouble on that head,' wrote Governor Phillip. For him, clearly, they were there for life.

With hot-headed talk being reported from the forecastle, surly glances and resentment spreading among his men, Captain Aitken called on Governor Phillip for help. It was decided that the women and stores going north to Norfolk Island would sail aboard the *Surprize*. The *Lady Julian* would not even touch at Norfolk; extra stores would be sent up on the *Justinian*. In January of that year, some of the Norfolk Islanders had attempted a mutiny of their own. Their plan had been to overpower the camp guards and make a break for Tahiti, every sailor's fantasy island. The Norfolk insurrection had been put down easily enough by the marines, but it would be folly to send up a ship whose men might feel sympathy for a Tahiti dash. The *Lady Julian* would sail for Canton on 25 July; the *Surprize*, with women from the *Lady Julian* aboard, would follow north at a safe distance of a week's sailing.

Despite these precautions, as the day planned for the *Lady Julian*'s departure approached, the officers realised they still had a serious problem on their hands. On the night of 24 July, either the women would not leave the ship or the men refused to go ashore and the marines were sent in. There was a scrum, as marines laid hold of the women and passed them down to the lighters, the seamen came down the ladders after them and carried the fight to the shore, the women tried to splash back out and the camp turned out to watch. Amid the shoves and taunts of the marines and the crying of bewildered babies, John took leave of his wife and son. 'We exchanged faith – she promised to remain true and I promised to return when her time expired, and bring her back to England.' He gave her his Bible. He wrote his name, hers and the baby's on the frontispiece and then he was pushed into a lighter and they were separated by the crowd at the waterline.

On 25 July 1790, John Nicol left Sarah Whitelam in the dirt camp at Sydney Cove. Six days later, the colonists of Norfolk Island sighted the sails of the *Lady Julian* on the horizon. The excitement which had stirred the inhabitants of Sydney Cove when the *Lady Julian* appeared off the headlands in June now gripped this frightened outpost, which had had no contact with their fellow colonists in over a year and feared itself abandoned once by London and again by Sydney. News of a sighting brought the island to a standstill. Tools were downed, people from every camp on the island were called to Cascade Bay to see the tiny squares of canvas on the western horizon. Even those in the hospital huts heaved themselves out of bed and limped to a vantage point. When darkness fell, fires were lit on the beach at Cascade to guide the ship in. She was within two miles of shore when the men, ankle-deep in the surf, realised that her crew was not reducing sail, but adding. 'All the harm I wish [the captain] is that I hope that he will goe to Hell for not calling when he could with so little trouble to himself,' wrote Ralph Clark that night. He expressed the feelings of all – sick of their posts, longing for news from home, they loathed the barbarous backwater to which they had been sent. The resentment of a year was aimed at the ship which failed to call on 31 July. The islanders did not know that there were men on board more desperate to stay than they were to leave.

The day the *Lady Julian* sailed past Norfolk Island, the *Surprize* left Sydney Cove for the same destination. She carried aboard about 150 of the *Lady Julian* women with their children. The great majority of them were still unspoken for, but some were already in couples or pregnant. Sarah and Thomas Gregory were there, reunited and accompanied by their little daughter Elizabeth. So was the newer couple of Charlotte Simpson and Superintendent Doidge. There was a clutch of *Lady Julian* wives: Sarah Dorset and baby Edward; Mary Barlow and baby Ann; Mary Flannegan and Elizabeth Gale, pregnant by *Lady Julian* seamen. Susannah Mortimore, already accompanied by one small daughter, bore another one on the voyage from Sydney Cove to Norfolk Island, fathered by a *Lady Julian* seaman, name unknown, heading for Canton a week's sailing north. Some of the early wharf brides sailed with their men: Mary Winsfield and John Young, Esther Thornton and William Sherberd were aboard; so was Nelly Kerwin and her new husband, Henry Palmer. One of the last aboard was Mrs John Coen Walsh, formerly Sarah Whitelam, who had already entered her new role as colonial helpmeet. The day after John Nicol sailed out of Sydney Cove aboard the *Lady Julian*, Sarah married another man.

Chapter Fifteen

Love Pilgrimages

When Sarah Whitelam signed her cross to John Coen Walsh on 26 July, John Nicol was working the first day of a miserable passage to Canton on a ship full of ghosts. He took down his hammock and went to sleep in another part of the ship where he would not be haunted by Sarah. It did not work. Everything on board reminded him of her, everything 'brought her endearing manners to my recollection'. Presumably, other forecastle husbands were feeling the same, and it was a ship crewed by disconsolate seamen which, in October 1790, reached up the Pearl River to the Whampoa tea-hongs – the warehouses in Canton where tea merchants worked.

John Nicol had come full circle. He had sailed from these wharves to London two years before, alone and looking forward to retirement from the sea and a reunion with his family in Scotland. That had not worked; instead he had sailed from London to New South Wales with his hopes vested in a new life with Sarah Whitelam. He had been forced to leave Sarah in Sydney Cove and now he was back in Whampoa, once more alone. The life of the Chinese river which had captivated him on an earlier voyage was now tedious. Other seamen may have comforted themselves in the brothels of Lob Lob Creek, but John Nicol preferred to spend the hours of waiting in Canton laying plans for his return to Sydney Cove, along with Edward

Powell, who had left his own Sarah and her baby back in the colony. Both men were idle as the ship's company endured the endless bureaucracy of the hongs. It was a chance to talk obsessively about how to get back to the colony. John had been brought away from the Cove by force, but two months later he was still rebelliously considering the possibility of jumping ship in Canton. If he could find a ship to Rio or the African Cape, he would at least be on his way back south and would take a chance on picking up a ship for New South Wales. What dissuaded him from this plan was not the practical difficulty of escaping the *Lady Julian* and getting a berth elsewhere. It was the fact that neither he nor Powell could afford to forfeit the wages waiting for them in London at the end of the trip. If they were to bring their wives away from the colony, it would be at heavy expense, for the women would have no money to pay their own passage. The wages due at the end of an 18-month voyage were considerable, and passion gave way to prudence. The *Lady Julian* left Canton with both men still aboard, their plans for rescue deferred but not defeated.

They arrived back in London just after the next fleet of transports had sailed for Sydney Cove at the beginning of 1791. Aboard one was Mary Talbot, who had gone over the bow of the *Lady Julian* in the Thames in July 1789, been retaken and was now back on her way to the colony. This time round, there was no trip to Scotland to look up his family, no musing over which berth was likely to be more amusing. The hunt was on for the first ship back to New South Wales but all agents Nicol visited enquiring for a ship to the colony told him the same – 'there was none, nor likely to be soon'. He took the next best option – a cooper's berth aboard the *Amelia*, a South Sea whaler, which he was assured would touch at Rio. His plan was this: to sign on as though he intended to complete the round journey, then to feign sickness at Rio, be left behind and find his way however he could to New South Wales. He had enough cash to bring Sarah away with him when he got there. Before he boarded the *Amelia*, he converted his wage from the *Lady Julian* voyage into coin and sewed it into the seams of his clothes.

Until the departure of the *Amelia* in 1791, John Nicol and Edward Powell probably remained in touch, each encouraging the other in their search for berths back to the colony. When it became clear that no immediate return would be possible, they went their separate ways – Nicol on the first ship out he could get, Powell to execute a longer-term and more considered plan. Nicol was finally on his way south to Rio, thence Sydney Cove and Sarah. He got no further than Deal, on the Kentish coast, where the *Amelia* was blown on the sands, threatened by the wreckers, and had to be towed back up to the Port of London. Still there were no ships to New South Wales, or any with even a berth to Rio or the Cape, and so Nicol fumed in Deptford while the *Amelia* was refitted.

John's memories of the voyages he made over the early 1790s were confused by the time he came to dictate his memoirs in 1822. What emerges from his tangled recollection of the years is a telescoping of ships and contracts which had him back off Cape Town in about 1792 or 1793, biding his time for a ship heading for the colony. In fact, his Cape Town voyage must have been undertaken in 1796 or 1797. By this date, Edward Powell was already back in the colony. Somewhere in the intervening years, John Nicol had had news that he had succeeded in returning to Sarah Dorset in the colony, and 'when her time expired, brought her home, and married her'. He never heard the real end to the story.

Edward Powell, now 30, left England for Sydney Cove in July 1792, a passenger aboard the *Bellona*. Unlike John Nicol, who was trying to work his passage back aboard a series of vessels, Edward Powell had taken a passage back out as a free settler. His plan was no longer to bring his wife away and back to England, but to stay in the colony. The 1792 voyage was substantially different from that of 1789, which he had worked before the mast, a seaman who spent his off-duty hours canoodling with a convict in the forecastle. The 13,000 miles which the *Lady Julian* covered in twelve months the *Bellona* managed in five and a half, sailing with 13 settlers and 17 female convicts aboard. Presumably, Powell's intention in returning to Sydney Cove two years after he had left it was still to find and marry Sarah Dorset. She had served five years of her sentence and would be allowed to marry a free husband whose skills were of value in the colony. During his months at sea, Powell's plans changed.

Also aboard the *Bellona* was a large farming family from Blandford in Dorset. Thomas and Jane Rose were emigrating with their four children (one of them called Mary) and 18-year-old Elizabeth Fish, probably a niece, who came aboard with her one-year-old daughter. Possibly Elizabeth Fish had borne a child out of wedlock; this could have been the reason the family was leaving Dorset. Among the other free men were three who, like Powell, had already sailed this passage once: all three had been seamen on the ships of the first fleet and were now going back as colonists. One of them, Thomas Webb, had been living on Norfolk Island in August 1790 when Sarah Dorset and the others arrived on board the *Surprize*. He had remained there until February 1791. At that time the population of Norfolk had been about 550, small enough that everyone knew, or at least knew of, everyone else and Thomas could bring Edward Powell up to date as far as then. Perhaps he learned from Thomas what John Nicol still did not know, that Sarah Whitelam had married someone else.

Sarah Dorset, on the other hand, had arrived alone on the island with her baby. The *Surprize* landed her passengers where the *Sirius* had been swept on to the reefs a year earlier. It took five days for all the women to struggle down a lifeline through the surf on to the beach. Londoners Mary Chasey and Elizabeth

Johnson ended their colonial life here, drowned in the waves of Norfolk Island.

They had arrived in a colony run by Major Ross, who had his own idea of colonial development based on the pig. Pigs, he thought, would get convicts involved in the production of their own food and off the public store as quickly as possible. Unfortunately, there were not enough pigs for the convicts to have one each, nor even one per couple. A pig per three people was all that could be managed, and when the beasts were issued at the end of the year, Norfolk Island arranged itself into a bizarre society of *ménages à trois*, each based around the household pig. There was no clergyman on the island until November 1791, several months after Thomas Webb had left, when Richard Johnson came over from the mainland to perform a mass marriage-fest for upwards of 30 couples, baptising an estimated 100 babies at the same time. Only after Johnson's visit did more conventional family units emerge from the three-per-pig tangle. The lack of records on Norfolk and the particular difficulty of distinguishing couples amid the pig-keepers make it difficult to tell who was cohabiting with whom, and how soon these relationships started. Sarah Dorset was issued her pig in company with two male convicts. Although, unlike most of the other *Lady Julian* women, she did not marry, she became pregnant in March 1792, two months before Edward Powell left England aboard the *Bellona*. Webb could not have known of her pregnancy – he had already left the island; but if it was the result of a relationship initiated by February 1791, he could have known of this and passed his knowledge on to Edward Powell.

There was plenty of time for the settlers to get to know each other well aboard the *Bellona*. They shared ambition, and they were thrown together by proximity and events. Barely a week out from Plymouth, Elizabeth Fish's baby daughter started having fits. She died within days, and they buried her at sea. On the Tenerife to Rio run, scurvy took the same hold on convicts and passengers that Powell remembered from last time round. Edward Powell's knowledge of the colony, his farming background and his financial status as a man who could set himself up in New South Wales made him an attractive addition to the Rose family circle: a manly arm for Mrs Rose to cling to when she took a tottering constitutional on deck; a drinking companion for Mr Rose; a comfort to their bereaved niece. Somewhere between the Port of London and New South Wales, the tales which had seduced Sarah Dorset were recycled to seduce Elizabeth Fish. The *Bellona* arrived in Sydney Cove on 16 January 1793. By now, it was a town of decent appearance, unlike the collection of dirty huts Powell had seen last time round in 1790. There was even a small church instead of the tree beneath which the congregation had gathered in the early days and here, on 24 January, Edward Powell and Elizabeth Fish were married.

What had changed his plans? The month before the *Bellona* came in, Sarah Dorset had given birth to a baby girl on Norfolk Island. Edward Powell could not have known of this when he arrived in January 1793; convict babies did not make news in Sydney Cove, and it generally took longer than this for information to travel between the two settlements anyway. Either he had learned from Thomas Webb that Sarah Dorset had been living with another man and rejected her because of this or he had already decided to reject her anyway. Insidious doubt could have entered his mind on the voyage, creeping disloyal thoughts of the advantages offered by a free bride, possibly with a dowry, over a convict woman, penniless and likely to be a different woman from the sweet girl he had left three years before. Edward Powell would display great ambition later in his colonial life, becoming a prosperous landowner and a respected voice in local politics. A convict bride did not necessarily hold a man back, but she did not help him on either.

In February 1793, Mr and Mrs Edward Powell went to seek

out land from among the allotments on offer in the Homebush area. Powell was granted 80 acres, and their homestead was given the uneasy name of Dorset Green. It adjoined the 160 acres granted to Thomas Rose, father of four. Here the Powells and the Roses began a life which revolved around the homestead, the stores of Rose Hill (now renamed Parramatta), the settlement's church and markets and the company of the settlers whose land adjoined theirs. Edward Powell would soon come across familiar faces at divine service, or doing business at the commissariat, or selling produce on the Kissing Point wharves. Women who recognised the latest settler as Sarah Dorset's lover might have asked him a few pointed questions and turned their backs on his bride in loyalty to their old shipmate; they might have shrugged and displayed indifference. Sarah Sabolah Lyons would shortly turn up nearby, back from Norfolk Island. She might have had a caustic comment or two. Ann Mash, another *Lady Julian* wife, was a couple of miles up the track. Surgeon Alley had gone back to England; Ann had moved in with John Irvine, the Lincolnshire quack transported for the theft of a silver cup, who, as there were not enough free surgeons to go round, had been appointed surgeon of Parramatta. Mary Stewart, Sarah Varriner, Mary Williams and Ann Young were all *Lady Julian* women living close to Edward Powell's 80 acres in the early 1790s, ready to remind him of his early days if his free settler status should go to his, or his wife's, head.

Sarah Dorset herself came back from Norfolk in 1794 with two children but no husband. She settled in Sydney. It may have been only on her return to the mainland that she learned Edward Powell had come back and asked for news of her – and that he had married another woman. A broken heart, a vow of revenge, so much water under the bridge? We know what she had done by about 1800 – she had settled with a Sydney butcher by whom she had three more children – but not what happened in the intervening years. The colony was still small enough in the 1790s that a man living in Homebush and coming downriver to the wharves of Sydney Cove every so often stood a good chance of bumping into a woman he knew who lived around the Rocks. Edward and Elizabeth Powell's first child, a daughter, was born in April 1794 and baptised Sarah. Maybe the relationship between Sarah Dorset and Edward Powell did not end with his marriage to Elizabeth Fish, but sometime later. However, two years after baby Sarah's birth, the Powells baptised their second child Edward and this effectively annulled Powell's relationship with his first son, the Edward born five years before in Rio de Janeiro.

While Edward Powell was becoming a Homebush yeoman, John Nicol was still at sea. It was during his time aboard a South Sea whaler that his hopes of ever seeing Sarah again reached their highest and their lowest points. Off Cape Town sometime in the mid-1790s, his goal seemed finally attainable. Sarah was at the end of her sentence and he was two months' sailing away. His ship wallowed in the Cape waters, harpoons whistled, decks ran with whale oil and John Nicol packed his trunk below. And then the sails of the *Venus* were sighted to the east. Signals were exchanged; both ships hove to and longboats were hoisted for the captains to exchange news. Captain Coffin of the *Venus* was returning to Britain having left a cargo of convicts in Sydney Cove.

The two ships remained in company for some time in and out of Cape Town, and John Nicol became friendly with several of the *Venus* men. At some point, he confided his Sydney Cove love affair, and the next time they appeared the sailors brought along a stowaway convict who had popped up somewhere in the Southern Ocean. The stowaway had been persuaded to speak on the understanding that Nicol would not inform on him to Captain Coffin and had news not only of progress in the settlement but of Sarah Whitelam personally. She was in good health, she had a fine son and she had left the colony some months previously, bound for Bombay. The pain this news caused the other ship's eager cooper must have persuaded the stowaway to withhold the details he suspected would be most hurtful: 'how she got away, he could not inform me.'

Sarah Whitelam had done well in the colony. She had left Sydney Cove on 31 August aboard the *Surprize*, bound for Norfolk Island with Sarah Dorset and her other shipmates. Her new husband, John Coen Walsh, had remained in Sydney Cove for several months, earning money to set up his family on Norfolk shortly afterwards. He joined her in 1791. They had two sons together. When Walsh was pardoned, Sarah became a free woman in an automatic recalculation of her status according to that of her husband. Their Norfolk farm was prosperous, and six years after their wedding they paid passage for themselves and the three boys aboard the *Marquis Cornwallis*, which left Sydney Cove for Bombay in June 1796. This was how she got away from the colony.

Where many men would have given up on the chase, particularly one which had grown cold with years, John Nicol seemed almost revitalised at this point: 'my love for her revived stronger at this time than any other since I left her. I even gave her praise for leaving it. She did so to be out of bad company, my mind would whisper, and I resolved to get to Bombay as soon as possible.' It might have been better if the convict stowaway aboard the *Venus* had told him the whole truth: that she had left the colony a prosperous young matron with a family, in the care of a faithful husband. Had John known this, he might have resigned himself to her loss. Instead, his imagination conjured up pictures of a single, young and pretty woman, the Sarah he remembered, reduced to using whatever means she could to escape the colony because she believed her lover had forgotten her. Like Governor Phillip, John could not conceive of women getting out of the colony other than by selling themselves to passing sailors, like the two women who disappeared aboard the French ships which arrived in Botany Bay just after the first British ships. In fact, about 25 of the *Lady Julian* women who arrived in 1790 eventually left the colony, most of them to return to Britain, some of them even before Sarah Whitelam boarded the *Marquis Cornwallis* with her husband. Mary Kimes quietly disappeared from the records in the same year as her husband completed his sentence and sailed for England; she probably went with him. The ones who got out early were, almost without exception, those who did not contract some alliance with a male mate within the first months of colonial life. Ann Bone, alias Smith, literate, 19 and single, maintained herself on land granted to her in own right on Norfolk Island, returned to Sydney on the first possible ship and left the colony. Amelia Harding, also young and literate, also given a plot of land to cultivate in her own right, had no children and left for Sydney, thence England, in 1794.

Other women left later, sometimes leaving behind colonial husbands and families. Abandonment, like victimisation, was intricate, practised by women on men as well as by men on women. More men passed through the colony than women ever did, so the number of men leaving and women staying is skewed towards a suggestion of base male treachery. Individual stories suggest that a different truth lurks. Surgeon-General John White spent four years in domesticity with *Lady Julian* maidservant Rachel Turner and left her a generous settlement when he departed, which continued even after she married an up-and-coming boatbuilder in Sydney. Sarah Young seems to have ditched her husband, who had petitioned Lord Sydney from his Portsmouth hulk to join his beloved wife, shortly after he arrived in Sydney Cove on the *Scarborough*. She moved in with a marine lieutenant instead and later paid her passage home, presumably from the money the lieutenant left her when his corps sailed from the colony.

Some men simply walked out on their *de facto* wives and families: midshipman Henry Waterhouse seems to have abandoned Elizabeth Barnes, six months pregnant with his daughter, when he returned to England in 1792. But some women did the same: Grace Brown, London shoplifter, now 38 and mother of five children, walked out on a *de facto* marriage of nearly 20 years' duration when she sailed from the colony in 1809. Two other wives of colonial marriages were sailing alone for home on the same ship. Elizabeth Gosling dumped her husband, Daniel Brewer, when they failed to make a go of their land grant on the Northern Boundary Farms just outside Parramatta and went home in 1799, aged 42. Elizabeth Gale, superior maidservant – and literate, like Elizabeth Gosling – also ditched her colonial partner in 1809 and returned to England; it is unclear how many of her children she took with her. Hannah Pleasant Jones was on HMS *Kangaroo* in 1814, leaving her fishmonger husband and teenage daughter behind her.

Nelly Kerwin neatly turned on its head Governor Phillip's satisfaction at not receiving details of the women's sentences. Her life on Norfolk Island was eventful – her husband was killed by a falling tree and she bore a stillborn baby within three years there. Even these experiences did not defeat her. Nelly's capital conviction had been commuted to transportation for the term of her natural life after George III recovered from his madness; in 1793, seven years after she was first sentenced, she sailed for England a free woman. The government in New South Wales had been bamboozled.

John Nicol knew none of this. In his recollection, the disorderly girls he had left at Sydney Cove were still females in distress. The hunt for Sarah Whitelam now became an obsession. From the Cape, he crossed the Atlantic to Rio and jumped ship to sail for Europe aboard a Portuguese merchantman. He went from Lisbon to Portsmouth, hiding from the press gangs who were searching out men to fight the French, and took a coach to Lincoln to visit Sarah's parents. They had no more news of her than he – or so they said; the last they had heard of her was John's own letter, posted before he left on his last voyage, announcing he would soon be bringing her back from New South Wales. If they were withholding something from Nicol through kindness, they, too, did him a disservice.

In London, once more he trudged about the docks looking for a suitable berth. Nearly a decade had passed since he left for New South Wales with his cargo of disorderly girls. He was no longer a lad. Years of service at sea, with the usual variety of seaman's accidents and diseases, meant he was not the catch he had once been to a recruiting captain. The Indiamen turned him down; the whalers had no berths. At length, dispirited and on the point of giving up, he accepted work on a ship back to China, 'depending on Providence if we were ever to meet again'. It was a dreary voyage. After China, the *Nottingham* sailed slowly south to the fever-struck Dutch at Batavia, and John Nicol was nearer the colony than at any point during his long quest.

He considered jumping ship and finding a passage south to ask after Sarah in the colony. However, the fever in Batavia, the 'European's grave', was so virulent that he stood a real risk of illness if he stayed to wait for a ship south, and if he did not catch the fever the Dutch press gangs would get him. John found he was no longer prepared to take such risks to find Sarah again. He was hurt by 'her leaving [the colony] so soon, without waiting for me', which 'showed she cared less about me than I cared for her'. Rather than continue chasing a ghost from port to foreign port, he would return to Britain and this time, as he had planned years ago when he returned from his first China trip, he would go to Scotland and settle. He would call once more at Sarah's family house in Lincolnshire on his way, 'and be ruled by the information I there obtained'. If there was still no news, he would accept that she was lost.

But fate remained against John Nicol until the last, for it was several years before even this more modest plan could be realised. He did return to Britain from Batavia, but rather than taking the coach for Scotland, the press gangs caught up with him and he was swept into the maelstrom of the French wars, the blockades at Malta and Cadiz, the siege of Gibraltar, the battle off Cape St Vincent. It was a blistering final chapter in his career at sea. At the turn of the century, he finally limped off his last man-of-war in Portsmouth and took a coach north. Even now, Sarah was still on his mind, although he accepted the search was over: 'I was now too old to undertake love pilgrimages after an individual as I knew not in what quarter of the globe she was, or whether she were dead or alive.'

When John Nicol dictated his memoirs to an Edinburgh bookbinder in 1822, he was living pathetically off scraps and charity on the streets, an old man whose memory of dates, names and the sequence of events was growing cloudy, but whose memory of Sarah Whitelam was glowing and tender. 'Old as I am,' he said, 'my heart is still unchanged.' He never forgot the elusive convict lover he left in Sydney Cove.

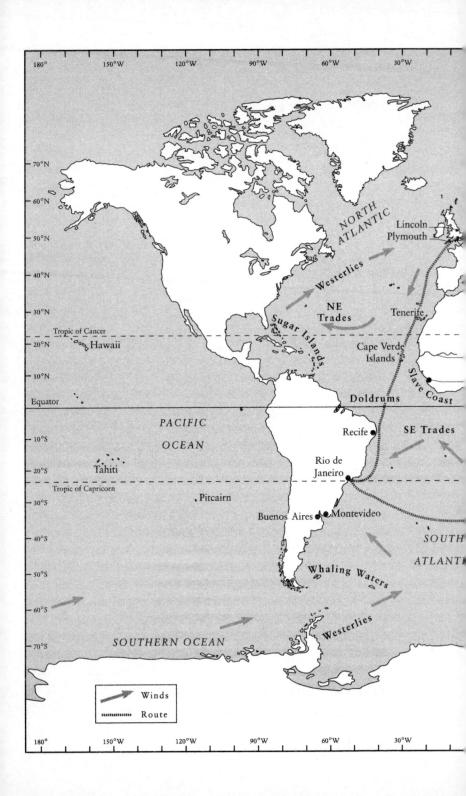

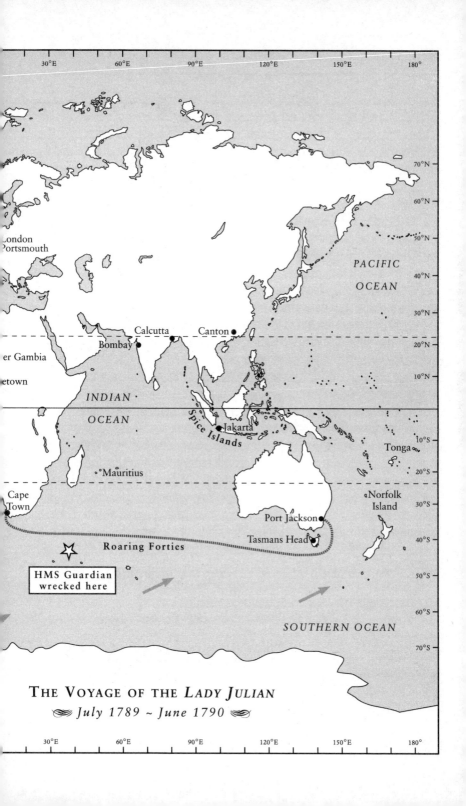

THE VOYAGE OF THE *LADY JULIAN*
July 1789 ~ June 1790

Select Bibliography

Aitken, Dr John *Principles of Midwifery; or, Puerperal Medicine* (Edinburgh, 1785)

Anderson, C. L. *Lincolnshire Convicts to Australia, Bermuda and Gibraltar* (Lincoln, 1993)

Archenholz, Baron Johann Wilhelm von *A Picture of England: containing a description of the laws, customs and manners of England* (London, 1789)

Austen, Jane *Pride and Prejudice* (London, 1813)

Banks, Sir Joseph *Journal of the Right Hon. Sir Joseph Banks . . . during Captain Cook's first voyage* (ed.) Sir J. D. Hooker (London, 1896)

Barrington, George *A sequel to Barrington's Voyage to New South Wales* (London, 1800); and *A Voyage to Botany Bay* (Philadelphia, 1793)

Bateson, Charles *The Convict Ships, 1787–1868* (Sydney, 1974)

Beaglehole, C. J. *The Life of Captain James Cook* (London, 1974)

Beattie, J. M. *Crime and the Courts of England, 1660–1800* (Oxford, 1986)

Bland, Dr Robert *Some Calculations of the Number of Accidents or Deaths which happen in consequence of Parturition* (London, 1781)

Bligh, Captain William *A Voyage to the South Seas, undertaken by command of His Majesty . . . including an account of the mutiny on board the said ship, etc.* (London, 1792)

Bloxhame, Marion – unpublished research

Bradley, Lt William *A Voyage to New South Wales . . . with a portfolio of charts* (Sydney, 1969)

Buchan, Dr William *Advice to Mothers, on the subject of their own health; and on the means of promoting the health, strength, and beauty of their offspring* (London, 1803)

Carpenter, Kenneth J. *The History of Scurvy and Vitamin C* (Cambridge, 1986)

Cioranescu, Alejandro *Historia de Santa Cruz de Tenerife 1494–1803* (Santa Cruz de Tenerife, 1976)

Clark, Lt Ralph *The Journal and letters of Lt Ralph Clark, 1787–1792* (ed.) Paul G. Fidlon and R. J. Ryan (Sydney, 1981)

Cobley, John *Sydney Cove in 1788* (London, 1962) and *Sydney Cove in 1789–90* (Sydney, 1963)

Collins, Judge-Advocate David *An Account of the English Colony in New South Wales* (London, 1798)

Colquhoun, Patrick L. L. D. *A Treatise on the Functions and Duties of a Constable, etc.* (London 1803); *A Treatise on the Police of the Metropolis* (London, 1797); *The State of Indigence, and the Situation of the Casual Poor in the Metropolis* (London, 1799); and *Observations and Facts relative to Public Houses; interesting to Magistrates, the Clergy and Parochial Officers* (London, 1794)

Cook, Captain James *A Voyage to the Pacific Ocean* (London, 1784); *The Journals of Captain James Cook on his Voyages of Discovery with Charts and Views* (ed.) J. C. Beaglehole; and *The Voyage of the Endeavour 1768–1771* (Cambridge, 1955)

Cuppage, Frances E. *James Cook and the conquest of scurvy* (Cambridge, 1994)

Dos Santos, Lucio José *A Inconfidencia mineira. Papel de Tiradentes* (Sao Paulo, 1927)

Easty, Private James *Journal of a First Fleet marine* Dixon Papers (Mitchell Library, Sydney)

Finch, Bernard and Green, Hugh *Contraception through the ages* (London, 1963)

Flynn, Michael *The Second Fleet: Britain's Grim Convict Armada of 1790* (Sydney, 1993)

Fowkes, Francis – collection of maps and drawings in Mitchell Library, Sydney

Freund, Bill *The Making of Contemporary Africa* (London, 1984)

Gardner, James Anthony *Above and Under Hatches* (ed.) Christopher Lloyd (London, 1955)

Gentleman's Magazine

George, Mary Dorothy *England in Transition: Life and Work in the eighteenth century* (London, 1931); and *London Life in the eighteenth century* (London, 1925)

Gillen, Mollie *The Founders of Australia – a Biographical Dictionary of the First Fleet* (Sydney, 1989)

Golding, William *Rites of Passage* (New York, 1980)

Green, Shirley *The Curious History of Contraception* (London, 1971)

Hamilton, Dr Alexander *A Treatise on Midwifery, comprehending the management of female complaints* (London, 1781)

Hickey, William *Memoirs of William Hickey 1749–1809* (ed.) Peter Quennell (London, 1960)

Historical Records of Australia (Mitchell Library, Sydney)

Holford, George P. *Letter to the Rt Hon. The Secretary of State of the Home Department . . . on the propriety of taking other measures for the supply of women to the settlements in New South Wales, than that of sending thither all the female convicts sentenced to . . .* (London, 1827)

Hughes, Robert *The Fatal Shore* (London, 1987)

Hunter, Captain John *An Historical journal of events at Sydney and at sea, 1787–1792* (Sydney, 1968); and *An Historical Journal of the Transactions at Port Jackson and Norfolk Island* (London, 1793)

Jackson, Stanley *The Old Bailey* (London, 1978)

Kelley, Hugh *Memoirs of a Magdalen, The History of Louisa Mildmay* (London, 1767)

Levy, M. C. I. *History of Ryde and its Districts 1792–1945*

Lincolnshire, Rutland and Stamford Mercury

Lind, Dr James *A Treatise of the Scurvy* (Edinburgh, 1753)

Maitland, William *The History of London from its foundation to the present time* (London, 1775)

Nash, M. D. *The Last Voyage of the* Guardian, *Lieutenant Riou, Commander, 1789–1791* (Cape Town, 1990)

New South Wales Historical Records (Mitchell Library, Sydney)

Newgate Prison Books (PRO, London)

Nicol, John *The Life and Adventures of John Nicol, Mariner* (ed.) John Howell (Edinburgh, 1822)

Nihell, Elizabeth *A Treatise on the art of midwifery* (London, 1760)

Noah, William *Voyage to Sydney aboard the* Hillsborough, *1798* (see Frank Clune *Bound for Botany Bay*, London, 1965)

O'Brian, Patrick – Jack Aubrey/Stephen Maturin series

Old Bailey Sessions Papers (Corporation of London Records Office)

Pardons and judges' correspondence – unpublished (PRO, London)

Place, Francis *Autobiography of Francis Place* (ed.) Mary Thale (London, 1972); and *Illustrations and Proofs of the Principle of Population . . . Together with unpublished letters of Place on birth control* (ed.) Norman E. Himes (London, 1930)

Portlock, Captain Nathaniel *A Voyage Round the World . . . in 1785–1788* (London, 1789)

Poultry Charge Books (Corporation of London Records Office)

Rodger, N. A. M. *The wooden world, an anatomy of the Georgian navy* (London, 1986)

Rumbelow, Donald *The Triple Tree, Newgate, Tyburn and the Old Bailey* (London, 1982)

Ryan, R. I. *The Third Fleet Convicts* (Cammeray, 1983)

Scott, Sergeant James *Diary*, Dixon Papers (Mitchell Library, Sydney)

Searing, James F. *West African Slavery and Atlantic commerce, the Senegal River Valley 1700–1860* (Cambridge, 1993)

Smith, Dr William *State of the Gaols in London, Westminster and the Borough of Southwark* (London, 1776)

Stone, Lawrence *Road to Divorce* (Oxford, 1990)

Tench, Lt Watkin *A Narrative of the Expedition to Botany Bay, with an account of New South Wales* (London, 1789)

The Times

Thompson, George *Slavery and Famine, punishments for sedition; or, an account of the miseries and starvation at Botany Bay* (London, 1794)

Watling, Thomas – collection of drawings (Mitchell Library, Sydney); and *Letters from an exile at Botany Bay to his aunt in Dumfries* (Penrith, 1792)

Watson, Robert *The Life of Lord George Gordon* (London, 1795)

Welch, Saunders *Proposal to render effectual a plan to remove the nuisance of common prostitutes from the streets of this metropolis* (London, 1758)

West, Peter *A History of Parramatta* (Kenthurst, 1990)

White, Surgeon-General John *Journal of a Voyage to New South Wales* (London, 1790)

Yarwood, A. T. *Marsden of Parramatta* (Kenthurst, 1986)

Acknowledgements

Tom, Jeanne and Christopher Rees; Pat Patterson and Michael Snowling for sharing their knowledge of sailing and navigation with me; Marion Bloxsome for sharing her research with me; Isobel Dixon and her colleagues at Blake Friedmann for taking me on and giving me every encouragement; Doug Young and Angela Mackworth-Young at Headline, London; Lisa Highton and Pauline McGuire at Hodder Headline, Australia; Tristan Palmer; Martin Banfield for hospitality in Sydney; the staff at the Public Records Office in Kew, the Corporation of London Records Office and the Plymouth Records Office; and the guides at Old Government House and Elizabeth Farm, Parramatta.

Index